Richard Foreman

and the Ontological-Hysteric Theatre

Theater and Dramatic Studies, No. 2

Bernard Beckerman, Series Editor

Brander Matthews Professor of Dramatic Literature
Columbia University in the City of New York

Other Titles in This Series

Richard Foreman
and the Ontological–Hysteric Theatre

by
Kate Davy

UMI RESEARCH PRESS
Ann Arbor, Michigan

Produced and distributed by
UMI Research Press
an imprint of
University Microfilms International
Ann Arbor, Michigan 48106

Library of Congress Cataloging in Publication Data

Davy, Kate.
Richard Foreman and the Ontological-Hysteric
Theatre.

(Theater and dramatic studies ; no. 2)
Revision of the author's thesis, New York University,
1979, under title: The ontological-hysteric theatre.
Bibliography: p.
Includes index.
1. Foreman, Richard, 1937-   —State history.
2. Ontological—Hysteric Theatre.   I. Title.   II. Series.
PS3556.O7225Z63 1981   792'.023'0924   81-10380
ISBN 0-8357-1220-6   AACR2

For Arnold Aronson

Contents

List of Plates

Preface

Because Richard Foreman's Ontological-Hysteric Theatre has never seated more than seventy spectators at a time, under the best of circumstances, only a limited number of people will ever have the opportunity to see a production. Consequently, many of those interested in Foreman's theatre will have to rely on studies such as this one to understand what his plays look and sound like in performance. For this reason, I have included seventy-eight photographs in this work, and attempted not only to elucidate what Foreman is trying to accomplish, but also document the visual and aural characteristics of his productions.

In addition to the fifteen pieces presented under the appellation of Ontological-Hysteric Theatre since 1968, Foreman has been involved in writing and/or directing a dozen projects that do not fall under this title. Among these are: (1) four original, commercial, musical productions done in collaboration with composer Stanley Silverman; (2) two video pieces; (3) one feature length film; and (4) two Broadway shows (see the introduction that follows). This book concerns itself with Foreman's avant-garde theatre work, however, which necessarily limits its scope to those productions identified as Ontological-Hysteric Theatre.

Beginning with *Sophia = (Wisdom) Part 3: The Cliffs* in the winter of 1972, I have attended eight Ontological-Hysteric Theatre productions. In discussing the seven pieces I did not see—the five that preceded *Sophia* and the two presented in Paris in 1973 and 1976—I have depended upon the playscripts, photographs, and especially my interviews with Foreman and others. I am grateful to Jonas Mekas for having the foresight to gather several people together following Foreman's second production in 1969 to tape-record a discussion with Foreman of the first two Ontological-Hysteric pieces, for which there are no photographs and only one short newspaper review. This lengthy group discussion was extremely helpful in documenting particular aspects of the earliest work.

Like this group discussion, many of the sources cited in the text are not available to the reader. Nearly a third of all the footnote references are derived from these unpublished sources, which include interviews, lectures, and panel presentations. In order to minimize possible confusion, I have divided the bibliographic entries into four categories (books, magazines and journals, newspapers, and unpublished material), primarily to separate the sources available to the reader from those that are not.

Although the study does not analyze the commercial productions and work done in other media, several of the newspaper entries in the bibliography are reviews of this work, as well as that of the Ontological-Hysteric Theatre. I have also included many of the reviews and articles on the two productions mounted in Paris that appeared in French publications.

While the bibliography lists the major reviews of Foreman's productions, no claim is made for all-inclusiveness—not every review of every production appears. Also, because I obtained several of the newspaper reviews in photocopy form from a variety of sources, not all of the page numbers are cited. However, all other relevant information appears, and the reader should have no trouble locating these reviews in the newspapers themselves or on microfilm.

Interspersed throughout the text is material of mine that has appeared previously in published form. For the most part, I have indicated this by citing the reference in the footnotes just as any other source. The exceptions to this are chapter 2, a large portion of which appeared in *Twentieth Century Literature* as my article entitled "Richard Foreman's Ontological-Hysteric Theatre: The Influence of Gertrude Stein," and the descriptions of *Book of Splendors: Part II (Book of Levers) Action at a Distance* and *Blvd. de Paris (I've Got the Shakes)* in chapter 3 appeared in my *Theatre Crafts* article on Foreman's scenography (see bibliographic entries).

Since this study has depended to such a great extent upon information obtained from unpublished sources, I am thankful to many people for their help in my research, particularly those who granted interviews —especially Richard Foreman, Kate Manheim, Jonas Mekas, and Amy Taubin. Mimi Johnson, at Art Services in New York, was kind enough to allow me to disrupt an entire afternoon shuffling through files on every aspect of the operation of Ontological-Hysteric Theatre, and making copies of anything I wished. I am also appreciative of Jonas Mekas's help in giving me access to his personal files at the Anthology Film Archives, in which I found, among other things, copies of Foreman's early notes on his work.

Finally, I am most grateful to Michael Kirby and Arnold Aronson for their help, encouragement, and patience in the process of writing this book.

Introduction

Stage directions from the text of Richard Foreman's first Ontological-Hysteric Theatre production, *Angelface* (1968), indicate how the "celestial being" in the performance appeared on the stage:

> (The front door opens revealing WALTER I, who now has a pair of gigantic wooden wings strapped onto his back, angel fashion. He stands—)
> ....
> WALTER I
> I can't get in—
>
> (He thrusts his body forward, banging the wings with a loud smack against the doorposts.)[1]

Although the scene has obvious slapstick qualities—and Foreman's plays, while not put-ons, are not humorless—such a moment has implications beyond its obvious theatricality. For example, are the wings supposed to make the spectator think that the character is an angel, or is the idea to stress the awkwardness and, hence, humanness of the actor who cannot walk through the doorway because he is wearing them?

The answer lies in not making a choice at all. The spectator is meant to "vibrate" between alternatives—the imaginative (angel) versus the concrete (actor). In every moment, Foreman attempts to present the elements of the performance in such a way that the spectator is never quite certain of what category to place them in. In so doing, Foreman hopes to refocus the spectator's attention on that which is not ordinarily noticed, but present, and capable of being noticed nonetheless.

For instance, when asked what his 1976 French production, *Le Livre des Splendeurs,* was all about, Foreman replied, "books, obviously." But because all of Foreman's plays, in a sense, are "about books" in one way or another, does this mean that in the Paris production book themes and imagery recurred more frequently, or that books played a more important role in this particular piece? "No," Foreman explains, "books show up often, just as in a normal, or Ibsenite, play other ordinary actions are repeated. Like when a new character enters and says 'hello' and then shakes hands—it's the glue holding things together."[2] Of course, Ibsen did not title any of his plays "Shaking Hands" and, indeed, that is the difference. While most playwrights focus on the things held together or pulled apart—dramatic confrontations among characters— Foreman focuses on the glue itself, or the everyday banalities and objects of life that hold experience together, transforming them theatrically so that we see them fresh.

Foreman's work involves a certain perceptual and intellectual "syncopation." He places the elements of his performance in a context where more than one possibility for combining them exists but, at the same time, the combining, or matching, process among these alternatives does not quite work. "To me," he states, "what is noticeable is what doesn't match in a matching, and I'm only interested in what is noticeable."[3]

In the fourteen Ontological-Hysteric Theatre productions presented over a ten-year period following *Angelface,* the near-matching and mismatching dimension of Foreman's plays became increasingly complex, generating ever more intricate relationships capable of existing on many different levels simultaneously. The ultimate goal was, and continues to be, the breakdown of habitual, passive ways of perceiving, processing, and knowing phenomena— an altering of the very structure of consciousness. Just how Foreman goes about accomplishing this end is the subject of the following study.

In the United States during the sixties, many people experimented with drugs as a means of altering consciousness chemically, and many of the plays written during this era by new American playwrights reflected the drug experience, not only in their content, but also in the way they were structured. Reflecting the experience, however, is not the same as inducing the experience, and it is an art-induced, rather than drug-induced, form of consciousness altering that Foreman wants to achieve. To accomplish this, he began creating theatre pieces designed to change the structure of consciousness itself. Instead of introducing changes in the "content" of consciousness by focusing on *what* is perceived in the theatre, Foreman is interested in changing how we perceive. The premise is that if the "way of seeing" is altered, a concomitant change in the organization of consciousness will result, not merely a change in what the consciousness contains. Foreman is not so naive as to believe that such a radical change will occur as a result of exposure to any one work of art. But he does feel that the cumulative effect of art experiences of a certain kind could cause individual changes in the limits, nature, or character of consciousness.

It is, in part, this concern for the directionality of both consciousness and art historically that places Foreman's Ontological-Hysteric Theatre work in the realm of the avant-garde, separating it from the work of many of his contemporaries, as well as from a good deal of his own work. Richard Foreman has been involved in many commercial theatre productions, but the difference between these and his avant-garde works is both striking and significant. Although there are definite stylistic similarities between *any* two productions that Foreman directs, the motivations and impulses behind each kind of work are entirely different and , most importantly, Foreman himself understands, accepts, and acknowledges this difference.

In the following chapters much is made of Foreman's rejection of traditional, commercial theatre—an ostensible contradiction, since he is often actively involved in it. This does not invalidate the point, however, for in making Ontological-Hysteric Theatre Foreman rejects the goals, premises, and most of the procedures that distinguish commercial theatre from avant-garde work. Moreover, that this study does not attempt to analyze the commercial work is not an indication that the commercial work is not as good—many people prefer Foreman's commercial pieces. A case could be made, however, for the significance of Ontological-Hysteric Theatre histori-cally, and Foreman certainly considers it more important than his other theatre work. Regardless, an understanding of Ontological-Hysteric Theatre is not dependent upon an analysis of Foreman's other work (although the opposite is not true).

Foreman is an entertainer who, when he creates Ontological-Hysteric Theatre, holds in check that tendency to basically please and amuse an audience. While he believes that a continuous diet of entertainment is not, ultimately, healthy for the head, he does not feel that it is necessary to avoid it at all costs. He readily admits that

> I do like entertainment. When I make the commercial shows I hope to entertain myself in much the same way that I would be entertained if I went to see a Cary Grant movie from the thirties. But that's a different concern than I have when I make the serious work of Ontological-Hysteric Theatre.[4]

The major commercial pieces have included five musical productions done in collaboration with composer Stanley Silverman, whom Foreman met in 1968 through Silverman's wife, Mary Delson. Silverman had been commissioned by the Fromm Music Foundation to do a music-theatre piece for presentation by the Berkshire Music Festival at Tanglewood (Lenox, Massachusetts). After reading one of Foreman's scripts, Silverman asked him to write the libretto for what would eventually become the opera *Elephant Steps*. Foreman reminisces,

> I must give Stanley tremendous credit. I had never directed so much as a teatime in my own apartment at that point. Stanley said, "Who should we get as a director?" And I said, "Stanley, I can direct it. I should do it." And Stanley said okay.[5]

Elephant Steps was presented at Tanglewood in 1968 during July and August, and again in April, 1970 at the Hunter College Opera Theatre. The opera was conducted by Michael Tilson Thomas who also played the Archangel role. The production was reviewed by *Time Magazine, The Village Voice, New York Magazine, The New York Times,* and *The Chicago Tribune,* among others. *The New York Times* critic stated, *"Elephant Steps* earned rave notices, and so did its actor-conductor."[6] In 1974 Columbia released a recording of the music as a two-album set, under its "Masterworks" logo.

While Silverman and Foreman were waiting for a New York production of *Elephant Steps,* Lyn Austin asked Silverman to be the music director for the Lenox Arts Center. By that time Silverman and Foreman had collaborated on a number of songs, which they then decided to string together and mount as a musical production for Austin's first year at Lenox. Titled *Dream Tantras for Western Massachusetts,* it was presented in July and August of 1971, and, although well-received by the few critics who saw it, the production was never opened in New York.

The following summer, Austin presented another Foreman/Silverman collaboration that became the hit of the 1972-73 Off-Broadway season, playing at the Mercer Arts Center theatre in New York from November through April. The production was *Doctor Selavy's Magic Theatre* and while it was conceived, staged, and designed by Foreman, the lyrics were not his. Several years earlier Silverman had collaborated with Tom Hendry on the score for a musical version of the Satyricon of Petronius, for the Stratford (Ontario) Festival. The production was unsuccessful and, Foreman recalls, the idea to use the songs again was Mary Silverman's.

> They [Silverman and Hendry] had twenty songs which they liked very much and I liked very much. And they came to me and said, "Richard, could you imagine taking these twenty songs . . . and making a different play around them?" So . . . I listened to the tape, and I started . . . just inventing a dream play in which they all occurred, a dream narrative.[7]

Like the response to *Elephant Steps,* the critics raved about *Selavy,* but this time the exposure was much greater. In 1974 United Artists Records released an album of all the songs from the musical.

Hotel for Criminals, commissioned by the National Opera Foundation and presented in New York in January, 1975 at the Exchange Theatre in Westbeth, was a critical failure. Composed by Silverman, the opera was conceived, written, directed, and designed by Foreman, who felt that it was by far the best of the four pieces he had done with Silverman. The critical response was disheartening but not altogether unexpected. While *Selavy* was done in the spirit of an entertaining nightclub revue, *Hotel for Criminals* was more enigmatic, based on the crime serials of the French silent filmmaker, Louis Feuillade. Of the daily critics, Foreman remarked:

> They liked *Doctor Selavy,* but they thought that it was nonsense, that it was kookie, that it was "what young people do, so we'll buy that." But this piece is much more sophisticated,

subtle, serious, and I think they're frustrated because they think the technique is preventing them from seeing the real story that they want to be seeing. They feel frustrated whereas in *Selavy* they thought there was no story anyway so they could just pick up on the pretty girls dancing across the stage.[8]

The last successful Foreman/Silverman collaboration to date was on Joseph Papp's production of the Bertolt Brecht and Kurt Weill *Threepenny Opera,* which opened May 1, 1976 at the Vivian Beaumont Theatre at Lincoln Center. Foreman directed the production and Silverman was its musical director and conductor. The reviews, for the most part, were extremely favorable, and the production enjoyed an extended run. Because of its popularity, Papp reopened it at the Delacorte Theatre in Central Park in the summer of 1977.

Finally, Silverman composed the incidental music for Stuart Ostrow's play *Stages,* and Foreman directed. It opened on Broadway at the Belasco Theatre in March, 1978 and closed the same evening. Interestingly, although the daily critics obviously panned it, a couple of them noted that Foreman had done an imaginative job of directing what they considered to be an "impossible" script.

Over the same period of time that Foreman was involved in these commercial ventures, he was also writing and mounting his Ontological-Hysteric Theatre pieces, for which he also received a great deal of attention. As early as May of 1972 his fifth piece, *Evidence,* was covered by Jack Kroll in *Newsweek* magazine. Before that, a few reviews had appeared on *Total Recall (Sophia = (Wisdom): Part 2)* (1970-71), *HčOhTiEṅLà (or) HOTEL CHINA* (1971-72) in publications with smaller circulations, such as *The Village Voice* and *Changes.* Arthur Sainer wrote the initial reviews of some of the earliest pieces in his column in the *Voice.* He raved about *Total Recall* and in a subsequent article reported: "On the strength of my notice, a close friend . . . went to see it. She managed 10 minutes of it and then split, bored out of her mind."[9] He then went on to explain how it is necessary to be "in patience," as he put it, to experience Foreman's work. More than anyone else, Sainer is responsible for persistently and enthusiastically covering Foreman's early work, encouraging his readers to see it.

By 1974, Foreman's Ontological-Hysteric Theatre work was receiving almost as much exposure, if not acclaim, as his successful commercial productions. Perhaps because of the nature of his avant-garde theatre pieces, the critics seldom attempted to interpret them, or make negative value judgments about them. Curiously, even when a reviewer reported being bored during a performance, he or she usually described the event as "fascinating," or at least "intriguing," nonetheless.

Gertrude Stein once made a remark to the effect that "nobody needs criticism, only appreciation." With regard to his avant-garde work, Foreman has been very fortunate in this respect. For the most part, his work has been appreciated rather than criticized. It is hoped that the following chapters will contribute to the already significant, and ever-growing body of appreciation for the Ontological-Hysteric Theatre and the work of Richard Foreman.

1

Foreman as Producer: The Origins and Founding of the Ontological-Hysteric Theatre

In describing his life as a playwright, Richard Foreman states:

> . . . bear in mind that [my] life has, for many years, been adapting itself to a certain obsessional need to get something onto paper, to AMASS a certain kind of material on paper, which would, hopefully, as the MASS grew, suck the life itself into the orbit of the being-style manifest in the writing . . . so the process is circular, spiral, pulling oneself up by the bootstraps.[1]

This process has produced well over forty playscripts in ten years, some twenty-five of which Foreman has mounted, directing and designing them himself. Celebrated as one of the most important avant-garde artists working in theatre today, Foreman began "pulling himself up by the bootstraps" in his individual, novel way in 1968 when he founded the Ontological-Hysteric Theatre. Foreman was involved in theatre for many years preceding this juncture in his career, but a theatre of a different kind.

Born in New York City on 10 June 1937, Foreman was raised in Scarsdale, a suburb in Westchester County, New York. A performance of Gilbert and Sullivan's *The Pirates of Penzance,* by the D'Oyly Carte Opera Company, introduced him to the theatre when he was nine years old. He recalls that the fictional world of the theatre so enticed him that he began "making and staging and starring in my own copies of Gilbert and Sullivan, discovering . . . a world in which I could both 'dream' (escape) and at the same time function with an AUTHORITY (as director-producer) not available to me in other aspects of my kid-life."[2]

Foreman rapidly progressed from his "kid-life," unilateral approach to production and began to specialize in his early teens. In fact, he began his theatre career in the early fifties as a teenage scene designer, working in community theatre while attending junior high school.

His activity in theatre continued at Scarsdale High School where he was president of the drama club. He feels his drama teacher was especially important to his development because he not only allowed but encouraged Foreman to follow his inclinations—which sometimes meant accepting surrealistic set designs for bedroom farces. By the time he graduated Foreman had participated in dozens of school and community theatre productions. Although he performed in numerous productions, he functioned primarily as a set designer during his pre-college years.

In high school, sometime between 1952 and 1954, Foreman came upon the chapter on Bertolt Brecht and the alienation effect in Mordecai Gorelik's book *New Theatres for Old*—an experience Foreman describes as "like the scales falling from my eyes."[3] Foreman explains that he spent the next ten or twelve years "worshipping Brecht" and immersing himself in whatever he could find on Brecht's theory, plays, and productions.[4] The influence is evident in Foreman's later work.

While at Brown University (1955 to 1959) Foreman became interested in film, assuming the role of film critic and writing a regular column published in the school newspaper. For many years he attended films with Amy Taubin, a young actress he met in 1955 when she joined a summer theatre that Foreman helped operate at Scarsdale High School. Taubin remembers that during college, "Richard taught me all about European art films . . . he was insane for Cocteau."[5]

Film, however, would remain an avocation for during the same period Foreman began to take playwriting seriously. Why did he turn to writing when he had previously functioned primarily as a set designer? "Because I basically wanted to justify myself by becoming 'famous,' and being a famous playwright seemed O.K.,"[6] he explains. In these first attempts he admits that he imitated Arthur Miller, Jean-Paul Sartre, Tennessee Williams, or whoever was fashionable at the time.

An important event for Foreman was his introduction to the work of Ortega y Gasset by a Brown professor who was a former student of Ortega's. While Ortega's ideas introduced Foreman to the realm of intellectual rigor, it was the *experience* of reading Ortega that produced in him an emotion with which he was not familiar. Later, he would describe this emotion in terms of an "ecstatic state" and attempt to create a kind of theatre capable of eliciting an "emotion of the mind" akin to that he experienced when reading philosophy and other nonfiction.

Recognized as "professionally promising," Foreman entered Yale when he finished his baccalaureate degree at Brown. He studied under John Gassner at Yale, and graduated with an M.F.A. in 1962. Although he did not always agree with Gassner's opinions on drama, Foreman respected him for his diligent approach, describing it as "dealing with texts inch by inch, and discussing, inch by inch, the justification for what was there."[7]

The analysis and writing of plays became Foreman's sole pursuit following an embarrassing and suppressive experience in a directing class at Yale. The assignment was to create a stage tableau, which Foreman accomplished by arranging four or five of his classmates on the stage, sitting in chairs placed at slight angles to each other, holding their hands up in different ways. When the scene opened there was silence, and Foreman remembers the director, Nikos Psacharopoulos, saying sarcastically, "Oh, it looks like a Bufferin commercial." "The class went into hysterics," Foreman says, "and I was inhibited from ever doing anything else."[8]

In 1962 Foreman and Taubin married and moved to New York City.[9] There Taubin pursued an acting career, culminating in a major role on Broadway in *The Prime of Miss Jean Brodie* (1968), and Foreman joined both the New Dramatists and the playwriting unit of the Actors Studio. His play, *Harry in Love* (1965), was optioned by a producer, Helen Jacobson, but the project was abandoned after a year. Although Foreman has no copies of his work prior to 1968, the following anecdote concerning the outcome of the optioned *Harry in Love* suggests the nature of the material:

> The best thing I had to show from that was a very nice letter from Alec Guinness, saying that he loved the play, but that he didn't think he was right to play a New York Jewish-overweight tormented soul.[10]

Foreman says that his early works were similar in some respects to the plays of Murray Schisgal and Clifford Odets.

Whatever their precise style and content, it is clear that the plays written before 1968 were not avant-garde. For four or five years after arriving in New York, Foreman engaged in the routine of a beginning professional playwright aspiring to become the next "Arthur Miller" of the American theatre. As Foreman reports, years later, the method of writing was quite orthodox:

> . . . my writing habits were to get an idea (after searching around for the right combination of theatricality and political or psychological or sociological relevance), then do an outline, then do a first draft, then rewrite and rewrite again until a) the style seemed polished and strong and b) the plot line seemed efficient and rose to the proper climaxes. . . .[11]

Until 1968 the major, if not only, relevant question for Richard Foreman as playwright was, what will *work*? In other words, what can the playwright write that, when staged, will elicit a predetermined, predictable response from the spectator?

The change in the direction of Foreman's plays in 1968 was decidely radical and, ostensibly, quite sudden. There was, however, a gradual shift in Foreman's sensibilities that began when he attended a Living Theatre benefit program shortly after he arrived in New York. At the benefit, he stumbled upon *The Flower Thief,* a film by Ron Rice. This event was crucial in that it exposed Foreman to what was then labeled "underground film," and today is widely known as the New American Cinema movement. *The Flower Thief* impressed Foreman tremendously, and he saw hundreds of such films in the following years.

While the New American Cinema played a significant role in Foreman's transition from commercial to avant-garde theatre, there were other influences as well. With the exception of Jack Smith's work, however, the experimental theatre of the 1960s was not one of them. Foreman was familiar with the work being done in experimental theatre; but, although he was not content with commercial theatre, he preferred it to the expressionistic tactics of "audience assault" he sensed in much experimental work. Given the amount of film he saw and his relationship to the filmmakers themselves, it seems reasonable to consider the New American Cinema a major influence and examine in what general ways the events, films, and artists contributed to the eventual founding of the Ontological-Hysteric Theatre.

Of Taubin and Foreman, film scholar P. Adams Sitney recalls, "They were the most regular and faithful attendants of avant-garde film shows."[12] They attended films at Cinema 16, the Bleeker Street Cinema, and the Charles Theatre. Cinema 16 was a precursor of the Film-Makers Cooperative and its showcase, the Film-Makers Cinematheque (housed at the Gramercy Arts Theatre in 1964). In addition, filmmaker Ken Jacobs invited them to screenings at his loft in lower Manhattan beginning in 1962. As Taubin recollects, "the experience of going to Jacobs' loft for an evening was, at a certain point, extraordinary and terribly important for Richard."[13]

Taubin accounts for the impact of underground films by explaining that when she and Foreman arrived in New York they had been strictly disciplined academically in the European intellectual tradition.

> The Charles had open screenings which included a lot of "junk." It was the junk aspect of it that interested us at first. . . . it was so different from the art we had been accustomed to.[14]

Foreman feels that he might have ultimately dismissed these films as "too amateurish—not sophisticated, professional and high-powered enough to interest me"[15] had it not been for the weekly film columns by Jonas Mekas published in *The Village Voice*. Foreman read what the filmmakers were thinking about as Mekas, a filmmaker and editor of *Film Culture* magazine, guided the reader toward a different way of looking at a new esthetic in film.

Although everyone involved in filmmaking was keenly aware of Taubin and Foreman's presence, it was not until March, 1964 that Taubin and Foreman began to meet the filmmakers. Taubin and Foreman called to offer their help after reading that some of their acquaintances had been arrested for screenings of Jack Smith's *Flaming Creatures* and Jean Genet's *Un Chant D'Amour*. Taubin began doing volunteer work for the Film-Makers Cooperative, and Foreman met Mekas and many of the other filmmakers through her. Foreman, too, worked for Mekas and the Cooperative at different times over the years. One job, in the midsixties, consisted of organizing a project involving twenty filmmakers for the purpose of raising money. Another job required suggesting, planning, and organizing film programs for rental to colleges requesting them. When Mekas rented a loft space at 80 Wooster Street to house the Cinematheque, Foreman was responsible for booking performers into the space during the first few months after it opened in the fall of 1967. Some of the artists he engaged included Trisha Brown, Philip Glass, Steve Reich, and the San Francisco Mime Troupe. He was paid on a free-lance basis.[16]

Foreman was initially intrigued by *The Flower Thief* "because it had obviously been made by some little guy like me in New York, with his own little camera and his own little friends."[17] Unlike the collaborative nature of commercial theatre, and the emphasis on group creation that would evolve in the experimental sector, *The Flower Thief* was clearly the result of the thought and effort of one artist. In 1967, five years after seeing *The Flower Thief,* Foreman began to consider such an approach to mounting a theatre piece.

While the connection between the method used in making *The Flower Thief* and his own work and was indirect and late in coming, Foreman sensed immediately the significance of Jack Smith's film, *Flaming Creatures,* and claims that it was a "major experience in my artistic change."[18] He understood that Smith's work was carefully wrought, and that Smith purposely created a "collision" between the formal aspects of the film and certain kinds of "personal garbage in the raw state."[19] Foreman saw the film in 1963 and in 1973 declared:

> *Flaming Creatures* was a relevation to me. It . . . allowed me to feel that I didn't have to be embarrassed by the roughness in my own work. Most of my work up to that point had been rewriting . . . to get rid of things in the language that sounded rough or corny or unsophisticated to my ears. What . . . [*Flaming Creatures*] did for me, primarily, was to make me realize that you could accept all that and show it for what it is.[20]

Actually, in 1963 this realization was in a germinal stage since it was not until 1966 that Foreman even began to change his writing procedures and style.

The problem of direct and specific influence is obvious. For example, Foreman credits Ken Jacobs's work, beginning with *Blonde Cobra* (1963), with helping to free him from the notion that he had to "come on" to the spectator and move him emotionally. He explains, "I still get sucked into the desire to knock the audience out," while Jacobs "let beauties just be there and define themselves."[21] While this is true of Jacobs's work, it is also true of other films Foreman saw during the same period. On the other hand, it is entirely feasible, and probably correct, that through Jacobs's work Foreman learned that a variety of seemingly peripheral material could be the subject or focus of a piece—the use of "light," for example, as subject matter. Foreman states, "I stole everything about 'lights' directly from Jacobs's work."[22]

The point here, then, is not to speculate on how individual films may have specifically influenced Foreman's work. Playwright and film critic Ken Kelman uses Louis Feuillade's *Vampires* to point out how a particular aspect of a film might appeal to Foreman in a highly idiosyncratic way: "After seeing *Vampires* he said to me, 'I liked those flowers.' Shortly thereafter, all these bowls of flowers appeared in a Foreman play."[23] Indeed, the use of flowers as a decorative motif remained in all Foreman productions, but the "influence" is hardly significant. Like any artist working in any medium, Foreman notices details that interest him and incorporates them into his work.

Sitney describes Foreman as having a "totally digested film consciousness" and stresses that there is no simple mode of transformation and translation, explaining that, "What Foreman sees in the cinema becomes something totally different in his work."[24] Mekas agrees that in Foreman's work the experience of viewing films is completely transformed into something that transcends the film influence. Mekas also acknowledges some confusion regarding Foreman's enthusiasm for certain films, recalling that Foreman "saw [Dennis] Hopper's *Last Movie* and said he saw one of the greatest movies—we hated it. So I went to see it [again] to understand why Richard would like it, and I have never understood it."[25]

Any interpretation of *why* Foreman was impressed by *Last Movie* is merely conjecture. In an attempt to demonstrate the general nature of the New American Cinema's influence on Richard Foreman, the task here will be to document, out of a great many films and a few performances, those that particularly impressed Foreman, as well as those he specifically disliked.

Michael Snow's films were especially important for Foreman, and some filmmakers believe that Foreman's work influenced Snow's later films. Foreman met Snow before a screening of Snow's early film *New York Eye and Ear Control* (1964) and asked him, somewhat facetiously, if it was a good film. "It's a masterpiece," Snow responded matter-of-factly. Stunned, Foreman recalls, "I was so amazed that he had the courage to say it was a great film— and it was!"[26] Foreman wrote the program notes on *New York Eye and Ear Control* for the *Film-Makers Cooperative Catalogue,* and Snow helped with lighting—operating a primitive light board—on Foreman's first production. Foreman has occasionally given talks on Snow's films, once for large audience at the Museum of Modern Art (1976) in conjunction with a retrospective of Snow's painting, photography, and film.

Both Taubin and Foreman recall being so excited by an untitled film they saw at the Gramercy Arts Theatre in 1964 that they rushed home and called Jacobs to find out who made it. It was Andy Warhol's *Haircut* (1963). Sitney remembers that Foreman was also very emphatic about liking Warhol's *The Chelsea Girls* (1966).

Despite widespread enthusiasm for Stan Brakhage's work, Foreman felt Brakhage's early films were overrated. He did not like them "because of what I thought was a lack of tension within the individual images. I've always been unable to relate to *Dog Star Man* [*The Art of Vision* (1961-1966)]."[27]

Although Foreman appreciated Jack Smith as a filmmaker, it was not until he attended the Cinematheque's month of expanded cinema events (November-December, 1965) that he became an admirer of what he considers Smith's revolutionary theatre work. Foreman remembers the Expanded Cinema Festival vividly. He saw works by Robert Rauschenberg, Claes Oldenburg, Robert Whitman, Andy Warhol, Dick Higgins, Ken Dewey, and John Vacarro. The works that particularly impressed him include: (1) *The Rites of the Dream Weapon* by Angus MacLise; (2) a piece by Jerry Joffen; (3) Piero Heliczer's *The Last Rites;* (4) the music of LaMonte Young; (5) Ken Jacobs's "shadow play;" and (6) Jack Smith's *Rehearsal for the Destruction of Atlantis.* In his *Village Voice* column Mekas described Smith's piece as:

> an orgy of costumes, suppressed and open violence, and color. The center of the piece was a huge red lobster, a masterpiece creation of costume and character. . . . Smith's piece was loose and relied on chance, on coincidences, on conglomerations.[28]

In the following years, Foreman attended a few of the midnight performances that Smith presented in his loft.

For audiences at Smith's midnight shows, the greater part of the performance was waiting for it to begin. Taubin explains that what intrigued Foreman was Smith's "calculated strategy of everything going wrong and falling apart."

> He might be looking for something during the piece. Or he would have the text on a single sheet of paper, and he would have to walk it around so the actors could say their lines. Then, as though he were going to reshoot a scene, he would physically regroup the actors on the stage. Sometimes he recruited audience members to work the lights, etc., during the performance.[29]

Sitney stresses Foreman's fondness for the "totally unprepared" aspect of Smith's work. In his book *Visionary Film*, Sitney states:

> Richard Foreman was the first to observe . . . a different level of dialectic in every presentation by Smith. His plays, slide shows, and even film screenings . . . invariably start late, break down several times, and involve Smith himself rushing out, instructing actors, fixing equipment, and suddenly changing the course of the work, until these activities assume the center of attention and the work which initially attracted the audience seems one prop among others, mostly junk.[30]

Kelman maintains that Foreman "admired Smith as a real genius and was intrigued by the 'openendedness' of the work."[31]

Between 1962 and 1968, Foreman relied on film viewing, and a well-developed habit of prodigious reading, for the energy, inspiration, ideas, and strategies he could not find in most theatre. Other films Foreman considered important include: *Heaven and Earth* or *The Magic Feature* (1950-60) by Harry Smith; *The Queen of Sheba Meets the Atom Man* (1964) by Ron Rice; *Christmas on Earth* (1964) by Barbara Rubin; *Diaries, Notes and Sketches* (1964-69) by Jonas Mekas; Michael Snow's films *Wavelength* (1967), and [*Back and Forth*] (1969); all of George Landow's films, especially *The Film That Rises to the Surface of Clarified Butter* (1968); and Ken Jacobs's *Tom, Tom the Piper's Son* (1969).

Foreman has often stated that the experience of seeing these films altered his attitudes about what constitutes art. His ideas changed gradually as he watched what independent filmmakers were accomplishing within their medium. An important factor, he believes, was "the notion that here were people just by themselves, with their home-movie cameras, making things on their own terms, exactly the way they wanted to make them, not depending on anyone else."[32] Eventually Foreman would abandon the standard of collaboration in theatre and begin to direct his own plays, building the sets and props as well as designing them.

In addition to the filmmakers' way of working, the self-conscious, self-aware, self-referential nature of the films had a profound effect on the formation of Foreman's artistic consciousness. Through the filmmakers' phenomenological approach, Foreman discovered what he describes as "a new esthetic, built upon a truthfulness in attempting to catch the natural rhythms of the individual artist—come-what-may as a result."[33] He considers this discovery, or realization, a turning point in his art.

> It was mostly coming to terms with all those "home movies" and accepting things that . . . were akin to things that embarrassed me in my own work.[34]

As a writer, Foreman had expended a great deal of energy "polishing" or rewriting his scripts to eliminate the rough and unsophisticated elements that embarrassed him because they smacked of immaturity and amateurishness. He contends that

> it was through seeing these films that I realized I had to radicalize exactly those elements which had . . . bothered me about my work . . . radicalize what was my personal awkwardness, my personal stress. . . .[35]

For Foreman, to "radicalize" is not only to accept but ultimately to "make central to my work the very elements which I had heretofore tried to suppress and exorcise as not being 'weighty, serious, impressive' enough."[36]

Foreman's first attempt to incorporate this new approach into his writing resulted in a play entitled *Good Benny*. He asked Ken Jacobs to read it. Jacobs remembers disliking it because "it was being informative in a way that wasn't plastic . . . things were getting in the way of the play of energies."[37] Foreman was very upset by Jacobs's response, but not completely discouraged.

In his subsequent writing, he continued in the same general direction as *Good Benny*. In writing his next play, Foreman again employed his new approach to and method of writing. This time, however, the result was far more developed and more advanced.

The play was *Angelface,* and Foreman gave it, with some trepidation, to both Jacobs and Snow to read in the summer of 1967 during a period when he and Taubin, Flo and Ken Jacobs, and Joyce and Michael Snow all rented a place in East Hampton. Foreman reminisces, "If they had thought it was terrible and hated it, I may have waited even longer before doing a production."[38] They liked it, but, although *Angelface* would be the first Ontological-Hysteric Theatre production, Foreman had only begun to consider the possibility of mounting it himself.

During the same summer, Foreman took it upon himself to renovate the ground floor of a building at 80 Wooster Street in New York's Soho district that was to house the Cinematheque in the fall. Because of trouble with the police and building departments, the space was closed the following summer but, for some reason, it was closed only to showing films. Of Foreman and this event, Jonas Mekas recalls:

> His involvement was very physical in preparing that space for us. So when it became vacant, it developed very naturally that Richard wanted to do a play there. This was the chance to do a production since he was talking about it at the time. So the space becoming available at that time helped him to make up his mind and brought on his first production.[39]

Both Kelman and Sitney agree with Mekas that this renovation work was a turning point for Foreman since he had been thinking about mounting a production and the labor made him feel at home with that particular space.

Foreman agrees that the space was a factor in his decision, especially since one of the reasons he had not done a production earlier was fear of being laughed at. He felt "safer" and more comfortable taking this first big step in a space he helped to build. He is certain, however, that he built the set and rehearsed *Angelface* while movies were still being shown in the space.

Foreman is correct in maintaining that he probably was thinking about using the Cinematheque for a production from the beginning of his work on the space. *Angelface* was presented on four successive evenings (to audiences ranging from about half a dozen people to twenty or so) in April, 1968, while the building was not closed to showing films until July. It is understandable that his friends would remember these events as coinciding for, although Foreman may have had the space in mind from the beginning of construction, it was several months after the Cinematheque opened before Foreman, as he describes it quoting Shakespeare, "screwed my courage to the sticking point"[40] and asked Mekas if he could mount a play in the space. Until early in 1973, 80 Wooster Street was the home of the Ontological-Hysteric Theater. Foreman appreciatively affirms that "my first four years of existence were made possible by Jonas Mekas, who gave me his then-closed Cinematheque ... and just let me use it, though he kept on paying the rent. . . ."[41] After Foreman acquired his own theatre loft, the space was further renovated and reopened as the Anthology Film Archives.

Besides the filmmaker's influence and the availability of working space, there was at least one other significant factor contributing to Foreman's decision to produce his own plays. Through the New Dramatists, the Actors Studio, and Taubin's work in professional theatre, Foreman was becoming more familiar with commercial theatre, and more alienated from it as the familiarity grew. The *Harry in Love* project was Foreman's last attempt to enter the commercial theatre world. The reason, according to Taubin, was not because the project fell through but because the experience of having a play under option was so awful—"He didn't want to live his life that way."[42] Despite appearances and regardless of the impetus, the fact is that for Richard Foreman the transition from behind-the-scenes commercial playwright to avant-garde producer/playwright/director/designer was an arduous one that spanned a period of six years.

The choice of "Ontological-Hysteric" for the name of his theatre was prophetic but not well thought out. In March, shortly before *Angelface* opened, the "Orgien Mysterien Theater" of Hermann Nitsch, an Austrian artist, was performing at the Cinematheque. Foreman felt his theatre needed a name and remembers thinking, "Hey, that's a good name; Orgies-Mysteries, umm, orgies, mysteries, what about, umm . . ."[43] and ontological-hysteric was chosen. It was an expeditious decision. Unfortunately, until Foreman acquired a reputation this title kept some people away because it seemed indicative of tendencies in the experimental, "audience confrontation" theatre well-known at the time. Considered in the context of Foreman's work, however, "ontological-hysteric" can be seen as an appropriate choice of terms.

Foreman's goal in founding his own theatre was to replace the theatre of confrontation, emotion, and "ideas" with what he calls a "mental," nonemotional, yet sensual theatre.

> I wanted a theatre that did the opposite of "flow"—a theatre that was true to my own mental experiences, i.e., the world as being pieces of things, awkwardly present for a moment and then either re-presented by consciousness or dropped in favor of some other momentary presentation.[44]

Consequently, the functioning of the consciousness became his preoccupation, resulting in work that deals directly with the nature of thought itself. He discarded the conventional dramatic attributes of plot development and character interaction, replacing them with a kind of "atomic" structure. He explains that this structuring involves the breaking down of all the theatrical elements (story, action, sound, light, composition, gesture) into the "smallest building-block units, the basic cells of the perceived experience of both living and art-making."[45]

It is in this approach to theatre that the use of the word "ontological" becomes clear. Ontology is "the science of being or reality; the branch of knowledge that investigates the nature, essential properties, and relations of being." In his theatre, Foreman takes the fundamental conflict (hysteric) basis of most traditional theatre and renders it phenomenologically—retarding and breaking up the hysterical situation or state, and focusing on the moment-to-moment reality of things-in-and-of-themselves.

> . . . I'm taking nineteenth-century naturalistic triangles and other psychological situations, which I believe are basically hysterical at their roots, in terms of classical psychiatry, the hysterical syndrome. And I'm trying to redeem them, and open up holes by which more— well, it sounds pretentious—more *cosmic* perceptual concerns bleed through, that are really ontological concerns in the Heideggerian sense.[46]

For the most part, Foreman's avant-garde theatre contemporaries during the sixties were striving to develop a theatrical language or style that, while different from traditional theatre, would nonetheless be easily accessible to large numbers of people, in some cases "the masses." Foreman confesses that he is involved in making "coterie art" but feels that, for him, there is no other alternative. Stating, in 1969:

> . . . the avant-garde theatre in this country generally says "we want to exploit the body and release the inhibitions of the body, because the mind is no longer of any use." But in emphasizing the body and having the actors do all kinds of physical things, the mind takes a violent step to defend itself. I think the only way to transcend the mind is to find a way to confront it, to baffle it—you must deal with *it* if you want to get past it. I think you have to get past the mind as it is now. The way we are using it now.
>
> The New American Cinema films were the first things I saw that were doing that sort of thing. I hope that my plays are the beginning of that same tradition for the theatre.[47]

2

Foreman as Playwright: The Structure and Method of Generating Texts

Because Foreman is involved in every aspect of theatre art, his plays are sometimes regarded as mere background for his visual work. Foreman, however, considers himself fundamentally a playwright and places his texts firmly at the center of his theatre work.

In the midsixties, as he tired of commercial theatre, Foreman became increasingly discontent with the approach to playwriting he had faithfully employed since he left Yale.

> . . . like most professionally oriented playwrights, [I] delighted in my ability to not-so-much write as REWRITE plays so that they would "work" on stage (i.e., so the actors would find the kind of material with which they—and the director—could manipulate the audience through a desired sequence of emotions and emerge at the end with a nice, not too simple but not too subtle, "meaning").[1]

He began to consider a radically different approach but was not certain of how to go about it until he was introduced to Gertrude Stein's work "through all the filmmakers and poets and nontheatrical people in New York who . . . were very influenced by her."[2]

Foreman maintains that Gertrude Stein's theoretical writings were the primary influence on his writing method, technique, or style. Her literary and theatrical theory, therefore, can be examined as an historical precedent for his work. Stein's approach functioned as a prototype for Foreman. This does not imply, of course, that Foreman imitates Stein. He begins with her, shares the same goal, works from the same impulse, struggles with the same problem, but, indubitably, the results are entirely different; as Stein so accurately expressed it in her chapter "The War" in *The Autobiography of Alice B. Toklas:*

> Another thing that interested us enormously was how different the camouflage of the french looked from the camouflage of the germans, and then once we came across some very very

neat camouflage and it was american. The idea was the same but as after all it was different
nationalities who did it the difference was inevitable. The colour schemes were different, the
designs were different, the way of placing them was different, it made plain the whole theory
of art and its inevitability.[3]

It is equally inevitable that an innovator like Foreman would assimilate
Stein's theory, bringing her sense of "contemporariness" into the present—
extending and expanding its perimeters.

By the spring of 1969, Foreman had mounted his second play, *Ida-Eyed,*
and, like *Angelface,* it passed virtually unnoticed. There were only a few
performances, a few audience members, one review, and no photographs. His
friends, artists and writers active in the New American Cinema movement,
convinced that this theatre work was extremely important, decided it must be
documented, in some manner, for the future. Hence, when *Ida-Eyed* closed,
seven people met with Foreman to discuss and record, via a group interview,
his work to date. During this discussion Foreman explained that while he had
only read Artaud's theory, for example, once, "I have returned to Gertrude
Stein's theoretical writings on literature and the theatre at least twice a year,
and continually ponder, and am troubled, and am led, and ruminate[on]it."[4]

In precisely what ways did Foreman's reflections on Stein affect his
work—how exactly did her writing trouble and then lead him? Rather than
imitate life as it was known and lived during the first half of the twentieth
century, Stein focused on the timeless qualities of the human mind,
relentlessly documenting through her work the progressive stages in the
evolution of consciousness, always concerned with the "next" evolutionary
phase. Stein was convinced of the ongoing and inevitable "directionality" of
the human mind and, therefore, art. The key word is "consciousness."

As a student of William James, Stein's notion of what constitutes
consciousness was realized through James's ideas on psychology, which
formed the basis of his pragmatic philosophy. Stein understood the esthetic
ramifications of James's pragmatism and made concrete his concept of the
"stream of consciousness" by translating its principle into her literary genre.
Stein is not a "stream-of-consciousness" writer as the phrase is popularly
understood. When James described consciousness as a "stream," he was using
introspection as a tool for psychological investigation. "Introspective observation," he maintained, "is what we have to rely on first and foremost and
always."[5] If, as he explains, consciousness is examined mainly by "looking
into our own minds and reporting what we there discover,"[6] then it cannot be
understood as consisting of a mosaic of discrete thoughts, perceptions, and
sensations. Instead, he concluded that "within each personal consciousness,
thought is sensibly continuous," and interruptions or time-gaps "no more
break the flow of the thought that thinks them than they break the time and
the space in which they lie."[7] In relation to Stein and Foreman, it is crucial to

note that James did not necessarily characterize the uninterrupted "flow" of thought as proceeding by association. The "stream" is merely going on—intentionally or unintentionally, and by any number of means—continuously.

From this premise emerged one of Stein's most important innovations—her esthetics of the "continuous present." This concept emanated from her meditations on the nature of experience itself, the function of consciousness, and the relation of consciousness to its own mental states. These ruminations led her to postulate an ontological dualism of "being" and "existence"—each an irreducible element or mode composed of inherent, discrete attributes. These attributes, in turn, are the result of her thoughts on the subjects of time, knowledge, and audience. In her book *The Geographical History of America or The Relation of Human Nature to the Human Mind,* she equates "being" with the human mind, and "existence" with human nature.[8]

For Stein, the human mind (being) is eternal or timeless, while human nature (existence) is time-bound. From this distinction in time sense, she differentiated between the attainment of knowledge and the condition of knowledge, or "remembering" in relation to "knowing." Remembering is successive in that it involves the assembling or "re-collection" of past events, ideas, facts, thoughts, or experiences, establishing a continuity and an associational relationship between past and present. Although knowledge is acquired, figuratively, over a period of time by memory, Stein contends that "when you know anything, memory doesn't come in. At any moment that you are conscious of knowing anything, memory plays no part."[9] Thus, knowing is the condition of knowledge as a state of consciousness. It can be described as immediate or direct because its "time" is in any present moment when the mind is aware of knowing—it is not dependent on appendages of associational process—it is complete in itself. Remembering, on the other hand, can be described as a "re-calling" and, therefore, indirect and complete only in relation—past to present.

Taken a step further, the state of knowing can be discerned as any present moment in which the mind is aware of itself knowing—the consciousness thrown back on itself, as it were. It is this intentional state of mind that Stein employed in all the work she labeled "entity writing," which she placed in opposition to "identity writing." For Stein, entity is the "thing-in-itself" detached from time and association, while identity is the "thing-in-relation," time-bound, clinging to association.

By definition, identity writing is audience writing—intended to be popularly understood by a reading audience. Because it is conferred on an individual from the outide and depends upon "the other" or an audience, Stein links it to existence or human nature, stressing her point in sentences like, "She knows her name is Rose because they call her Rose."[10] She considers it *external* in that it involves an individual's functions and relationships in society. In the process of writing, identity entails a time sense that is successive (past, present, future) and relationships that are causal (beginning, middle, end).

Entity is linked to being or the human mind which is *internal* and has no identity—any sense of audience is absent. At any moment, as Stein explains, the human mind "knows what it knows when it knows it." Hence, entity writing focuses on knowing or the immediate present and "actualities" while identity writing deals with remembering and "reconstructions." In the process of writing, entity is a state of mind characterized by organic process and relationships that are dissociated or discontinuous (the continuous moment-to-moment *present*).

The following chart outlines the attributes of being and existence, indicating the opposing characteristics in this philosophical system.

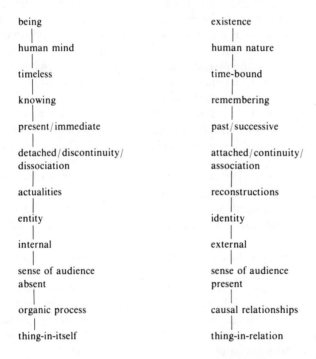

being	existence
human mind	human nature
timeless	time-bound
knowing	remembering
present/immediate	past/successive
detached/discontinuity/ dissociation	attached/continuity/ association
actualities	reconstructions
entity	identity
internal	external
sense of audience absent	sense of audience present
organic process	causal relationships
thing-in-itself	thing-in-relation

At the same time, by beginning at the end of each list and reading to the top, one can discern the constituent elements of two different kinds of art, leading to Stein's dualistic ontology. The chart is not meant, however, to imply that one approach is better or worse than the other. While most of Stein's work falls into the entity category, a few of her titles, including *The Autobiography of Alice B. Toklas,* for example, can definitely be classified "identity writing." Stein, unquestionably, preferred entity to identity writing and considered the latter her secondary work.

Of identity writing as a work of art, Foreman makes an unequivocal value judgment when he describes it in terms of

> works of art which occasionally have their moments but which basically both bore me and (I would maintain) are subtly enslaving those who "make the effort" not to be bored by what they already know to be true (i.e., their own emotional responses to murders, loves, betrayals, righteous indignation in the face of injustice, and all those other fine things that classical art is always "about").[11]

He is aware, of course, that *Harry in Love, Fat Rubinstein*—all of his early plays—are examples of this kind of identity writing. There are many other types, however, and Stein's lectures and theoretical writings are among them. Foreman, too, has published several articles and manifestos "delineating and figuring out for myself the theoretical implications and next steps for the kind of art I found myself in the middle of making,"[12] he writes. Identity writing in any form or style is easily recognizable, while entity writing is more difficult to describe. Beginning with *Angelface,* all of Foreman's plays belong to the "entity writing" category, which Stein refers to as "really writing" or "pure writing." In practical terms, what precisely are the characteristics of "entity writing," what are its methods, and why can Foreman's plays be labeled as such?

The "continuous present" is not only one of Stein's most significant esthetic theories, it constitutes the basic structural dimension of all Richard Foreman's plays, as well as her own entity writing. The content of the continuous present is, in one sense, itself. Because Stein was concerned only with reality as she perceived it, final, complete reality was "now," the present moment of perception. "The business of Art," she explained, "is to live in the actual present, that is the complete actual present, and to express that complete actual present."[13] Her goal was to capture and express this present reality or what she termed the "excitingness of pure being." If the form of the composition is understood as an extension of content, then it must adhere to the same present time sense. Stein equated composition with "things seen" or the way of seeing. When she observed a difference between "the time of the composition" and "the time in the composition" she was referring to the actual historical "time of" composing (the time in which the author lives, writes or "sees") in relation to the "time in" or to which the composition addresses itself (the time in which the "things seen" exist). If this distinction results in a double time sense, it is not consistent with Stein's notion of content. It is in the continuous present that the "time of" and "in" the composition are united and become one and the same thing since, as a compositional device, it becomes the continuous, moment-to-moment progression of the writer's own thinking process while concentrating on any facet of reality, or the present moment of perception.

Stein concluded that, "at present composition is time . . . the time-sense in the composition is the composition that is making what there is in composition."[14] Here "time-sense" actually refers to a negation of time for, she explains, "as a person writing . . . you have to denude yourself of time so that writing time does not exist . . . and if you are writing about the present, the time element must cease to exist."[15] In place of this obliterated sense of time, Stein calls for "an existence suspended in time," which is the result of what Donald Sutherland has described as "the isolation of present internal time."[16]

This isolation of internal time can function as a method of generating texts when perceived as a form of contemplation or meditation. For both Stein and Foreman, meditation exists on an "esthetic" plane (rather than in the sense of hypnotic trance), involving a deliberate detachment of oneself from the external world while documenting one's own consciousness in the act of writing. In this meditative, dissociated state, memories, past associations, and identity slip away, and one experiences moments of mental suspension or Stein's "existence suspended in time." The writing is not "about" consciousness; on the contrary, it *directly* reflects the workings of the author's mind employing a meditative, introspective process in composition, producing texts that are personal, self-referential entities rather than reconstructions.

Foreman points out that his scripts "read like notations of my own process of imagining a theatre piece."[17] This is true because, in the act of writing, Foreman incessantly documents his own effort at writing a play in an attempt "to notate at every moment, with great exactness, what was going on as the 'writing was written.' "[18] The result is related to Stein's work in that it deals directly with the nature, process, and activity of thought itself. Although Stein, unlike Foreman, did not bring her work into another medium—literally staging the process of writing—her conception of "play as landscape" was as instrumental as her writing technique in the development of Foreman's work.

Stein maintained that life experiences and art experiences are not the same. She was, therefore, concerned with the functional differences of art and life in relation to the entire range of experience or emotional response. She focused her attention not only on what the human mind knows at any moment of knowing but *how* one knows what one knows. In her lecture, "Plays," she relates her experience of theatre art and explains why this experience caused such a state of nervousness that she stopped attending the theatre altogether.

In early childhood, Stein attended a great many plays and operas in Oakland and San Francisco, where she grew up. At that time, her experience of the theatre event was primarily one of sight rather than sound.

> . . . a child's feeling of the theatre is two things. One which is in a way like a circus that is the general movement and light . . . and a great deal of height in the air, and then there are moments, a very very few moments but still moments.[19]

She experienced the space, movement, and light of both the theatre auditorium and the stage—the "moments" she refers to were visual. In *Uncle Tom's Cabin,* for example, the only moment she remembered was "the escape across the ice. I imagine because the blocks of ice moving up and down naturally would catch my eye more than the people on the stage would."[20] While a child certainly perceives sound in a theatre, Stein contends that, "One must be pretty far advanced in adolescence before one realizes a whole play."[21] In other words, a child does not really "hear" a whole play, that is, understand what it is "about" and experience it on all possible levels. Before adolescence, the theatre consisted for Stein "of bright filled space and usually not more than one moment in a play."[22]

When Stein began to "realize a whole play," she became troubled by "sight and sound," she explains, "and its relation to emotion and time, rather than in relation to story and action."[23] She felt it was impossible for her emotion to be "in time"—proceeding on a one-to-one basis—with the action on the stage. The relationship between the emotion of the spectator and the action of the play existed in what she called "syncopated time."

> Your sensation . . . in relation to the play played before you . . . your emotion concerning that play is always either behind or ahead of the play at which you are looking and to which you are listening.[24]

Because a syncopated tempo in jazz exists as a thing-in-itself, listening to a jazz band did not make Stein nervous, but, as experienced in the theatre, syncopated time exists as a thing-in-relation and thus created a great deal of internal confusion or nervousness.

"Syncopation" is related to the memory/expectancy structure of most plays. When the curtain opens, the spectator is introduced to any number of characters and situations, usually through expository dialog, and then placed in a position of remembering past information or events while anticipating future events, climaxes, or resolutions. This position made Stein nervous because she was given little control—the play's structure was forcing her to "read" the performance in a specific way, manipulating her emotions unnaturally. After all, in life, one's emotions nearly always match the situation one is involved in at the moment. While Stein did not expect the theatre experience to be the same as life experience, she felt the performance was attempting to imitate and evoke emotional experiences familiar in life, failing by the very nature of the spectator/performance situation, and thereby creating internal confusion via the existence of more than one time sense. During a performance that progresses by means of a more or less linear information structure, syncopation occurs whenever the spectator stops (whether to remember, reconsider any number of variables, doze, or check the program for an actor's name), while the play continues. Having stopped or paused, the spectator must then "catch up," emotionally, in an effort to match the emotional movement of the event on stage.

In addition to following the story or plot of the play, Stein had difficulty seeing and hearing the performance at the same time. She explains that she "stumbled" over such details as "clothes, voices, what they the actors said, how they were dressed and how that related itself to their moving around."[25] She wished she could simply pause and look at the costumes or hear the actor's voices, without the play running on ahead without her. At sixteen, she experienced a production she describes as "a very simple direct and moving pleasure" when Sarah Bernhardt performed a play in French. Since Stein was not familiar enough with the language to follow the plot, she said, "I could rest in it untroubled. And I did."[26]

It was this simple and direct pleasure Stein was aiming for when, many years later, she began writing plays. As playwright, she was not concerned with the text solely as literature, but with its capacity to function as a vehicle for establishing a time sense in the experience of theatre similar to that she had known as a child. To remedy syncopation, Stein abandoned the conventional narrative attributes of drama and conceived the static or "landscape play." In a landscape composition each element has equal weight and is as significant as the whole. She states:

> . . . to me one human being is as important as another human being, and you might say that the landscape has the same values, a blade of grass has the same value as a tree. Because the realism of the people who did realism before was a realism of trying to make people real. I was not interested in making the people real but in the essence or, as a painter would call it, value.[27]

Using the continuous present as a means of structuring a play in the absence of a developing narrative, story, or plot, Stein created a static composition, eliminating progression. She originated plays that are continuously present—the elements of the play, like the features in a landscape, are equal in value and always remain, objectively, "there" or present.

The "movement" in a play with a narrative structure is progressive (going somewhere), and in order to move forward with the action, the play must first provide the spectator with the appropriate information concerning the various relationships of characters and situations essential to story development. Unlike a narrative composition, the "movement" in a landscape play is not forward and backward but "in and out," the way one "reads" the elements in a landscape setting as the eye moves from object to object, perceiving the relationships between individual elements presented simultaneously. Because the landscape play is not "going anywhere" or progressing, the spectator can move "out" of the composition, or stop, at any moment without creating syncopated emotional time. Furthermore, the possibility of syncopation occurring is minimized by the fact that a landscape play is not compelled to begin by providing information designed to acquaint itself with the spectator. If a play were perceived like a landscape, then, Stein felt, "there would be no difficulty about the emotion of the person looking on at the play being behind or ahead of the play because the landscape does not have to make acquaintance. You may have to make acquaintance with it, but it does not with you."[28] A play as a landscape provides an example of the concreteness of experience versus the imaginative, intellectual qualities of a narrative, for a landscape play has no beginning, middle, and end—it is simply there, it is continuously present.

It is in the relationship of the text to the stage production that Foreman begins to elaborate on Stein's basic theory, manifesting his own unique esthetic. Translating Stein's notion of landscape into the theatrical event, for example, does not imply the composing of a single, silent stage picture that the audience contemplates for hours at a time. On the contrary, in staging a play Foreman employs a device that Stein invented and used in her writing called "beginning again and again." This device is one means of creating a continuous present within a landscape setting. A series of beginnings can create a picture in words, or a total situation on stage, eliminating memory since a "beginning," by definition has no history—it is concrete because it is simply "there"—and a series of beginnings strung together do not go anywhere. In staging, Foreman focuses on the flow of individual "moments" or images, concentrating on the momentary intensity of each image, and placing them next to each other in a sequence. The result is the presentation of a stream or flow of concrete present moments, arrived at by beginning again and again, creating a continuous present on the stage.

Foreman's moment-to-moment writing process, like Stein's, cannot be reduced to a simple notating of a passive, meditative state. However, while complex, certain aspects of this process can be demonstrated both literally and metaphorically, as in the following passage in which Foreman answers, very specifically, the question "How do you write?"

I take naps during the day. To "clear" my mind, so that I can "begin again"—start a new day, as it were—whose writing will come from a new place. It's as if my writing were trying to define some "unseeable" object whose outline can only be traced through a one-step-removed method akin to the physicists's method of firing electrons at a particle and catching the electron's patterns of deflection on a photographic plate. So I "fire" bursts of writing at an invisible particle (a certain state of being, a certain dreamed of, intuited, level of consciousness or attention) and the writing, some of it, hits the page. But then, to avoid being dragged into the river of that "discourse which has just gotten under way" I need to move back to the firing area—I SLEEP, I NEGATE THE DRIFT of the writing burst I've just fired, its tendency to live its own life and write its own development—I wake up cleansed, and fire again.![29]

This "firing again," although a literal "beginning again," is related to esthetic meditation by virtue of the way it is achieved. Foreman stresses that he cannot make a decision to start again—he cannot will a new beginning, explaining that "Sometimes I try to—

> I think, "O.K., that scene seems good and enough of that, now I want to start from another place in such a way that the reverberations between the two will be productive. . . ," and I make the attempt to "begin again," but it never works. I have to wait for the next day, or go to sleep, or hope that I will be "distracted" and then, not willed, something else gets scribbled on the page, and, having forgotten the context of surrounding pages, the new item is the one I've been waiting for and produces the proper reverberations.[30]

This "waiting," of course, is passive. Foreman's literal approach to Stein's "beginning again and again" is a method for placing, and keeping, the consciousness in the proper passive state in order to obtain the results desired.

Once the writing has begun, the ending to each "burst of writing" takes various forms. In a passive state, Foreman describes the writing as a "documentation of the exploratory will, which 'receives' ideas, turns them over to look at them, subjects them to its very personal and idiosyncratic method of investigation, and, in so doing, EITHER receives another new idea for investigation. . . or does not."[31] He admits that, occasionally, he employs the usual active mode: "I begin a sequence 'willfully'. . . and then, if it tends to 'lose the energy' and peter out . . . that truth of process must be allowed to stay in the text. . . ."[32]

> . . . another "ending" for a unit which I frequently experience is a kind of premature closure in which I start with an impulse which I have the feeling opens a potential "world" for exploration—and then, somehow, after a few sentences or exchanges, I am already at the other side of the territory, having the feeling of "covering it in a single step": O.K.—begin again!)[33]

For Foreman, esthetic meditation generally involves alternating passive (waiting) and active (writing) states. The waiting, however, is not for inspiration, which Stein described as a kind of "blowing into you by someone else." Waiting for inspiration, as it were, is focused, centered—waiting for something in particular. For Stein and Foreman, the idea is to keep oneself unfocused, off-center so that, as Stein believed, the writer is unaware of what he knows the moment *before* writing but it flows down the writer's arm onto the page, surprising him at the moment of writing. Foreman describes the same phenomenon as a technique for maintaining a particular psychic state:

> My habit is to try to write BEFORE writing, to make the writing the preparation BEFORE writing. Pen always in hand, paper ready to catch its scribble . . . "Humm . . . I *MIGHT* write such-and-such . . ." And through that "I *MIGHT*" . . . of writing, the rest of the world of the not-written is still somehow available, and the writing . . . is a training in a certain psychic

posture of keeping all alternatives and departures from THAT moment and THAT impulse available. To "MIGHT write" is to stay in the center of where writing arises. . . . Only it's not a center . . . it's an everywhere. [34]

To sustain this state of passive "centerlessness" Foreman uses a specific, well-developed device—his reading habit. Foreman has always read philosophy, criticism, and both art and scientific theory insatiably. Just a few names on a list of hundreds would include: Henri Bergson; Kenneth Burke; Paul Dirac; Anton Ehrenzweig; Max Ernst; Buckminster Fuller; Eric Gutkind; Martin Heidegger; Edmund Husserl; Max Jacob; Carl Jung; Vasili Kandinsky; Paul Klee; Jacques Lacan; Stéphane Mallarmé; Vsevolod Meyerhold; Robert Musil; Friedrich Nietzsche; Oliver Reiser; Arnold Schönberg; Paul Valery; Simone Weil; Alfred North Whitehead; and Ludwig Wittgenstein. Reading as a part of writing is, for Foreman, a means of psychic orientation used to thwart habitual tendencies to write "out of a highly active mode of self."

> . . . my "writing-habit" of reading is to use the reading as a tuning mechanism—NOT to be tuned to what I am reading, but to keep myself "widened" and available (to what is not present). To make all the "readings"—in collaboration with what else is happening in the space where I am—keep me from being in a "center," which would deny, for the moment, the reality of things in OTHER centers. [35]

Foreman uses reading, and dozing, as techniques for invoking a passive mode that will "allow in everything that I was originally conditioned to KEEP OUT!" [36]

During each moment of writing, Foreman finds that he must consciously resist this conditioning or what he calls the "habits of early training" and "that effort sometimes bleeds onto the page on which I am writing as a little injunction or reminder to myself, and I allow that to stay in the writing (the play)." [37] In the following scene from Foreman's *Rhoda in Potatoland* (1974), one can perceive these admonitions, discoveries, assertions, and deflections as they are captured on the page in the process of, as Stein phrased it, "talking and listening" to oneself simultaneously in the act of writing:

VOICE
(As scene is shifting to grove of trees.)
Only being a tourist. Can you experience a place.

RHODA
I said go to the same place but it's different.

SOPHIA
Be Careful.

RHODA

Of?

SOPHIA
(Pause)

It's pretty isn't it.

RHODA

Yes.

SOPHIA

In ten minutes or less you'll want something different.

RHODA

Oh look.

(She points).

SOPHIA

You imagined it.

RHODA
(Pause)

I wrote it.

(Pause)

I didn't want to imagine it. I didn't want to explain it.
I just wanted to experience it.

SOPHIA

There it is.

RHODA

What.

SOPHIA

Wait.

RHODA

What.

SOPHIA

I said in ten minutes or less and it happened.

RHODA

What.

SOPHIA
(Pause)

It was there.

(Enter Agatha in woods.)

AGATHA

First it was Max here, but it was only imagined.
"Written."

AGATHA

Then it was me but I was visible.

RHODA
(Pause)

I'm going to change places.

AGATHA
(Points.)

I've had enough of you, Rhoda.

RHODA

That was me talking.[38]

It can be said that any Foreman script appearing in printed or typescript form, like the preceding scene here, is significantly different from the original version because Foreman's handwritten texts include graphic illustrations of various kinds (drawings, diagrams, sketches) that are deleted in the mediating step of "typewriting," radically altering the fullness or completeness of the initial physical object or handwritten play. Writing, for Foreman, is "INSCRIBING mind into matter," which includes "markings" of all and any kind, so that the absence of his "non-word" graphics in printed form eliminates, he explains, a "certain wideness of texture which, in the original manuscript represents for me a very special 'wideness' of mental posture."[39] The textual void created by the typewriter is filled during the process of staging through a conscious effort, he states, "to rewrite the text back into manuscript (the imprint of the personal hand) style." Hence, the staging embodies, in a highly specialized way, the idiosyncratic nature of the handwritten work (play), which is the evidence or unmediated expression of each moment of writing. Foreman states: ". . . the staging is a series of problem solving tasks which 'reconcretizes' the text. It's a matter of finding equivalencies for the densities and special 'auras' established by the graphics—typological as well as drawn—of the original manuscript."[40] The "equivalencies" Foreman invents in staging his plays demonstrate his novel, ingenious rendering of the materials of the theatre (see chapter 4).

Some of the drawings and sketches in the original manuscript indicate the "setting" he imagines or projects for the writing. Even though the writing consists primarily of dialog, his concentration is not focused on the characters who speak the lines. When he writes, Foreman thinks about the "kind of room" and the "feel of space" that the play exists in. He sees the props and other things in the room and "the activities of the body." He does not think of the characters' personalities or faces, because "I really think they are all me." The characters are shades, "like De Chirico figures with the faces wiped out," that come and go in his consciousness. In one line, a character may be a "real flesh-and-blood Rhoda, who is someone I know, saying a real thing to me" and in the next line "Rhoda may become an echo, sort of a memory in my mind, of a certain aspect of the woman."[41] Often, a line spoken by a character is actually Foreman's reaction to the line he has just written, as in this excerpt from *Vertical Mobility* (1973):

VOICE

Oh, it says what happened to Max's red feet.

RHODA

—Why am I thinking about it now.[42]

As Michael Kirby suggests, the plays can be regarded as "thought plays" or monodramas "representing the inner workings of one person's mind. . . . The characters can be seen to represent the various aspects of one person, to personify his attitudes and desires."[43] This quality is emphasized when a character refers to himself in the third person. Foreman states:

> . . . often to "shock" the writing back into alertness I will shift the grammatic "person" reference in order to angle the active-in-the-scene perspective differently. . . . Rhoda is saying things referring to herself in the normal first person, and then she will suddenly shift to self-reference in the third person. . . . this shift is not to imply something about HER psychology or aim within the scene, but is an articulating of the writing itself. . . .[44]

This "third person reference" also functions as one of many means employed to distance the viewer from the work so that he might savor it from afar rather than become involved in it as he is involved with events in life. Indeed, a certain psychic or "esthetic distance" is crucial to the elimination of syncopated emotional time in the experience of theatre art.

Like Stein, Foreman rigorously rejects "identity" or the desire to coerce, impress, persuade, or beguile the audience—no attempt is made to seduce or lure the spectator into an illusionary emotional milieu of the stage. Both artists avoid "emotional traps" or the intentional manipulation of an audience's emotional responses by eliminating the "lifelike" qualities of drama (clearly developing situations involving imaginary people in imaginary places), thereby creating a world into which the spectator has great difficulty projecting himself. (For example, the status of Foreman's characters is comparable to that of the main character in Stein's novel, *Mrs. Reynolds,* in which the reader is not privy to such basic information as the origins of Mrs. Reynolds, nor anyone else in the book.) Although many of the same characters reappear in all Foreman's plays, it is extremely difficult to identify with any of them. They function more as self-enclosed units than characters responding or reacting to climactic situations. Every effort is made to resist psychic projection on the part of the spectator by reducing the possibility of emotional involvement in terms of identification, sympathy, and empathy. As writers, Foreman and Stein do not think our thoughts for us, inducing us to believe in, think about, or feel predetermined emotions, ideas, circumstances, or relationships. Instead, we are thrown back on our own resources in an attempt to generate or awaken certain ways of perceiving and experiencing hitherto unsuspected and unexplored.

Stein was concerned with the condition in which human beings are governed by particular, irrational ways of knowing and believing. Foreman contends that this state of knowing is the result of habitual ways of perceiving, that is, the way we see things is learned—we learn to "see" or experience phenomena in whatever way makes us feel most secure.

> One always begins with the desire to write a certain kind of sentence . . . to put on stage a certain "kind" of gesture . . . The key . . . is in this sentence (gesture) cell. Most people don't see the cell, are perceptually unable to see small enough (ephemeralization). Because their LIFE training is that to "see small" means to enter the realm where contradictions are seen to be at the root of reality—and that disturbing realization they would avoid at all costs.[45]

The premise here is that man is innately a "centerless" being striving for equilibrium and harmony to the point of entropy or inertia. Unable to accept mortality, or the state of discontinuity, human nature clings to identity as a means of reassuring the self of "centerhood" in relation to the world. As Stein stated, "I am I because my little dog knows me." The "I" depends on the focus of an "other" to confirm its position in time and space—recognition (the perception or acknowledgment of something as true or valid) is sought, and recognizing, without confusion or question, is comforting.

Manipulative art, or art that imitates life as we know it, hypnotizes the viewer, reaffirming culturally conditioned ways of perceiving and responding, further subjugating the perceiving mechanism to the grooves of preestablished ideas and emotions. The audience of life-simulating art desires a recognizable content to relate to and rest in—an experience that requires a relaxed, passive, receptive mode of perception.

The art experience Foreman calls for demands an intentional, directed, active mode of perception, the beginnings of which are evident in Stein. By eliminating internal punctuation in long complicated sentences, Stein challenged the reader to participate actively in the experience of her work. She maintained that each sentence should impose itself upon the reader, forcing him to notice himself working at comprehending the whole.

> A comma by helping you along holding your coat for you and putting on your shoes keeps you from living your life as actively as you should lead it . . . a long complicated sentence

should force itself upon you, make you know yourself knowing it . . . [a comma] lets you stop and take a breath but if you want to take a breath you ought to know yourself that you want to take a breath . . . you are always taking a breath and why emphasize one breath rather than another breath.[46]

Having to be told when to "take a breath" is, for Stein, the epitome of passivity. Language, English vocabulary, is the raw material of her medium, and if we cannot even "breathe" for ourselves, how can we be expected to perceive words in any manner other than the way we have learned them? As James observed:

We ought to say a feeling of "and," a feeling of "if," a feeling of "but," and a feeling of "by," quite as readily as we say a feeling of "blue" or a feeling of "cold." Yet we do not: so inveterate has our habit become of recognizing the existence of the substantive parts alone, that language almost refuses to lend itself to any other use.[47]

Stein's objective is to erode the habitual patterns of reading by severing individual words, and events of ordinary living, from the contexts in which we customarily associate them. In so doing, she hoped to make the activity of perception present to the reader, throwing him back onto himself, startling him into a fresh awareness of his own mind. Like Stein's attempts to alter the experience of reading, Foreman's goal is to alter the "looking and listening" experience of theatre through dissociation in the "Steinean sense of letting an image arise, stopping, wiping it out, starting again."[48] It seems clear that, for both artists, some kind of mental awakening or "consciousness altering" composes the desired effect.

The description of an image as arising, being erased, and then being replaced by some new "arising," characterizes the activity of the conscious-ness. It is this activity that Foreman's texts both discuss and directly reflect: "the writing is generated in a certain way which ends up producing structures with a form and texture which is the very embodiment of the theories and goals which are the 'reasons for doing the writing.' "[49] The subject of the plays is the process of making the plays which "continues over the days and weeks and does not stop and begin for each 'play' but is a continual process."[50] While the writing is "continual," Foreman stresses that it is "NOT a continuation, but a change in direction" achieved through a deliberate form of inattention or "beginning again and again."

When asked by a publisher to produce a "comprehensible thing the public can understand," Gertrude Stein replied, "My work would have been no use to anyone if the public had understood me early and first."[51] Thirty years later, the influence of her thought is evident in the development of Richard Foreman's esthetic. Like Stein, Foreman believes the "experience" of reading and viewing his plays is more important than "understanding" them.

Although the plays provoke thought, they neither discuss "ideas" nor draw conclusions. Foreman's texts document the workings of the consciousness; they do not explain it. Foreman's plays are, as P. Adams Sitney suggests, "like rivers"—"they simply repeat their existence."[52]

3

Foreman as Scenographer: The Design and Use of the Physical Theatre

When Richard Foreman maintains that the various steps involved in creating a theatre piece (from the moment of pen-in-hand writing to opening night) are part of the writing itself, it is not an attempt to elevate the position of playwright by debasing the other roles he assumes in the process. On the contrary, the intent is to equalize the elements of theatre art by insisting that every phase of the production is an extension of the writing in a substantive sense—the production does not exist merely to complement the text. For Foreman the handwritten play, with its scribbling and sketches, is an object that is lost, as a physical object, in performance. His desire is to return the text to concrete physical reality, albeit in a different form, in the staging—the production does not "present" the text, it "embodies" the text. In such a scheme, each element and process of theatre art carries equal "weight" and shares the same significance.

It can be said, then, that Foreman is as much a set designer as he is a playwright and director. Yet his scenography has received little attention, despite the acclaim bestowed by the critics on his "visual" work. Much more attention has been paid to the scenography of Foreman's contemporary Robert Wilson—perhaps because of the grandiose spectacles Wilson some-times stages. Even Bonnie Marranca, who included a Foreman play in her anthology entitled *The Theatre of Images,* discusses some of Foreman's staging techniques in her introductory essay but virtually ignores him as designer.[1] (Presumably physical design has something to do with theatre "images.")

Another reason Foreman's design is generally overlooked may have to do with the traditional function of theatre design. Whether a stage setting is primarily functional or decorative, represents a specific place and historical period, or emphasizes a particular theme, it usually exists to serve the text in a complementary manner—it is the visual background of the staged play. As such, it cannot distract from the script nor overwhelm the action, as illustrated by the standard joke of the critic leaving a musical production "whistling the scenery." Foreman's designs neither dominate his performances, nor function merely as background. Instead, like Stein's attempts to erode habitual patterns of reading, Foreman's physical theatre is designed to assist in altering the experience of "seeing" itself.

While Foreman's use of space has changed markedly over the years from an essentially simple, static arrangement of set pieces and furniture to a highly complex system of movable scenery, the impulse behind the design and the basic approach have remained noticeably consistent. A setting designed by Richard Foreman is unmistakable—certain features and qualities in every setting are immediately recognizable.

Total Recall (Sophia = (Wisdom): Part 2) was the third Ontological-Hysteric Theatre production and the first to be photographed. An analysis of these visual documents of the production reveals the fundamentals of Foreman's design and the characteristics of his personal style. Presented at the Cinematheque on Wooster Street (December, 1970—January, 1971), *Total Recall* had more in common with traditional than experimental theatre in its design but was unlike both in overall effect. By placing plates 1 and 2 next to each other it is possible to see the full extent of stage space from left to right, as well as the position of the spectators in relation to the performing area.

Unlike much experimental theatre of the time, no attempt is made in *Total Recall* to alter the traditional audience-presentation relationship. The spectators all view the performing space from the same direction, as they would a proscenium stage production. However, there is no front curtain, no raised platform for the stage, no conventional lighting instruments, and, most notably, no attempt to mask the walls and ceiling of the building. Perhaps the most striking feature of the set for *Total Recall* is not the setting itself but its relationship to the loft space it occupies.

Clearly the play's decor was built so that the architecture of the loft would be visible. The back wall of the stage is a brick wall of the building. The arrangement of set pieces indicates two "places"—one interior and the other exterior. The interior is a perfectly rectangular area or "room" delineated, or "enclosed," by four imaginary walls. The rear wall is indicated by a "cabinet" or closet and a window placed next to each other in the same horizontal plane, parallel to the back wall of the stage. The invisible wall "fills in" the space betweeen the cabinet and window and extends to the right and left of them until it intersects the imaginary side walls defined by the doors on either end of the space, placed at right angles to the back wall and parallel to each other. While there is no proscenium arch as such, the fourth wall is suggested by two pillars that are architectural supports of the building. These two posts divide the space across its width, separating stage and auditorium areas, and thereby creating a picture plane stage arrangement. The picture plane is divided into thirds by the pillars and intersects the side walls (indicated by the doors) at right angles—the room is complete. Because the walls of the room are invisible, though clearly projected, three "places" are evident onstage simultaneously and overlap each other: (1) inside the room or "house;" (2) outside the house; and (3) the actual loft space or building that contains the setting. The ceiling and floor of the room, the "sky" and ground of the outdoors, and the ceiling and floor of the audience area are all the same—the ceiling and floor of the loft itself. Verisimilitude is not the intent—the play's space is deliberately superimposed on the architecture of the loft or given, actual place.

This superimposition of "place" in a picture plane arrangement of space is characteristic of every Foreman design and stems from his desire to force the spectator to notice that he is sitting in a theatre. During a radio interview with Michael Kirby in 1974 Foreman explained,

> If you go to a normal proscenium theatre, the emphasis is all on making you *forget* where you are and making you think that "ah" you are indeed in Greece, or wherever the play happens to be taking place. I don't want the spectators to believe for a moment or even entertain the notion that they might really be in Greece. The spectator must wake up to where he is.[2]

During the same interview Foreman explained the impulse behind another distinctive feature of his design—the use of right angles to delineate stage space:

> Being a person who had been involved in theatre all of my life, one thing that I had grown to hate was theatre scenery. Theatres are so designed that the stage space is always flared out at the sides, so that the people sitting on the sides can see the walls. I felt that that raked space was a subtle distortion of real space that the audience doesn't generally notice—it makes the space ambiguous. If there's one thing I want to do it's to clarify the space my play is taking place in so that when I put an actor in a certain position, you know just where he is in spatial relation to all the other features of the set. So I rigorously moved all those raked lines in so that everything was at right angles to the audience, so that when my actors look at each other across the stage, profile to the audience, the strength of their looking at each other would be reinforced by the right angles of the walls behind them, not made ambiguous by a wall that came in and made less than a right angle or more than a right angle.[3]

While the interior walls in *Total Recall* are not solid or tangible, they are reinforced visually by the walls, or opaque material, a few feet behind and parallel to the major set pieces: the upstage brick wall; the Cinematheque's white movie screen stage right (plate 1); and the dark rectangular material hanging stage left (plate 2).

The placement of furniture and props within the playing area emphasizes the basic design of the space. In plate 1 the position of the actors, chairs, table, rug, and radio follows strict rules of alignment and divides the depth of the stage into three horizontal planes, emphasizing the picture or proscenium plane of the fourth wall. The radio on the floor downstage left, like the cabinet and window upstage, faces the audience directly and is parallel to it. The edges of the long narrow rug behind the radio are parallel with all four sides of the space. Like the doors of the side walls, the actors face each other in strict profile to the audience. The formal relationship among visual elements is accentuated by their placement in the space.

Foreman constructed the set pieces and props for *Total Recall* himself. They have a homemade appearance not only because Foreman is not a skilled carpenter, but because he is not at all concerned with whether or not an object appears "slick" or professionally built. He states, "I want everything to look as if I myself made it."[4] His interest lies in the process of building so that when he constructs a door or bed, he wants the spectator to be able to notice how they were put together and just what decisions were made in the building process. Another factor contributing to the homemade appearance of the *Total Recall* setting is the obvious lack of concern for congruous proportion among the major set pieces—the window is considerably taller and wider than the doors, and the piece referred to as a "cabinet" (cupboard) in the script is the size of a standard clothes closet. In addition, while a stage direction states that the cabinet revolves on a "turntable" revealing a "secret panel in the back," plate 3 shows that it rests on a dolly with a rope to "pull" it around. This is not a sophisticated device and there is no attempt to conceal it.

Another identifiable feature of Foreman's scenography involves the simultaneous presentation of different versions or renderings of the same object or image. Against the brick wall, behind the cabinet (plate 1) is a flat painted to represent a three-dimensional landscape with clouds, trees, and a stream in the foreground disappearing into the hills in the background. Placed behind the window (plate 2), it suggests a "vista." Adjacent to the flat, a few feet away, is a variation of it, described as follows in a stage direction:

> (LEO in the window. Behind him a platform rolls into place, set with a small replica of a country scene as a three-dimensional backdrop-shadow box kind of affair. With realistic little trees, a river, etc. . . . [plate 4.][5]

Note that in this second version the tree is actually three-dimensional while the rest of the landscape is painted to *appear* three-dimensional. The widest point of the painted river begins at the front edge of the platform and curves or "winds" to the back edge where it meets the backdrop and continues "winding its way" up to a vanishing point in the picture. A performer standing on the platform (plate 5) is standing "in" the river—contradictory elements are fused in the image as the actor and tree become part of a two-dimensional portrayal of a three-dimensional landscape.

When the "scenic shadow box" is rolled behind the window (plate 4), two additional renderings of the image are present onstage, described in the text as:

> Two tables, like card tables. Each with a small curtained proscenium across the center of the tabletop. Like a small puppet stage. After the tables are set, . . . the crew opens the table-stage curtains revealing a shadow box behind each opening with a miniaturized built landscape.[6]

The table-stages are replicas of the "scenic shadow box" behind the window, but rendered on a smaller scale. Like their larger counterpart, each tabletop shadow box includes three-dimensional objects, placed in front of a two-dimensional representation of a three-dimensional landscape. Hence, four versions of the same landscape image are present onstage simultaneously and rendered in differing scales and dimensions: the painted flat; the large shadow box; and the two smaller tabletop shadow boxes.

The spectator may become aware of the more subtle duplications of the picture frame—the pillars of the loft frame the center of the stage; the window frames the large shadow box; the "proscenium across the center of the tabletop" frames the miniature landscapes of the table-stages. There are other possibilities. For example, if the table-stages appear as they do in plate 6 with their curtains open and shadow boxes removed, and if the cabinet appears as it does in plate 4, turned around with its "secret panel" made of curtains facing the spectators, then the curtains of the cabinet could be pulled back and the front door opened so that the cabinet becomes a frame for the landscape (flat) behind it, while the table-stage frames the cabinet, and so forth. Although this did not occur in the production, Foreman feels it is important for the spectator to understand the possibilities inherent in the design. The point is that the multiple perspectives Foreman does present imply other relationships that the spectator may entertain in the imagination. Space is divided and redivided, defined and redefined, and relationships in the space are reemphasized until space itself becomes as "plastic" as the objects, people, and activities in it.

Foreman's props and performers often seem to defy gravity as he attempts to present ordinary objects in out-of-the-ordinary positions. Tables, with the cups and saucers on top glued securely to the surface, are tilted toward the spectator, presenting an overhead view from a horizontal vantage point. In plate 6 the bed has "collapsed," according to the stage directions, and "SOPHIA gets back on the bed, slides to floor. Pause. Repeat onto bed but this time she holds herself suspended in place on the tilted mattress."[7] Foreman has stated that his use of space can be described as "cubistic" insofar as the conscious rationale behind his manipulation of space, performers, and objects is to "tilt things" or display a variety of angles and perspectives, not ordinarily perceivable from the vantage point of the audience, both sequentially and simultaneously.[8]

Finally, and perhaps most noticeably by virtue of quantity, is the lavish display of lights. In the ceiling there are three varieties of light, each with a different function. The hanging lights, with cone-shaped aluminum shades that direct the beam downwards, provide general illumination. They are bright, flat, and "spill" or overlap each other, eliminating shadows and, hence, the subtle effects of "mood lighting."

One of these lights hangs only a few feet from the floor and marks the center point, from left to right, of the space framed by the two pillars. In this position the light cannot represent the "overhead light" of the room since it would not be over the heads of the performers except when in prone or sitting positions (plates 1, 4, 5, and 6). The spectator must look "through" or past this light whenever it interferes with the line of vision to objects and activities occurring upstage of it. By interfering with the line of vision, it calls attention to itself and its position in the space. It not only functions to illuminate the space, but becomes as much a part of the setting as the major set pieces.

The two brightest ceiling lights—upstage right (plate 1) and downstage left (plate 2)—are aimed directly at the spectators. These lights are glaring— uncomfortably bright and shining in the spectator's eyes—and as such, function primarily a a means of distancing the spectator from the work. Light aimed directly at the audience from the stage is characteristic of every Foreman production and one of the many ways of identifying a Foreman design.

A careful examination of the ceiling lights reveals a small, suspended table lamp with a shade, above and downstage of the window, and partly blocked by another light in front of it. Two stage directions indicate how this lamp was used in the performance:

> A rope pulls the tablecloth off the table. . . . The lamp has been set on a wire so it remains there hanging a half inch above the tabletop.[9]

> (From above . . . a lamp is lowered to her, on a string, to the floor.)[10]

Because the lamp is lit when it is raised and lowered, it, too, calls attention to itself. After all, it could be turned off before it is raised to the ceiling, and turned on once it is lowered, but in every photograph it remains lit in its ceiling position (plates 1, 2, 4, 5, 6).

The "levitation" of the lamp to "a half inch above the tabletop" is reminiscent of the power Foreman confers on objects in all of his productions. A stage direction in *Total Recall* states: "The cabinet rear opens. SOPHIA is revealed standing inside, holding a lamp [plate 3]." A few moments later, when the cabinet opens again: "SOPHIA gone. Her lamp just hangs where she would have been holding it. Pause. It gets brighter."[11] While there is no attempt to conceal "how" the lamp manages to "hover" over the table and "stand" in the cabinet, the implication is that it is somehow animate and has a "mind of its own"—"SOPHIA lets go her lamp . . . it swings into the room and hangs there."[12]

The four pairs of light bulbs attached to each of the four set pieces (plates 1 and 2) function as: (1) focal points which, by their nature and numbers, lead the eye about the room from one to the other; (2) emphasize the rectangular shape of the objects and precise position in the space by defining their upper and outer edges; and (3) because they appear in approximately the same position, relative to each piece, the lights invite the audience to make comparisons among the set pieces (similarities in shape, differences in scale, similarities in function—all can be "walked into" or "through"). The lights atop the prosceniums on the table-stages are toy versions of life-size lamps in the production. (In plate 4, the miniature versions, stage right, are fused in one image with the "original," or life-size lamp, placed beneath them.) Their position accentuates the "framing" nature of the miniature prosceniums and, by extension, the framing nature of the other features of the design and space—the pillars, doors, window, and cabinet. In a Foreman design, the setting itself suggests alternative ways to perceive or consider it.

After *Total Recall,* before moving into the first theatre of his own, Foreman presented five more Ontological-Hysteric Theatre productions. Like the first and third pieces—*Angelface* and *Total Recall*—the fourth and sixth productions were mounted at the Cinematheque: *HċOhTiEňLâ (or) HOTEL CHINA* (December, 1971–January, 1972), and *Sophia = (Wisdom) Part 3: The Cliffs* (December, 1972–January, 1973); two were staged at Theatre for the New City: *Evidence* (April, 1972), and *Particle Theory* (April–May, 1973); and *Classical Therapy or A Week Under the Influence . . .* was presented at the Festival d'Automne in Paris (September–October, 1973).[13] The photographs of these productions show that the scenography became more complex as grant resources became available (from the National Endowment for the Arts and the New York State Council for the Arts), and Foreman continued to investigate new ways of achieving his artistic goals. Although the individual designs are distinctive, and it is easy to discern one from the other, the basic approach and principles underlying the design for *Total Recall* are evident in each subsequent piece.

Two of the major differences in the productions following *Total Recall* are the use of stage depth and the gradual narrowing of the spectator's field of vision. In general, the stage space for *Total Recall* can be described as wide and shallow—the picture plane is divided into thirds by the pillars because the setting extends beyond them. During the following four years, the tendency would be to "bring the setting in" so that it is completely contained within "proscenium arch" boundaries, and significantly decrease the distance scanned by the eye, from left to right.

The most dramatic difference between *Total Recall* and Foreman's next production, *HOTEL CHINA,* is the rearrangement of the space (plate 7). The audience faces a deeper playing area as the brick back wall of *Total Recall* becomes the stage left wall and the pillars, that divided the picture plane horizontally in *Total Recall,* appear stage right marking divisions in stage depth. Near the top of a pipe that is flush against the stage left wall, opposite the downstage right pillar, is a constructed inverted arch extending to the ceiling—this pipe and the pillar parallel to it designate the proscenium plane. The area in front of them can be considered the apron of the stage.

The back wall of the interior, or room, is comprised of a curtain and three doors (one stage right and two stage left) that face the audience directly and are parallel to it (plate 8). When the curtain is drawn open, the doors designate another proscenium plane, framing a little "stage within a stage" delineated by fabric or canvas walls that extend from doors, at an angle (like the "flared out" raked walls of traditional design), meeting another back wall (plates 9 and 10). While it appears that most of the play is performed within these two "places," the setting extends a short distance beyond the stage right pillars, defined by a slanted section of roof made of thin, trellis-like beams (plates 7 and 10), and described as a "balcony" in the text.

The space in *HOTEL CHINA* is divided not only by furniture, props and set pieces, but also through purely formal, nonfunctional, and nonrepresentational means—white boards or beams cut through the space, literally connecting performers and objects in different positions (at different points) in the space by "drawing" white lines between them. At the same time, the beams create varying angles and geometric shapes where they intersect. The stage directions indicate how these beams are incorporated into the performance, changing the "shape" of the space:

> . . . crew lowers a large white beam over the table, perhaps a foot above its surface. . . . [Later] . . . a second beam lowers. This one angled from above so it comes down into BEN's eye.) [Later] . . . They move it so it goes from his eye to a white dome which they place on a second table [plate 8]. [Later] . . . The crew comes and gives her a beam to hold. The beam is like an extension of her outstretched arms [plate 11].[14] Pause. BEN crouches so she can turn and make the beam revolve, which she does. She now stands in profile [plate 7].[15]

Most of the white ropes and strings that hang from the ceiling are functional—lights or other objects are attached to the ends of them, or they are used to raise and lower beams, lights, and other objects. Not all of the white ropes visible in the space serve such utilitarian purposes. In plate 12, much of the stage is dark; a rope runs across the width of the space (upstage of the downstage pillar) calling attention to the picture plane of the "stage within a stage" area where the scene is taking place. It also tends to divide the stage picture into top and bottom halves, purposefully emphasizing that "the house in the distance" visual effect is achieved partly because the house is at the top of the picture or the "horizon."

There are other reasons why the house appears further in the distance (or further back in the space) than it actually is: (1) the house is much smaller than life-size; and (2) the "road" (fabric) that leads to it is wider at the bottom, narrower at the top. A stage direction states that ropes are "hooked to make a line network, triangular, between two trees [the flowerlike cutouts, on each side of the fabric road, painted white and "potted" in white buckets—plates 12 and 13] and house."[16] These ropes "draw" six lines, or two triangular shapes, from the trees that converge at the vertex of the triangle at the top of the house. These limp, sagging lines stress the contrived perspective of the "road." In other words, the line (rope) that divides the picture in two, and those that connect the trees to the house, underscore the incongruities in the image. This, too, is typical of Foreman's visual work, that is, the stage picture suggests an illusionistic "little house on the horizon" image but various devices, like the ropes, are used to undermine any temptation to consider it as such, and emphasize the very means used to create the illusion of linear perspective.

A final feature of the scenography of *HOTEL CHINA* is the incorporation of words or written material into the design. This is accomplished in two ways: (1) handwritten phrases painted on movable set pieces (plate 9); and (2) typewritten sentences projected on a white, stationary screen (plate 8), placed unobtrusively near the ceiling stage left, behind (or very nearly so) the furthest back wall of the set (see chapter 4).

Compared to *HOTEL CHINA*, the white screen assumes a position of prominence in *Sophia = (Wisdom) Part 3: The Cliffs*. As Michael Kirby points out, it is the only element of the setting that is neither facing the audience directly or placed at a right angle to it—it appears "tilted forward at the top and angled across the upper corner of the space [plate 14]."[17] Kirby also notes that, "Cords loosely hanging from the four corners of the screen come together, like misplaced lines of perspective, at a point on the right wall, and a thin line stretches across the space from that point like a false horizon."[18] This line is a white string, tied around the downstage right pillar (plate 15), that remains throughout the performance. It calls attention to an important feature of this particular setting—in front of it are the posts of the picture plane, consciously constructed this time to suggest a proscenium arch.

Kirby describes two posts at each side of the stage with "thin frame arches" that "curve up from the top of the posts." He suggests that these arches "could be thought of as inner prosceniums that framed the action and divided the depth of the stage box into clearly defined planes."[19]

At the right, the effect of each arch is emphasized by a small curving railing that rises from its base and also runs parallel to the spectators; each railing is topped with a small shaded lamp. At the left, there are no railings, and the arches are incomplete, the closer one being suggested by a curving strip of wood.[20]

In contrast to *HOTEL CHINA,* this setting, for the most part, is contained within these proscenium arch boundaries. Occasionally, however, a performer can be seen to the stage right side of the arch, and Kirby mentions this indeterminate stage space, parenthetically, in describing the space behind the canvas "wall" hanging at the back (plate 14):

> Eight-foot-high boxes (or "cliffs," as they are called) slant back somewhat as they rise [plates 15 and 16]. The rear wall of cliffs is parallel to the curtain line and to the audience, but the left section, which joins it, is angled back as if in perspective. The wall on the right does not continue to the rear and allows a space for entrances and exits. Like dormer windows, five small peaked boxes (or "houses") stand at regular intervals on the left and rear cliffs. Thus . . . an exterior scene is established in addition to the interior room. (There is, however, some ambiguity about the room: On the left, behind the incomplete arches, is a wall of the same brown slanting boxes that make up the cliffs.)[21]

In *HOTEL CHINA* an entire "balcony scene" appeared to the stage right side of the pillar, but then the pillar only "seemed" to indicate the proscenium *plane* while in *Sophia* a proscenium *arch* is purposely suggested by a separate, constructed post in front of the pillar. That the setting extends beyond the arch, therefore, creates ambiguity in the stage space, that would not be as noticeable, perhaps, were it not for the rigorous attention to placement within the rest of the setting, emphasizing the picture-frame stage.

If there was any doubt about Foreman's conscious "proscenium plane" uses of space, it is dissipated by the design for *Classical Therapy,* presented in a conventional proscenium stage theatre in Paris, with fixed, numbered theatre seats in the auditorium (plate 17). The familiar white strings "draw the lines of vision," as it were, to center stage where Foreman has constructed an inner proscenium wall, with a complete proscenium arch in it, framing a smaller stage-within-a-stage, referred to as the "inner stage" in the text. At the bottom of the inner proscenium wall, on each side of the arch—emphasizing it—are two smaller arches cut out of the wall and hung with "stage curtains" (plate 18).

Additional proscenium planes are defined—the railings downstage, and on each side, of the inner proscenium opening curve up from the floor suggesting the two sides of the top of an inverted arch-shape. This relationship is repeated by a curve of the same shape in front of the edge of the stage, on either side of the ramps that extend the stage floor (plates 17 and 19). The eye can complete the top of this inverted arch, imagining the meeting of the two curved shapes under the ramps, or "through" the floor, in the case of the railings. The shape is completed in the object behind the stuffed bird (plate 17) to which the four strings are attached at precisely the points that correspond with the points where the incomplete inverted arches terminate visually. The eye can also complete the forms vertically, imagining two additional proscenium walls. The depth of the stage is divided into thirds by a constructed proscenium wall and the suggestion of two additional proscenium planes—a stage-within-a-stage-within-a-stage.

A life-size cutout of a person's body in profile (plate 20), placed in front of a larger than life-size cutout of a person's head in profile (plate 21), placed under the inner arch, points up the "cut-out of vertical space" nature of the arch. Including the proscenium opening, there are three cutouts-within-cutouts which have the same relationships as the three stages-within-stages— in this sense, certain aspects of the scenography "comment" on each other metaphorically.

Upon returning from the 1973 Festival d'Automne in Paris, Foreman rented a fourth-floor loft, further north on Wooster Street, and presented *PAIN(T)* and *Vertical Mobility (Sophia = (Wisdom): Part 4,* there in repertory. For the first time, he hired two carpenters to help build the sets and a unit of bleachers for audience seating, explaining at the time, "Now that I have a little more money, so that I'm not too exhausted when the actual rehearsal rolls around, I've been getting some help in the physical building."[22]

Typically, he placed the bleachers at one end of the new space, behind and between two pillars—architectural features of the loft. While the setting for *PAIN(T)* is contained within the visual boundaries defined by the pillars (plate 22), the stage right side of the *Vertical Mobility* setting is extremely ambiguous (plate 23). Unlike any other Foreman set, there is no definite scenic boundary stage right. The wall of the building itself is the physical boundary but there is no indication of an edge to the setting separate from it and no attempt to incorporate it, scenically, into the design (unlike the stage left walls in *HOTEL CHINA* [plate 11] and "Sophia" [plate 15], which were incorporated scenically via small lamps, painted flats, and constructed posts). Two factors seem to explain this: (1) Foreman's desire to change his style somewhat at the time; and (2) the order in which the two sets were built.

During the radio interview with Michael Kirby, Foreman talked about his set design as "up to now . . . based on a kind of flat-footed, right angle setup," adding,

> I've thought for a long time of changing, but it's difficult for me. I do tend to think in a very frontal kind of picture-frame way. . . . I am this year especially trying to change my style slightly, but I've tried in the past, and chances are it'll end up the same stuff.[23]

In plate 23, Kate Manheim (Rhoda) is being carried in on a chair. This entrance started next to the bleacher section and a couple of rows back, where she began reciting her lines, thereby drawing the spectator's attention downstage, outside of the proscenium plane. Apparently, this "breaking out" of the picture plane, along with deliberately not delineating the stage right space, was part of Foreman's attempt to "slightly" change his "flat-footed" right-angle approach and his "very frontal picture-frame" style.

With this in mind, it is interesting to note that when the rehearsals for both plays began, the *Vertical Mobility* set had already been built, while the *PAIN(T)* setting, except for a few movable set pieces, had not even been designed. Foreman originally thought that *PAIN(T)* would be staged in a very unorganized, "gym-like" atmosphere, where the spectator could see the sets for *Vertical Mobility* shoved up against the walls. He soon decided, however, that *PAIN(T)* needed a setting of its own, and it took shape during the rehearsal period.[24] Because he had not designed *PAIN(T)* ahead of time but, instead, allowed it to evolve gradually, it would seem that Foreman intuitively returned to previous tendencies. Compared to *Vertical Mobility,* the *PAIN(T)* setting sharply limits the width of the field of vision from right to left, and there is nothing ambiguous about the use of stage space. *Vertical Mobility* was not only Foreman's last attempt, to date, to change his style by not defining the outer limits of his design, but also the last piece in which the width of the stage space is greater than the depth.

The white curtains that comprise the basic setting for *Vertical Mobility* illustrate an important point related to the homemade quality of Foreman's scenography. In all of his technical work, Foreman aims for *bricolage.* The term *bricoleur* is used by Levi-Strauss to define a kind of handyman who invents in the face of specific circumstances, using whatever means and materials are available. Having purchased a large quantity of white sheet material, Foreman devised several uses for it besides the curtains for *Vertical Mobility.* Manheim wore it as a headdress that trailed on the floor (plate 23). It was used to cover performers lying on the floor, as well as pyramids, tables, and other objects throughout both plays. In *Vertical Mobility,* long draping flags, a ghost costume (plate 24), a toga, a nightgown, and a nightcap were made from it. A stage direction at the end of *PAIN(T)* reads, "Enter people under white sheets."[25] These costumes resemble Ku Klux Klan outfits (barely visible upstage center in plates 22 and 25) with tall, pointed hats and masks, all made by Foreman and from the same white material.

The *PAIN(T)* setting is noticeably different from *Vertical Mobility* and the previous designs, although many features are, of course, recognizable. The chandelier hanging stage left (plate 22) is reminiscent of the light in *Total Recall* (plate 1) hanging too low to represent an overhead fixture. The spectator must look past or "through" it (plate 26) to read words presented in two different forms simultaneously—projected on a flat and individual letters cut out of wood. The projection falls directly on the back wall of a room, painted in perspective, on the flat (plate 27). The setting itself includes a door downstage right, and the painted flat is meant to represent the room it is in. In front of the flat, Manheim stands next to a miniature painting of the painted flat, resting on an easel. The implication is that the rooms-within-rooms extend indefinitely in both directions—larger and smaller than those presented.

PAIN(T) is in the same visual style as previous productions but has a different "look" or quality from the others within that style. The stage space is divided into much smaller areas (plate 28), and within these areas the stage seems "cluttered" in that there are more strings, set pieces, and objects (plates 22 and 29). Compared to the wide, stark, empty quality of the space in *Vertical Mobility* (plates 23 and 24), the *PAIN(T)* setting is more condensed and more detailed. Also, in another apparent attempt to alter the "right angle" approach in *Vertical Mobility,* a long narrow table is repeatedly placed at a diagonal across the space (plate 30). In previous productions, long, narrow pieces were placed horizontally across the space. In *PAIN(T)* this is also true but, in addition, a railing and table are placed to emphasize depth, running downstage to upstage (plate 31). This kind of emphasis on stage depth, as well as the narrowing of stage space and increasing complexity in detail, is typical of the productions following *PAIN(T)*. Although *PAIN(T)* and *Vertical Mobility* were presented in repertory and in the same space, there are significant differences in the qualities or "look" in their designs. *Vertical Mobility* was the last part of four in the *Sophia = (Wisdom)*[26] series and the last design that can be strictly characterized as in Michael Kirby's description of *Sophia*:

> The design is simple and straightforward, but its appearance is muted and subdued. Everything seems to be carefully chosen and necessary; nothing seems hidden. . . .[27]

Stylistic homogeneity can be the result of conscious choices made by an artist applying a consistent set of principles to his design. Another possibility can be attributed to an intuitive factor, beyond or separate from intellectual planning, operating in the development of the work, and resulting in stylistic continuity. Foreman feels that in the beginning it was "all intuitive but after four or five years, when one is reasonably intelligent, one begins to look at one's work as an outside critic might."[28] In purchasing a space to house his theatre after *PAIN(T)* and *Vertical Mobility,* Foreman chose a fourth-floor loft on lower Broadway, in the Soho district, measuring approximately 30 feet by 150 feet. His choice of a space with these dimensions indicates a conscious decision to work with space in a particular way. It would seem that Foreman had decided to proceed in the direction of *PAIN(T)* rather than *Vertical Mobility.*

To date, Foreman has mounted four Ontological-Hysteric Theatre productions in this theatre: *Pandering to the Masses: A Misrepresentation*

(January-March, 1975); *Rhoda in Potatoland (Her Fall-Starts)* (December, 1975-February, 1976); *Book of Splendors: Part II (Book of Levers): Action at a Distance* (1976-1977);[29] *Blvd. de Paris (I've Got the Shakes)* (December, 1977-April, 1978). In each of these productions, the basic arrangement of space is the same. The audience seating section consists of seven rows of steeply raked bleachers (from floor level to four feet from the ceiling) placed at one end of the space facing a maximum perceivable depth of about seventy-five feet, and sixteen feet across. The playing area is always clearly defined stage left by the architectural wall of the loft, and by curtains or flats on stage right running parallel to it.

In 1977, Foreman maintained that he would never consider working with the space horizontally by placing the audience section against the long wall. Although he realizes that he could create very interesting effects by spreading the spectators out forty feet across, they would not be the *same* effects for everyone since sight lines would be radically different.[30] He is not trying to achieve a disparity of effect for different spectators sitting in different places. Instead, he controls the visual field by placing audience members close together so that he can carefully determine the various perspectives to be presented. The audience is positioned so that all spectators see essentially the same visual field at approximately, or relatively, the same angle.

The major difference in the basic design for each production is in the construction of the stage floor. Because Foreman did not employ any means of concealing the setting before *Pandering to the Masses* began, spectators immediately confronted the space (plate 32). The playing area begins at floor level, directly in front of the first row of spectators, extending fourteen feet deep at which point the stage floor begins a steep rake upstage, twenty-eight feet long and six feet high, to six feet from the ceiling, where it levels off and continues several feet back. The image of the "little house on the horizon" brings to mind the same effect in *HOTEL CHINA* (plate 12) but is achieved by means of a raked stage. The miniature house is rendered more realistically, in much more detail, and the illusion of distance is more exaggerated. The three posts on each side running upstage, parallel to the side walls, built in diminishing scale, help to alter the perspective and, at the same time, emphasize the means by which the house is made to appear further away than it is.

In *Pandering,* the raked stage was used to achieve a number of specific visual effects: (1) croquet balls were rolled down the rake; (2) clutching stuffed toy animals, Ben and Max rolled down the rake; (3) Rhoda appeared sitting on a large rock as it slowly rolled downstage from the top of the rake; and (4) on the "horizon," Rhoda, Eleanor, and Sophia slowly rocked in oversize rocking chairs placed across the top of the rake. In addition, Foreman frequently altered the volume of the playing area during *Pandering,* by placing a variety of painted flats horizontally across both the floor (plate 33) and raked floor (plate 34) at right angles to the side walls and at various distances from the spectators. Two different effects were achieved: (1) when a flat is placed downstage so the spectators cannot see the space behind it, there is a telescopic effect—the space shortened and condensed; (2) when the spectators can see the length of the space with the raked floor unobstructed, there is a reverse telescopic effect—the space is visible beyond the top of the rake and gives the appearance of extending to a vanishing point.

The division of space for *Rhoda in Potatoland* is intricately organized and much more complex. The floor is divided into seven playing areas (plate 35). Beginning directly in front of the first row of spectators, at floor level, is (1) an area three feet deep, extending to (2) a raked floor three feet high, meeting (3) a platform fourteen feet deep, to (4) another raked floor, running down to (5) an area ten feet deep, at floor level, extending to (6) a steeply raked floor, six feet high and six feet from the ceiling, meeting (7) a level platform that extends several feet back. Again, the space is divided by flats into "shallow-space" and "deep-space" settings; although this is not an entirely precise description since the amount of space visible differs from setting to setting, depending upon which of several flats are drawn across the space and how much, if any, space behind them is visible through doors, windows, and other openings. In *Pandering,* the space behind openings in the walls is usually masked, frequently by curtains (plate 33). In this way, space is hidden and revealed sequentially. In *Rhoda,* often the openings are not masked so that the walls conceal and reveal space simultaneously (plate 36).

In Paris, explaining how he uses the flats and varying heights of the floor in his New York theatre, Foreman commented, "I bring in a wall to sort of push something in the audience's face. . . . I like to make certain things seem like they're tumbling right out into the audience, and other things seem like they're running away"[31] (plates 37 and 38). Because the flats or walls are moved in and out, at varying distances from the audience, during the performance and in full view of the spectators, the "background" of a scene can change at any point, radically altering the foreground of the stage picture in relation to its background. Hence, it is possible that at one moment objects and performers can seem to be "tumbling out" of the picture and, moments later, seem to be "falling back" into the picture.

In addition to multiple playing areas at varying heights, and the diversity in the dimensions of the space hidden and revealed, the *Rhoda* scenography is distinct because of the extraordinary amount of detail within each setting. In the downstage right corner of plate 36 is a miniature version of a setting seen earlier in the performance. It is inside a tall boxlike container, shaped to resemble a proscenium arch opening. Even the dotted black-and-white string, stretched across the stage space, is included in the stage replica. The object on the floor of the miniature set is a life-size model of a potato, which has the same proportional relationship to its smaller-than-life-size surroundings, or context, that the larger-than-life-size potato in the doorway upstage right has to its life-size context. Stuck in the "head" or top of the large potato is a small, round mirror. At the same time, Max has tilted a small, round table toward the audience—the two round shapes, in different sizes, like the two potatoes, echo each other. These relationships invite comparison from the spectator, leading the eye in a triangular pattern as it travels, in any order, between the three points—small potato, large potato/mirror, table. There is another miniature image-within-an-image in this set. Three swinging barroom-type doors are painted near the top of the painted back wall that supports the two swinging doors of the set—it is a painting of itself.

Details like this abound throughout the production. Above the stage right door of the painted flat in plate 39 is a miniature painting of the door, window, and stripes of the flat itself. Above that, placed across the top of the flat, at regular intervals, are a series of miniature Renaissance perspective paintings, indicative of one of the many ways Foreman manipulates his deep stage space to play with perceptions of proportion, scale, and perspective. When the space is cleared of major set pieces, the eye travels up the steeply raked ramp in the rear (plate 40) to the "horizon" of linear perspective. The vertical stripes painted on the side walls accentuate perspective since they gradually become shorter as the rake climbs higher. Foreman places objects and performers within this space to create multiple perspectives that destroy, rather than enhance, the illusion of linear perspective.

In plate 40, a toy miniature of a massive galleon appears near the top of the raked stage. Considered by itself, it might represent a boat in the sea, on the horizon in the distance. Behind it, however, rocking slowly back and forth, is a shoe—enormous (by comparison), two-dimensional, and rendered partly as a cutout and partly as a painting. Curtains frame the shoe on either side "blowing gently in the breeze" generated by two hidden fans. Any semblance of perspective is thwarted by the proportion of the objects relative to each other in position and distance, as well as the nature of the objects. Instead, the image invites comparison among its elements: a line from the text suggests that boats and shoes are "both elements of a journey;" the rounded shape of the bottom of a shoe is like the shape of the bottom of a boat; the shoe is rocking the way a boat rocks in the water; the curtains "blowing in the breeze" are reminiscent of the sails of a boat; the wind that propels the sails is like the "wind" the performer in the foreground uses to blow the horn.

In plate 41, the entire rear rake is transformed into an enormous face or head. Note that in this playing area the floor is not the same color as the rest of the floor but, rather, the same brown color as the large and small objects that represent potatoes. While the head is onstage, a line from the text states:

"In time, they grow much bigger
In America they grow much bigger
. . . ."32

but is is not clear "what" grows bigger—presumably, potatoes. Perhaps the huge face is like the child's game "Mr. Potatohead," in which various things are stuck into a potato to represent eyes, ears, nose, and mouth of a face, in much the same manner as a face is created on a snowman. In any case, it seems the face has some connection with potatoes and "potatoland." The design is not mere background for the text—it assumes an "active" role in the production in that it suggests alternative ways to consider visual material and its relationship to the text, as well as to other elements of the scenography.

Foreman always thinks in terms of creating a series of spaces within spaces, but the design for *Book of Splendors* is exceptionally complex in this regard (plate 42). Stationary and movable scenery is used to define simultaneously several smaller localized areas within a larger area. The fixed scenic structures that divide the space include: two ramps; three constructed pillars that divide the rear ramp, lengthwise, down the middle; a raised runway along the stage left wall, accessible by steps in the front and rear; and three railings, about three feet tall, placed horizontally across the space creating narrow alleyways. The performers not only moved through these downstage aisles, but climbed over the railings and stood, walked, or danced on top of them.

There is nothing avant-garde about Foreman's scenic constructions in themselves. As the engraving of the Mnemonic Theatre (from 1619) that appears as part of his poster and program designs (plate 43) suggests, Foreman's devices are adapted from seventeenth-century scenic conventions. What *is* innovative is the way he uses these old techniques for specific effects.

The three sliding walls used to alter the volume of the space (plate 42), like those in *Pandering* and *Rhoda* are reminiscent of the seventeenth-century wing-and-groove system in that they consist of two or three panels or painted flats that slide on- and offstage via tracks or grooves, and are always changed manually in full view of the audience. Unlike the two upstage walls and those in previous productions, the downstage wall cuts through the space on a sharp diagonal. A massive step unit rolls on casters across the stage and fills the space horizontally. When performers sat in two chairs at a small table on the top step, their heads almost touched the ceiling (plate 44). This step unit seemed to reflect or mirror the tiered audience seating and, indeed, the heads of the spectators in the last row also nearly touch the ceiling. Because the unit was only about twenty feet from the audience, the effect was one of a rather cramped, claustrophobic space. Other movable set pieces also functioned to define smaller areas, including: (1) a tent; (2) a Plexiglas box, that slid onstage via grooves in the floor, containing, at one point, a naked male performer pressing against its downstage side (plate 45); (3) a cagelike box, with a peaked roof, made of window-screen material, in which a performer appeared, fanning himself while striking a haughty pose (plate 46); and (4) the wooden frame of a boxlike structure, with Plexiglas sides and a canopied top, that became the body of a car when Manheim, donning a driving coat and cap, goggles, and a scarf, stepped inside it and "drove" it (holding a steering wheel attached to a stick with a caster at the end on the floor) down the full length of the runway (plate 47).

Foreman maintains that after he asks himself, "How can I make the space be the most efficient and exciting resonator for the particular kind of 'music' which is the produced play?" he then builds the set to be a "machine" that will serve the piece.[33] With the number of set pieces and flats moving on- and offstage, in different directions, during the performance, the *effect* is often one of a "machine" operating with its many moving parts.

There are other kinds of movement related to Foreman's scenography. In *Book of Splendors,* for example, a bizarre image of a man "leaning out the window" was achieved by a simple device for movement. As an actress repeated variations on the line, "He leaned out of the window at a certain angle," a man visible from the waist up, facing full front, appeared and disappeared from behind the stage right wall, tilting sideways back and forth at a forty-five degree angle to the floor—clearly he was not bending any part of his body (plate 48). The actor stood on a narrow platform—his back supported by a vertical board—that tilted sideways on a pivot operated manually offstage.

Foreman also works with optical illusions, related to movement, achieved with vertical stripes painted in a monochromatic color scheme. The entire step unit is painted in stripes, alternating three shades of brown— cream, brown, and dark brown. At one point the unit began to appear onstage, revealing Manheim, in profile, on one of the steps. She was facing in the direction the unit was rolling but walked a couple of steps backwards and then turned and continued walking forward (plate 49). Although the image was brightly lit, the combination of the stripes moving in one direction and Manheim walking in the opposite direction, produced an extremely ambiguous sensation of the direction of movement, forcing the spectator to concentrate in order to determine what was actually occurring.

A similar effect was achieved with the diagonal wall, which was painted in the same pattern of brown vertical stripes (plate 50). Manheim, standing near its exiting point as the wall began to move diagonally downstage and off, exclaimed, "It's the room coming towards me." The effect was a momentary sensation of the room closing in on her. This optical phenomenon is based on quantity—simple movement becomes complex as the eye scans numerous stripes, rather than focusing on a single object. The illusion is further enhanced by the alternating intensities of color.

In his new space, Foreman continued to work exclusively in white light (floodlights and PARs) but used the four or so lights aimed directly at the spectators to create particular effects. For instance, in *Book of Splendors,* as somewhat eerie music could be heard, the lights in the back of the space dimmed while those aimed at the audience became brighter. What appeared to be large, hulking, mysterious creatures could be discerned slowly lumbering down the rear ramp. Although a general shape and very peculiar movement could be perceived, it was not until the rear lights began to come up and the front lights dimmed that it was possible to see performers holding large, open umbrellas in front of their faces with square decorator pillows strapped to their ankles (plate 51).

One of the distinguishing features of Foreman's scenography since *PAIN(T)* is the increasing amount of, and attention to, detail. Foreman explains that a great deal of his effort in mounting his plays is "directed toward things that, if they weren't there, a large part of my audience wouldn't notice the difference."[34] Foreman, however, often does not make it easy for the audience to notice the results of his labor. For example, during a sequence in *Book of Splendors,* music played loudly while two pairs of men clasped hands "arm wrestle" style and, furiously pushing and pulling each other back and forth, danced atop the railings. At the same time, at the top of the large step unit behind them were two small doors that performers opened for a moment to reveal colorful, grotesque face masks inside little cabinets painted gold (plate 52). When the activity of opening the doors was repeated, again for just a moment, three women, naked from the waist up, were grouped to one side (plate 53). Hence, it would not be difficult to miss this small but striking image because of the vigorous movement, loud music, and seminude women. Of course, Foreman could focus the audience's attention differently, but he assumes that the spectator is continuously scanning the visual field subliminally, and it is this kind of "wide-angled" vision that he is aiming for. He does not want the eye to become fixed on one point to the exclusion of others.

Although his methods have changed over the years, Foreman's concern with a particular kind of attention spans all of his work. He distinguishes between two modes of vision: (1) focused, "you can imagine two eyes looking out and focusing on a point;" and (2) "a kind of relaxed, passive vision—the cliche might be the artist stepping back from his canvas and sort of letting his spirit go blank, as it were."[35] In 1972, after *Total Recall,* during a discussion led by Stephen Koch with Post-Modern dancers and Foreman, Yvonne Rainer spoke of the spectator having to make a choice between "two very different things in the same space." To which Foreman asked, "But were you always interested in people making that choice? Couldn't they change their mode of attention so that the conflicting events could be held simultaneously in a kind of meditative, nondirected attention?"[36] This nondirected, or "wide-angled," kind of attention is not bound to the narrow limits, or focus, needed to function in the everyday world. Foreman explains:

> I realize that most of my audience will choose at each moment to watch a particular portion of the total stage-event. But that is the opposite of what I hope for—I wish the audience would learn to see differently, to float at all times in front of the total field of the stage. The small adjustments of gesture, light, word, et cetera, that occur moment to moment—those should slightly redefine the field as a whole rather than cause attention to dart about from event to event.[37]

Foreman works monochromatically in color as one means to achieve this.

Until *Rhoda,* when he used three shades of light green for some of the stripes, and with the exception of *Vertical Mobility,* the dominant color of all the elements (stage floor, props, set pieces, curtains) in all Foreman's pieces was a deep but flat brown accented by white and a subdued gold. Foreman feels that a monochromatic color scheme promotes the meditative, unfocused kind of attention he is aiming for.

Decoration is another means Foreman employs to attain this goal, the beginnings of which are evident in *Total Recall.* There are artificial flowers, all painted brown, attached to the floor pole under the bare bulb (plate 2). This same decoration appears at the top, on either side, of the window. In *Sophia,* the stage left wall is covered with artificial flowers on a trellis and flowers appear by the small, shaded lamps right and left (plate 15). Flowers decorate a house stage right in *Classical Therapy* and climb two posts where they are visible across part of the "ceiling" (plate 17). The openings in the back wall of *Pandering* are adorned with flowers, as well as the post downstage right (plate 33). Foreman embellishes his design with ornaments to soften the "single-mindedness" of a piece of the set, props, walls, he explains, "to make everything bleed into, or suggest, other related things—rather than just having signs or statements, the whole thing is more fluid and open to alternate readings."[38] In plate 2, the spectator might notice that the window and light pole are similarly decorated and ponder the implications. If the light pole with its branches were placed in the window, would it suggest a tree? Does it echo the tree visible behind it? Often decoration, mostly artificial flowers, is barely visible since once it is attached to props and scenery, it is painted over, in the same color, blending into the piece. Hence, instead of calling attention to itself, the ornamentation bleeds into that which it adorns, suggesting the "wide-angled" kind of vision Foreman is concerned with.

The "attention" or vision Foreman strives for is, of course, not merely visual but also aural and, generally, a state of mind or being while looking, listening, and thinking. Taking the visual aspect and examining it alone, however, *Blvd. de Paris* incorporated the most elaborate scheme for bleeding or blending elements of the performance into each other.

The stage floor is flat, eliminating the structures (ramps, platforms, runways) that divided the space vertically in previous productions. While in *Book of Splendors* many of the movable pieces are transparent (Plexiglas, screen), the step unit and walls are opaque—they completely block the view to the space behind them. In *Blvd. de Paris,* with one or two exceptions, everything is either transparent or includes windows and other openings that it is possible to see, walk, or crawl through. Three of the four sliding walls that divide the space horizontally are made of white, see-through, gauzelike material providing differing degrees of visibility through them depending on how many are present onstage simultaneously (plate 54). The major set piece, an old-fashioned train compartment, includes several windows and two doors that, at one point, open wide revealing the interior (plate 55).

The dominant color is black, interrupted by an occasional set piece painted white. In this context, the recurrence of "splotches" of color became a dynamic visual motif. For example, a bright red was the color of a few props—a vinyl shopping bag; two sets of boxing gloves; a long, narrow carpet; and a hood with horns worn by a performer representing a devil. The spectator might become acutely aware of this color and its repetition.

Feathers, artificial flowers, and fringe are omnipresent, decorating nearly everything in the space. The same long feathers, for instance, not only appear on set pieces, but in a hat worn by one of the performers. Manheim wears a long, black dress with a small, colored, flower print in the fabric. This same fabric is draped across sections of the ceiling and along the stage left wall. It appeared in numerous places—as the jacket cover of a book in one scene, and in another, the dress worn by a female figure in a large, cubist-style painting painted to match the fabric in Manheim's dress. The curtains in the train compartment are also made from it. By simplifying certain aspects of the overall design of the space, Foreman was able to intensify variations on a limited number of visual motifs.

For each of the productions mounted in this space, Foreman employed three people for two-and-a-half months to build the sets and props. The cost for materials varied from $8,000 to $10,000 for each production—this figure does not include labor.

Foreman has written extensively on his theory, esthetic, and writing but has never attempted to analyze his scenography systematically, explaining, "It's my medium so I've never had the compunction to justify or explain or even figure out for myself what I'm doing visually."[39] It is indeed his medium; after all, he began his career in the theatre as a teenage set designer. Of those years, when he functioned solely as a designer in the process of making theatre, Foreman recalls, "I had the feeling I was controlling the whole piece, because I was creating the world through which you perceived things happening."[40] The key to Foreman's work in the last decade resides in the novel relationship of text and performer to a given architectural space and the milieu he constructs. This relationship, however, is linked intrinsically to the unique staging techniques that Foreman has developed, and these must be considered for a complete picture of Foreman's scenography.

Plate 1. *Total Recall (Sophia=(Wisdom): Part 2),* New York, 1970-71.
(Copyright © 1970 Babette·Mangolte, all rights of
reproduction reserved.)

Plate 2. *Total Recall (Sophia=(Wisdom): Part 2)*, New York, 1970-71.
(Copyright © 1970 Babette Mangolte, all rights of
reproduction reserved.)

Plate 3. *Total Recall (Sophia=(Wisdom): Part 2)*, New York, 1970-71.
(Copyright © 1970 Babette Mangolte, all rights of
reproduction reserved.)

Plate 4. *Total Recall (Sophia=(Wisdom): Part 2)*, New York, 1970-71.
(Copyright © 1970 Babette Mangolte, all rights of
reproduction reserved.)

Plate 5. *Total Recall (Sophia=(Wisdom): Part 2)*, New York, 1970-71.
(Copyright © 1970 Babette Mangolte, all rights of
reproduction reserved.)

Plate 6. *Total Recall (Sophia=(Wisdom): Part 2),* New York, 1970-71.
(Copyright © 1970 Babette Mangolte, all rights of
reproduction reserved.)

Plate 7. *HċOhTiEnLà (or HOTEL CHINA,* New York, 1971-72.
(Copyright © 1971 Babette Mangolte, all rights of
reproduction reserved.)

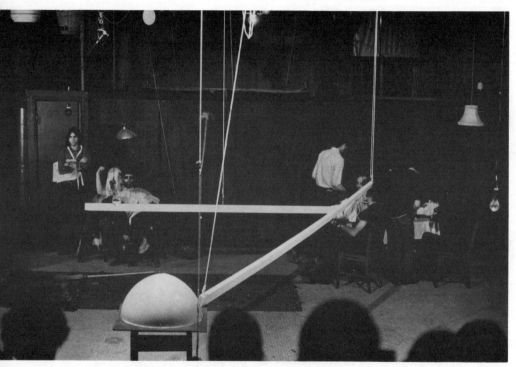

Plate 8. *HċOhTiEḣLà (or) HOTEL CHINA* New York, 1971-72.

Plate 9. *HċOhTiEnLå (or) HOTEL CHINA,* New York, 1971-72.
(Copyright © 1971 Babette Mangolte, all rights of
reproduction reserved.)

Plate 10. *HĊOhTiEṅLà (or) HOTEL CHINA,* New York, 1971-72.

Plate 11. *HċOhTiEṅLà (or) HOTEL CHINA,* New York, 1971-72.
(Copyright © 1971 Babette Mangolte, all rights of
reproduction reserved.)

Plate 12. *HċOhTiEṅLà (or) HOTEL CHINA,* New York, 1971-72.

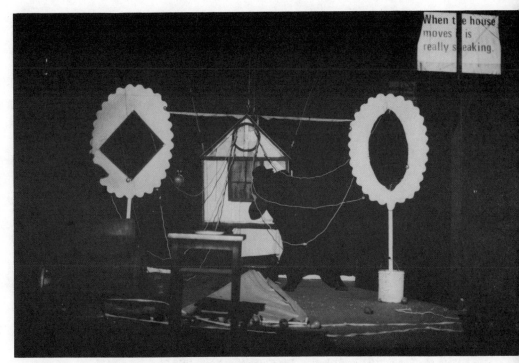

Plate 13. *HċOhTiEňLà (or) HOTEL CHINA*, New York, 1971-72.
(Copyright © 1971 Babette Mangolte, all rights of
reproduction reserved.)

Plate 14. *Sophia=(Wisdom) Part 3: The Cliffs,* New York, 1972-73.
(Copyright © 1972 Babette Mangolte, all rights of
reproduction reserved.)

Plate 15. *Sophia=(Wisdom) Part 3: The Cliffs,* New York, 1972-73.
(Copyright © 1972 Babette Mangolte, all rights of
reproduction reserved.)

Plate 16. *Sophia=(Wisdom) Part 3: The Cliffs,* New York, 1972-73.

Plate 17. *Classical Therapy or A Week Under the Influence,* Paris, 1973.
(Copyright © 1973 Babette Mangolte, all rights of
reproduction reserved.)

Plate 18. *Classical Therapy or A Week Under the Influence,* Paris, 1973.

Plate 19. *Classical Therapy or A Week Under the Influence,* Paris, 1973.
(Copyright © 1973 Babette Mangolte, all rights of
reproduction reserved.)

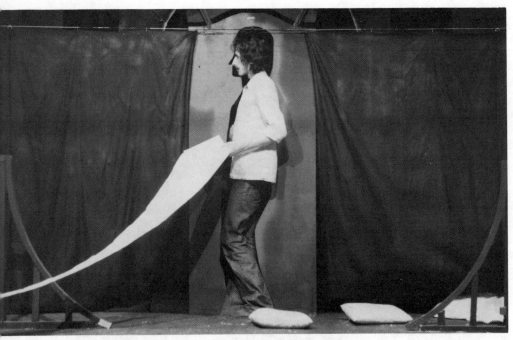

Plate 20. *Classical Therapy or A Week Under the Influence,* Paris, 1973.

Plate 21. *Classical Therapy or A Week Under the Influence,* Paris, 1973.
(Copyright © 1973 Babette Mangolte, all rights of

Plate 22. *PAIN(T),* New York, 1974.

Plate 23. *Vertical Mobility (Sophia=Wisdom): Part 4),* New York, 1974.

Plate 24. *Vertical Mobility (Sophia=Wisdom): Part 4),* New York, 1974.

Plate 25. *PAIN(T)*, New York, 1974.

Plate 26. *PAIN(T)*, New York, 1974.

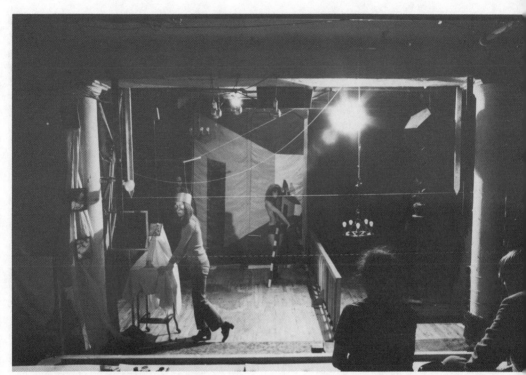

Plate 27. *PAIN(T),* New York, 1974.

Plate 28. *PAIN(T),* New York, 1974.

Plate 29. *PAIN(T)*, New York, 1974.

Plate 30. *Vertical Mobility (Sophia=(Wisdom): Part 4),* New York, 1974.

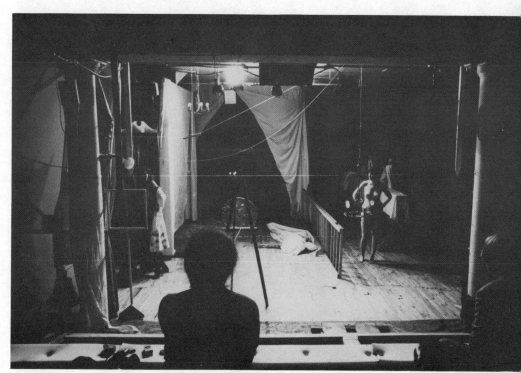

Plate 31. *PAIN(T),* New York, 1974.

Plate 32. *Pandering to the Masses: A Misrepresentation,* New
York, 1975.

Plate 33. *Pandering to the Masses: A Misrepresentation,* New
York, 1975.

Plate 34. *Pandering to the Masses: A Misrepresentation*, New
York, 1975.

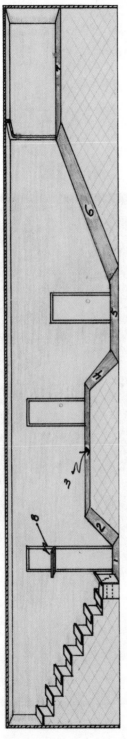

Plate 35.   Sketch of setting and auditorium (side view) for *Rhoda in Potatoland (Her Fall-Starts)*, 1975-76.

Plate 36. *Rhoda in Potatoland (Her Fall-Starts),* New York, 1975-76.

Plate 37. *Rhoda in Potatoland (Her Fall-Starts),* New York, 1975-76.

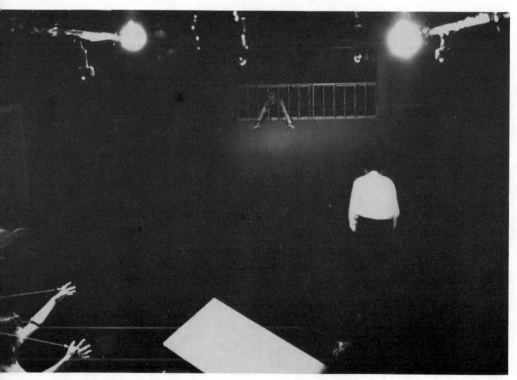

Plate 38. *Rhoda in Potatoland (Her Fall-Starts),* New York, 1975-76.

Plate 39. *Rhoda in Potatoland (Her Fall-Starts),* New York, 1975-76.

Plate 40. *Rhoda in Potatoland (Her Fall-Starts),* New York, 1975-76.

Plate 41. *Rhoda in Potatoland (Her Fall-Starts),* New York, 1975-76.

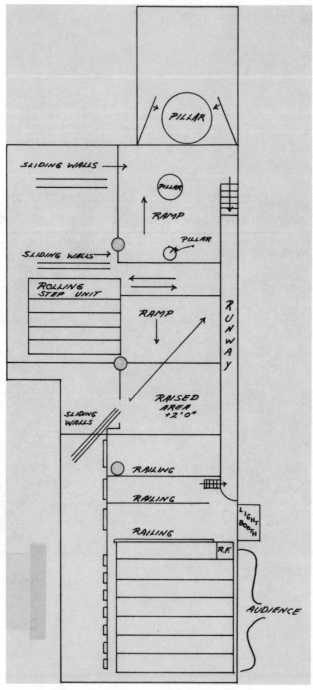

Plate 42. Sketch for setting and auditorium (floor plan) for *Book of Splendors: Part 2 (Book of Levers): Action at a Distance,* 1976-77.

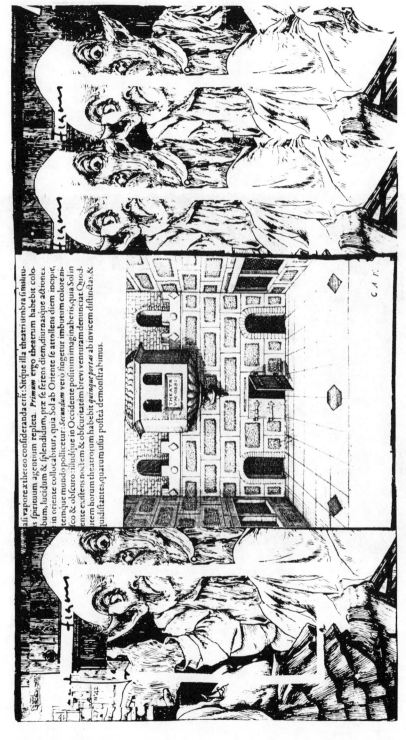

Plate 43. Program logo for *HOTEL CHINA*, including the Mnemonic Theatre.

Plate 44. *Book of Splendors: Part 2 (Book of Levers): Action at a Distance,* New York, 1976-77.

Plate 45.   *Book of Splendors: Part 2 (Book of Levers): Action at a Distance,* New York, 1976-77.

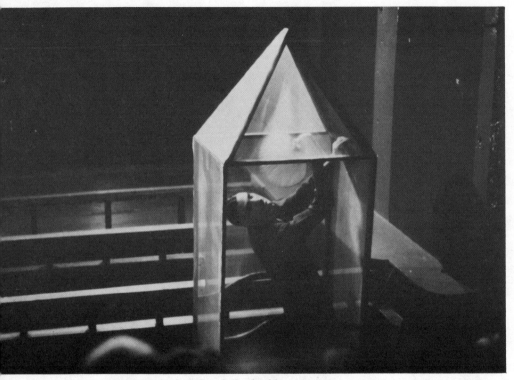

Plate 46. *Book of Splendors: Part 2 (Book of Levers): Action at a
Distance*, New York, 1976-77.

Plate 47. *Book of Splendors: Part 2 (Book of Levers): Action at a Distance,* New York, 1976-77.

Plate 48. *Book of Splendors: Part 2 (Book of Levers): Action at a Distance,* New York, 1976-77.

Plate 49. *Book of Splendors: Part 2 (Book of Levers): Action at a Distance*, New York, 1976-77.

Plate 50. *Book of Splendors: Part 2 (Book of Levers): Action at a Distance,* New York, 1976-77.

Plate 51. *Book of Splendors: Part 2 (Book of Levers): Action at a Distance,* New York, 1976-77.

Plate 52. *Book of Splendors: Part 2 (Book of Levers): Action at a Distance,* New York, 1976-77.

Plate 53. *Book of Splendors: Part 2 (Book of Levers): Action at a Distance,* New York, 1976-77.

Plate 54. *Blvd. de Paris (I've Got the Shakes),* New York, 1977-78.

Plate 55. *Blvd. de Paris (I've Got the Shakes),* New York, 1977-78.

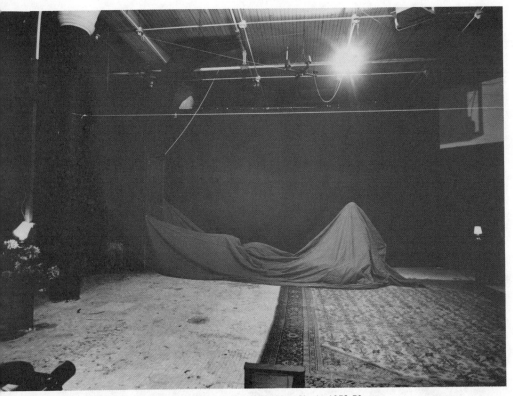

Plate 56. *Sophia=(Wisdom) Part 3: The Cliffs,* New York, 1972-73. (Photo © 1973 by Peter Moore.)

Plate 57. *Sophia=(Wisdom) Part 3: The Cliffs,* New York, 1972-73.
(Photo © 1973 by Peter Moore.)

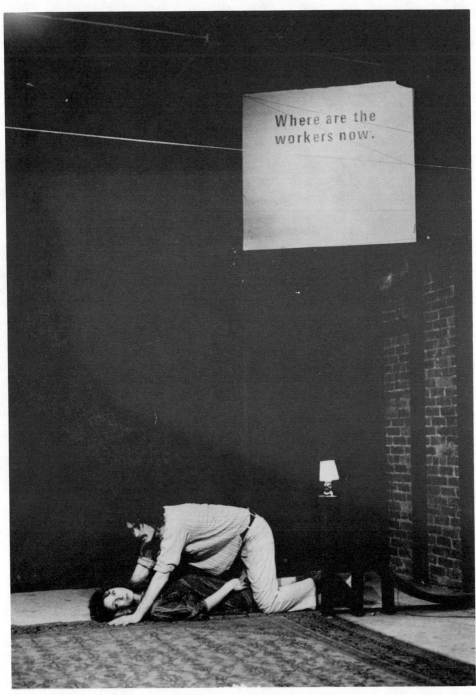

Plate 58. *Sophia=(Wisdom) Part 3: The Cliffs,* New York, 1972-73.
(Photo © 1972 by Peter Moore.)

Plate 59. *Sophia=(Wisdom) Part 3: The Cliffs,* New York, 1972-73.
(Copyright © 1972 Babette Mangolte, all rights of
reproduction reserved.)

Plate 60. *Sophia=(Wisdom) Part 3: The Cliffs*, New York, 1972-73.

Plate 61. *Classical Therapy or A Week Under the Influence,* Paris, 1973.
(Copyright © 1973 Babette Mangolte, all rights of
reproduction reserved.)

Plate 62. *Classical Therapy or A Week Under the Influence,* Paris, 1973.

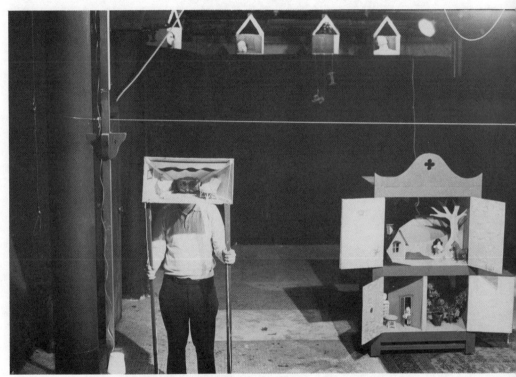

Plate 63. *Sophia=(Wisdom) Part 3: The Cliffs,* New York, 1972-73.
(Copyright © 1972 Babette Mangolte, all rights of
reproduction reserved.)

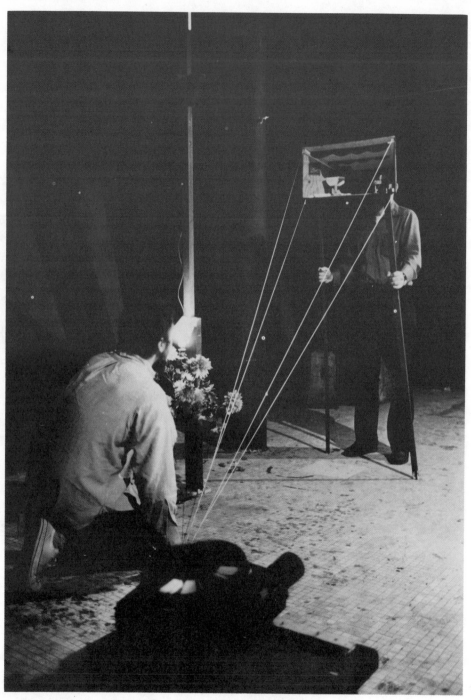

Plate 64. *Sophia=(Wisdom) Part 3: The Cliffs,* New York, 1972-73.
(Photo © 1973 Peter Moore.)

Plate 65. *Sophia=(Wisdom) Part 3: The Cliffs,* New York, 1972-73.
(Copyright © 1972 Babette Mangolte, all rights of
reproduction reserved.)

Plate 66. *Classical Therapy or A Week Under the Influence,* Paris, 1973.
(Copyright © 1973 Babette Mangolte, all rights of
reproduction reserved.)

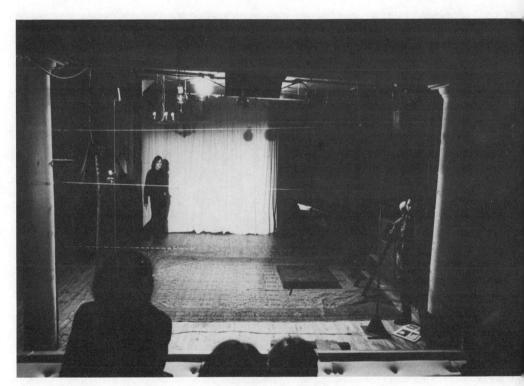

Plate 67. *Vertical Mobility (Sophia=Wisdom): Part 4),* New York, 1974.

Plate 68. *Sophia=(Wisdom) Part 3: The Cliffs,* New York, 1972-73.

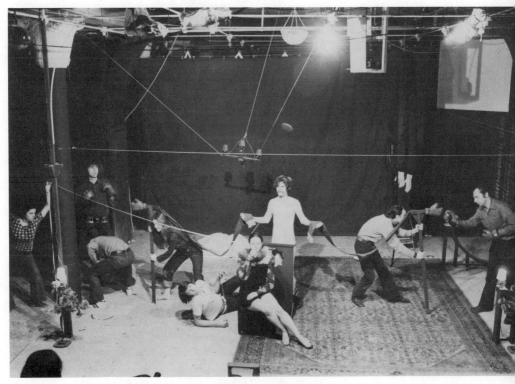

Plate 69. *Sophia=(Wisdom) Part 3: The Cliffs,* New York, 1972-73.
(Copyright © 1972 Babette Mangolte, all rights of
reproduction reserved.)

Plate 70. *Sophia=(Wisdom) Part 3: The Cliffs,* New York, 1972-73.
(Copyright © 1972 Babette Mangolte, all rights of
reproduction reserved.)

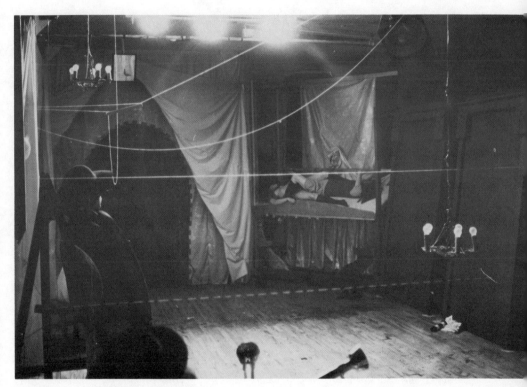
Plate 71. *PAIN(T),* New York, 1974.

Plate 72. *Vertical Mobility (Sophia=Wisdom): Part 4),* New York, 1974.

Plate 73. *Rhoda in Potatoland (Her Fall-Starts),* New York, 1975-76.

Plate 74. *Vertical Mobility (Sophia=Wisdom): Part 4)*, New York, 1974.

Plate 75. *Sophia=(Wisdom) Part 3: The Cliffs,* New York, 1972-73.
(Photo © 1973 Peter Moore.)

Plate 76. *Sophia=(Wisdom) Part 3: The Cliffs*, New York, 1972-73.

Plate 77. *Rhoda in Potatoland (Her Fall-Starts),* New York, 1975-76.

Plate 78. *Sophia=(Wisdom) Part 3: The Cliffs,* New York, 1972-73.

4

Foreman as Inventor: The Development
and Use of Staging Techniques

Before analyzing the unique methods Foreman has developed for staging his plays, it is important to have some understanding of what his performances look and sound like as perceived moment-to-moment. In the newspaper reviews that comprise the earliest accounts of Foreman's productions, the descriptions of his performances are somewhat misleading. Writing on *HOTEL CHINA* for *The Village Voice* in early 1972, Arthur Sainer describes the performance as follows:

> What are the events? Someone is in a room. An event. Someone is not in a room. Another event. A buzzer sounds. A third event. Someone falls through a doorway, dropping a platter of dinnerware, someone is covered with a newspaper, only his lit pipe continues smoking through the hole in the paper, someone puts both feet in buckets, someone is being hit by pebbles, someone is not being hit by pebbles, a rock is moved, someone peers halfway through a half-opened door, someone collapses on the ground, someone's teeth are connected to strings which are connected to the ceiling of the theatre, a rock is not moved, someone continues peering halfway through a half-opened door, someone is sweeping up pebbles, someone's feet in buckets are being dragged along the room, a buzzer is sounding, something is heard to crash, a rock is seen on film, in color, a rock is moved, a house is rocked, voices are heard on tape. . . .[1]

While this brief rendition of the "events" is intriguing, it is difficult to imagine precisely *how* they were staged. What kind of mental image is conjured up by a statement like "someone's feet in buckets are being dragged along the room?" Later in the same year, and for the same publication, Michael Smith described *Evidence:*

> Often it is almost a play. Max is at home alone, trying in a very spaced-out fashion to write a play. This is the play he is writing. Ben comes over, is thrown in through the window. They refer to Rhoda. The speeches are broken up, dialogue all but obliterated. Slow. Incongruities, Metronomes, a blinking light, a drum, a buzzer, quacks to set off time. A beautiful woman downstage petrified, pointing. Later a picture falls off the wall and engulfs Ben. Objects are shown to the audience. Music. . . . Long looks at the audience. More cords. Lamps. Tilting tables. Cigars. Cardboard boats. Meticulous craft, no illusion.[2]

Like Sainer, Smith tries to indicate "what happened" in the performance but, because of the space limitations inherent in newspaper publishing, the result is a rather disconnected, incomplete "list" of images, props, characters, and the elements and qualities of Foreman's style and staging techniques.

In an attempt to indicate both what "happens" in a Foreman production and the structural continuity of a production through time, Michael Kirby described, in detail, the two opening scenes and part of the third scene from *Sophia = (Wisdom) Part 3: The Cliffs.*

Sophia begins:

A buzzer sounds. A man walks into the playing area and sits in the chair, center. His head propped on his right hand, he gazes steadily toward the audience. He does not move.

At the left, in the same plane as the seated man, the door opens. It swings toward the spectators, concealing the person who has opened it. Part of the entering man's head appears as he stops and remains motionless. He, too, is facing the audience; his hand is on the edge of the door. Neither of the men move.

The door closes. The man who appeared to be entering has gone away without being seen completely. The seated man rises, turns, and stands looking at the door. He walks to it and stops. He passes both hands over the surface of the door without touching it; only his hands and arms move. He presses his body against the door, his head turned to one side, his eyes closed, his arms extended along the flat surface. He is motionless.

Speaking carefully and distinctly, a man's recorded voice says: "Not yet." The lights go out.

When the lights come on, the man is again motionless in the chair. Now he is sitting up straight, his hands on his knees. Relaxed ragtime jazz is heard; it is not very loud. Three people pull a large brown canvas in through the door and lift it over the man, covering him completely. Then they pull part of the canvas to the open door and attach it to the door frame at either side. They leave. The canvas hangs around the open doorway and extends to cover the motionless man in the center of the stage.

Now there is movement. It is apparent that someone has crawled unseen through the doorway and is moving under the canvas. Another indistinct figure and then another are crawling under the heavy cloth. Then the canvas is motionless. It forms a brown mass that rises into hills in several places. Nothing moves for quite a while. The music fades [plate 56].

Again, the recorded voice is heard: "Not yet." The lights go out.

A metronome above the playing area begins ticking in the dark. The lights come on. The canvas is still there, rising in its irregular mounds. Two people carry in pieces of furniture— an old wicker armchair painted white and a small brown table—and place them so that their rear legs are on the front edge of the canvas. The two people leave.

Carefully, without moving the chair and table, the performers who have been huddled under the canvas emerge. They gather up the canvas and exit with it, leaving the furniture in position and the man still seated in the center.

Slides are projected on the screen above the playing area at the right rear. They read:

IMAGINE THE CLOTH
SLOWLY DESCENDING OVER EVERYTHING

IT WILL NOT ACTUALLY HAPPEN, SO YOU
SHOULD IMAGINE IT IF YOU LIKE.

ASSERTION.

THERE IS NOTHING ELSE INTERESTING.
ONLY ASSERTION IS INTERESTING.

A tall, narrow, white screen is wheeled on and placed to the left of the seated man, who now has his head propped in his left hand and is still gazing steadily toward the audience. A printed message similar to the first is projected on the screen. It reads:

ONLY ASSERTION IS INTERESTING. THE
DANGER IS:
TRYING TO MAKE AN ASSERTION
DECORATED.
DO NOT FALL PREY TO THAT DANGER.
THINK OF AN ASSERTION.

When the slides go off, the wheeled screen is moved out of sight. A buzzer is heard. Again, the door opens. The voice on the tape says: "Not yet."
A different man's voice can be heard from the loudspeaker. During the speech, the seated man repeats several of the words quietly. The voices are the same. The recorded voice says:

Two simultaneous assertions, notice. (The performer says, "simultaneous.")
Now that painting ("Now" "that") is no longer interesting, perhaps
something else ("something") will be interesting in the same way.

A slide appears on the raised screen: "Painting a wall is still interesting."
The first voice heard from the loudspeakers says: "People are more interesting than props: Do you agree with that statement?"[3]

Most of the performance elements mentioned by Sainer and Smith also appear in Kirby's description, but in the latter the reader has a sense of how each element functions in relation to the whole. For example, Sainer reports that in *HOTEL CHINA* "someone peers halfway through a half-opened door." In the context of *Sophia,* this same image functions as a device for generating expectancy through the technique of "hiding and revealing."

The play has three "beginnings," the first of which is composed of three thwarted expectancies: two short-term, and one long-term. The opening of the door generates an obvious short-term expectancy—when a door opens into a room, we expect someone to enter through it. Someone does enter, but not completely—we examine that which is revealed and anticipate that which is not. Because the person leaves without completing the entrance, the original expectancy is thwarted. A second short-term expectancy is thwarted when the seated man crosses to the door and, instead of opening it, presses his body against it. The third expectancy is long-term because it is related to the very nature of a "beginning." At the sound of the buzzer that begins the play, the audience anticipates a performance of some duration to follow. The tape recorded words "Not yet," followed by a blackout, bring the first few minutes to an end, suggesting that the performance has not yet begun. It "begins again," and then ends again with the repetition of "Not yet."

The metronome, that Smith merely lists in his account, introduces the third beginning. The ticking sound of a metronome is traditionally used in the practice of musical pieces—it is set and begins ticking immediately *before* the musician starts to play. At the sound of a metronome, therefore, the spectator may anticipate the beginning of a musical piece. The end of this third "beginning," the buzzer, echoes the opening of the first beginning, combining it with the device for ending all three: "A buzzer is heard. Again, the door opens. The voice on the tape says: 'Not yet.' "

The structure of Foreman's productions is discussed in chapter 6. The point here is that, while his staging devices are interesting in themselves, they do not function in isolation; they are not "gimmicks" displayed for their own sake, as Sainer's and Smith's descriptions seem to suggest. Instead, when confronted with staging *Angelface,* Foreman, like his contemporaries in experimental theatre, wanted to alter the experience of theatre art but had little money to achieve this goal. Hence, he invented and developed novel techniques for staging his plays in response to both practical problems and esthetic concerns. They are significant in that they indicate new directions for examination and development in the art. The purpose here is to describe and discuss these techniques, answering the questions: How did they develop? What is the impulse behind them? How are they executed on the stage?

Some, though not all, of Foreman's staging techniques were developed as theatrical equivalents for the unique properties of his texts. In addition to English vocabulary in dialog form, Foreman's plays include diagrams, drawings, ideograms, charts, sketches, and the idiosyncrasies of handwriting, all of which he considers essential elements of the physical object or "play" (see chapter 2). The typewritten script prepared for rehearsals is merely an incomplete version of the original. In the staging, Foreman's goal is to complete the typewritten script, "re-concretizing" the original manuscript, by reinstating the scribbling of handwriting and graphic material of all kinds.

This is not literally the case, of course, but it is not merely figurative either; the staging does not recreate the text in an entirely emblematic, analogous, or metaphorical sense. Instead, using the raw materials of the theatre, Foreman devises "equivalencies for the densities and special auras" of the handwritten text. An "equivalent," by dictionary definition, is "equal in force, amount or value; corresponding or virtually identical, especially in effect or function."

Some of Foreman's equivalencies are evident in the scenography. One of the most obvious examples of a functional equivalent is the lights glaring in the spectator's eyes, which serve to distance the spectator from the work just as certain characteristics of the writing distance the reader (see chapter 2).

Although the function and results are the same, the *experience* for the viewer and reader is different because of the difference in the mediums. Equivalencies for the "densities and auras" of the original text can be found in (or deduced from) several facets of Foreman's visual work, from the homemade quality of the setting and props to the multiplicity of points of light within the settings (see chapter 3).

In terms of aural material, Foreman notes that "the sound-layering I use—tapes of repeated words, noises, music—also serves to reflect the multiple pulls of the visual and ideational aspects of manuscript."[4] This use of sound also functions as a staging technique and, while it can be considered an equivalent for certain aspects of the manuscript, it originated as an expedient solution to a practical acting problem, and subsequently developed into a highly complex technique for staging auditory material.

Unlike such groups as The Open Theatre and The Living Theatre, Foreman had no desire to work from an ensemble approach by placing the actor at the center of his theatre and developing the psychophysical resources of the performer. Instead, he deliberately cast nonactors to play the roles in *Angelface,* with no intention of training them in a method and style of acting. He wanted a certain quality—akin to what he had experienced viewing underground films—that he felt would come naturally from people with little or no performing background and, thus, no preconceptions of how to behave on the stage. At the same time, he realized that the script was long and it was not feasible for nonactors to memorize some twelve hundred lines, especially with only two weeks of rehearsal time. After contemplating a number of technical possibilities, Foreman finally decided that the extensive use of a tape recorder would provide an adequate and interesting solution.

In the text, the dialog is separated into units of varying lengths by the word "pause," which appears as a stage direction after a given number of lines—some units contain only one line, others five or seven lines. Foreman explains the procedure employed for *Angelface:*

> The actors recorded, monotonously and at a fairly quick speed, all of the lines. They read through the play with the pauses. In performance the tape was played and the actor, as soon as he heard one of his own lines coming over the tape, would start to repeat that line as soon as it began. But where the recorded line was spoken at normal speed, he would, in repeating it, delay after each word, so that he never got to finish the line. If on the tape, he started another line in that same unit, he could either continue his original line or pick up the new line. Another rule was that when they got to a pause, wherever they were on stage, when the tape stopped, all of the actors stopped.[5]

Speech, cues for movement, and the tempo of the performance were all dependent on the tape. Because he operated the tape recorder during the performance, Foreman could be considered the "conductor" of the piece, as well as its author and scenographer. "I controlled the length of the pauses. I would stop the tape recorder in the pre-set pause position and hold it for as long as I thought was interesting. The pacing of the play was different for each performance."[6]

Because he did not want to repeat himself, Foreman abandoned recorded dialog for his next piece, *Ida-Eyed,* and it was performed by experienced actors. At the group interview that followed this production, Jonas Mekas asked Foreman, "Now, you worked on *Angelface* with non-actors, and in *Ida-Eyed* with actors. Do you think *Ida-Eyed* would have been stronger if you'd done it with non-actors?" The phrasing of the question indicates Mekas's opinion but, probably because one of the actresses from *Ida-Eyed* was present during this discussion, Foreman evaded the question, answering, "I don't want to answer that question from the esthetic point of view. I didn't feel that I could ask non-actors to learn it. For me, that's an excellent reason for not using non-actors. Now I found that . . . I deeply mean that I have no opinion."[7] The fact that he returned to using taped dialog and nonactors in his next piece, indicates that he had some opinion. Although actors continued to work with Foreman occasionally, all subsequence pieces were cast primarily with nonactors.

In the production following *Ida-Eyed,* the dialog was recorded and played over loudspeakers during the performance, or some combination of live and recorded speech was used. Different rules were employed for delivering dialog and they varied within each production, as well as from one production to another. In *PAIN(T)* and *Vertical Mobility,* for example, the performers spoke their complete lines, live, from the stage. In other performances, when an actor heard one of his lines coming from the loudspeaker, he merely repeated a word or two quietly along with the tape, slightly echoing the line. Kirby describes the quality of speech in *Sophia= (Wisdom) Part 3: The Cliffs:*

> It is not merely the mechanical characteristics of recording and broadcasting that give the speech that is heard from the loudspeakers an unusual quality. Because the volume can be electronically regulated when the tape is played, the performers do not need to be concerned with projecting their voices; soft speech may be amplified. When recording, the actors speak slowly and clearly, reading their lines in a measured and uninflected manner. The sentences that are heard are loud but unemotional.[8]

While the voices of individual characters heard on the tape are those of the performers designated for each role, Foreman's own voice can be heard speaking the lines designated by "Voice," and "Legend" in the texts. Using the tape recorder as a vehicle, Foreman functions both as a commentator, by directly addressing the audience, and as a character, through the "Voice," speaking to other characters onstage. Beginning with *Particle Theory* (1973),

Foreman began to add more of his own voice to the tape, interrupting the performance to address the spectator with material not written in the text but added during rehearsals. He explains, "It's like sitting there next to somebody and saying, 'Look don't you see this?' and 'Are you overlooking that?' "⁹ Hence, even though the dialog was not on tape for *PAIN(T)* and *Vertical Mobility,* for example, the performances included a great deal of recorded speech which, with few exceptions, was Foreman's voice (see chapter 5).

There was an esthetic, as well as practical, reason for returning to recorded dialog after *Ida-Eyed.* Foreman explains, "I was very disturbed by the sound of the spoken American language on stage."¹⁰ He felt that the inflection of the language as it is spoken in America is too casual; it is spoken leaning "back on the heels," as it were, while he felt that French, for instance, is a "forward language: leaning forward, . . . your *mouth* is leaning forward."¹¹ He recalls, "I wanted a kind of dense language that implied the structure of the language, the structure of the consciousness, the structure of thought—I wanted to achieve that without sounding 'highfalutin' and 'arty.' "¹² He felt that he could accomplish this by removing the necessity for actors to project their voices, flattening out the delivery by eliminating inflection, and creating an echo effect—live voices heard against recorded voices.

Most importantly, however, in order to "complexify," as he puts it, the sound of the American language, Foreman adds a variety of sounds and noises both with, and against, the sound of speech. These sounds include the ticking of a metronome, buzzers, thuds, bells, drum rolls, slaps, foghorns, pings, boings, glass shattering, whistles, screams, and muffled explosions. Usually a few are chosen and repeated throughout a performance not only to add density to the sound of the language, but to function as "framing devices" by punctuating or emphasizing a particular word or action. Noises also provide cues for actors, indicating changes in scene, position, and movement.

Noises can serve as an explicit part of the action, as Kirby points out in describing a scene from *Sophia* that makes use of only vocal sounds:

> Motionless performers and offstage voices say, one after the other, the drawn-out, semi-musical word-sound "boing!" For a few minutes, nothing is heard but the sequential repetition of the sound in different pitches and voices from different parts of the space. In a parallel sound sequence early in the second act, actors beat on tin pots with spoons. They strike the pots rhythmically but in different tempos, and this action, too, continues without dialog for some time.¹³

The repeated use of one-syllable words, standing alone in the text, such as "Oh," "Shhhhh," and "Look" are the verbal equivalents of the noises that permeate Foreman's productions. The single most commonly used line of character dialog consists, in its entirety, of the word "What." The interjection "huh" is often tacked onto the end of a character's line for verbal punctuation. This excerpt from *HOTEL CHINA* illustrates:

MAX
(Pause, tiny bells tinkle.)
Take a load off my feet, huh.

BEN
Do that

MAX
What

ALL
(Pause. Tinkle stops.)
Shhhhh.

BEN
I could be quiet when I do that or else
(A thud.)
Try it again.[14]

The pauses and noises called for in the text reflect Foreman's desire to breakdown the syntactical flow of language and indicate a general staccato pattern for speech and sound. The techniques he employs for staging this sound pattern elaborate on it and intensify its effect. During the rehearsal period for *Vertical Mobility,* for example, four sounds, indicated by italics, were added to the following, final lines of the play:

RHODA
(Pause.)
He cannot speak only, huh.
(Pause.)
Oh, Max, I do not recognize—

MAX
What.

RHODA
the room.
A "ping" against the word "room."

MAX
Look.
(Pause.)
It became very beautiful. Oh, Rhoda.
A "thud" against the word "beautiful."

ALL
Shhhhhhh.

MAX
(Pause.)
We are now in Paradise.
                    A "thud" against the word "Paradise."

RHODA
I know it.

MAX
(Pause.)
Is it beautiful enough.

RHODA
No.
                    A loud "No!" immediately after RHODA's "No."[15]

Music, too, is an important part of Foreman's sound score. For instance, he often uses several tape loops that repeat a phrase of music or a single noise throughout a scene, creating a background of sound with a particular quality. During a rehearsal for *PAIN(T)*, Foreman made such a loop by placing the microphone of a tape recorder against the outside of a large glass bowl and then throwing two pennies into the bowl, against the side. When the sound was recorded, he spliced the ends of the tape together, making a "loop." This loop ran continuously between the two reels of a tape recorder, repeating the sound in a rhythmically precise way. Rather than develop melodically, the music or sounds on a loop regularly and mechanically "begin again." This technique has its sensory effect, but it also emphasizes the nonnarrative, continuously present nature of Foreman's plays.

Music also functions in traditional ways: as background for movement and the "dances" that usually occur in a Foreman production, and to create or suggest certain moods (like the eerie music that accompanied the mysterious, lumbering creatures in *Book of Splendors* [see page 55, chapter 3]. Foreman has described his musical selections as "obscure," that is, he does not choose songs, tunes, or melodies that are easily recognizable. The genres, however, are usually immediately identifiable and include, among many others, Dixieland, ragtime jazz, and limbo dance music. The music he used for a dance he entitled "The Old Right Left" in *Rhoda in Potatoland,* for instance, was taken from an album of selections by Tiny Parham—a Chicago "South Side Jazz" musician—originally recorded between 1928 and 1929.[16]

Just as Foreman's design became more elaborate over the years, his uses of recorded sound became increasingly complex. In the text of *Sophia,* one of Rhoda's lines appears as follows:

I/I ha/ad a/a fun/ny dre/eam/ las/st ni/ight a/a bou/ut th/he a/a bom/min/na/able sn/now ma/an.[17]

Kirby describes how this was realized in the performance. The same voice was usually heard from the two loudspeakers used for the piece, but occasionally a different voice could be heard on each speaker. Rhoda delivered only parts of each word in the sentence above while a man's voice coming from the other loudspeaker, completed each word:

> RHODA: I (voice: "I") ha(had) a(a) fu(funny) dr(dream) la(last) ni(night) a(a) bou(bout) th(the) a(a) ba(bom) ina(inable) sn(snow) ma(man).[18]

By 1978 Foreman had progressed from the effects possible with a single tape recorder and two speakers, to the use of multiple sound tracks on several speakers for simultaneity in auditory effects, or sound-layering.

For *Book of Splendors* there were four loudspeakers in the space: two small speakers were hung above and in front of the audience, one on each side of the bleachers; a large speaker was hidden in the pillar at the top of the rear ramp (plate 42), facing the audience; and another large one was placed on the floor behind the audience bleachers. This speaker system had seven sound inputs—the four tracks on a portable, but large, reel-to-reel tape recorder, and three small, portable cassette tape recorders. Through mixing, Foreman was able to produce different sounds on different speakers, thereby filling the space with sound coming from four directions simultaneously. Often the sound, especially dialog, seemed to be traveling through the space, since the spectator heard disembodied sentences, broken down into individual words that were projected from different speakers—the words "traveled" from one speaker to another around the space. At times, the speakers seemed to be talking to each other across the playing area, or a performer would be speaking a line from the stage while another performer's voice could be heard from the loudspeakers delivering a different line, at the same time. Thus, live and recorded voices, noises, and music were layered, one over the other, resulting in different kinds and qualities of sound heard simultaneously, coming from different areas in the space.

Because of his position and activity in the space during each performance, Foreman is present both as spectator and director/performer. In *Total Recall,* Foreman simply sat on the floor to operate the tape recorder for the piece (note the tape recorder in the front row of spectators in plate 1). For later productions, he usually sat behind a small table directly in front of the audience, house right, visibly running the sound and lighting equipment.[19] When he constructed the bleachers for his new theatre, he built in a permanent position for himself in the front row (plate 42), and the lighting booth became a space in the wall of the building that connects the door of Foreman's loft with that of the loft next door. Beginning with *Pandering,* a person was employed to run the lights from this booth. Until *Blvd. de Paris,* when another person ran the sound equipment from Foreman's front-row seat, Foreman "conducted" every Ontological-Hysteric Theatre performance. He not only monitored the electrical equipment, but participated in the performance by producing some sound effects live, such as clapping boards together or ringing bells, and occasionally calling out "cue," or counting out loud to indicate changes in activity. If someone would forget to come onstage, which rarely happened, he simply called out that person's name and the performance continued without a break. In Foreman's productions, the performers are almost completely dependent on the cues he generates and controls, both live and on tape, for delivering their lines and changing their positions. As Kirby points out, "Using these techniques, Foreman is able to control performances to a degree that is impossible with traditional methods."[20]

In addition to running sound and lights, Foreman operated the slide projectors he used for most of the eight productions from 1972 to 1975. Generally, one projector hung from the ceiling and one rested on the floor. The slides almost always contained only written material—the sentences labeled "legend" in the texts—and were usually projected on fixed projection screens (plate 13, 14, 19), but occasionally appeared on set pieces (plate 26) or on movable projection screens (plate 57). This written material functioned in several ways, one of them in keeping with Foreman's desire to add density to the experience of language.

Foreman particularly liked reading the subtitles that accompany foreign language films, explaining, "The language has a thickness because of that double process that to me is very exhilarating, and I'm trying to capture something akin to that experience in the theatre."[21] By presenting written material in his theatre, Foreman provides a reading experience for the spectator that overlaps the aural experience—two modes for experiencing language occurring simultaneously.

Foreman explains that the slides also function as

> a kind of running commentary on the play, as it is proceeding, to raise questions that I think might be interesting at various points in the action; to throw into doubt certain things that the spectator might be taking for granted; to introduce another angle of thought. There are many perspectives on any event, and I want as many of those perspectives as possible to be present to the spectator in all moments.[22]

In *Sophia* (plate 14), a grandfather clock appears in the window of the rear wall upstage left and the slide reads:

> The clock says
> "Can't you see me.
> Even if you can't
> see what time it is.
> See me anyway."

Using personification, Foreman asks the spectator, in essence, if he can perceive or comprehend the clock onstage apart or separate from its "time-telling" function, that is, as an object occupying space. Foreman addresses the audience directly, occasionally in the form of questions that (1) are purely rhetorical; (2) ask the spectator to remember past actions, characters, or bits of information; or (3) induce the "expectancy mechanism" to contemplate what might occur in the future. The question on the screen in plate 58, "Where are the workers now," functions in all three of these ways. Because the "workers" were not visible to the audience, the question invites speculation as to their whereabouts. It also brings to mind the workers from an earlier scene, and it suggests, "What will happen when they return?" (see chapter 6).

Often the slides provide expository information (plate 13): "When the house moves it is really speaking." Sometimes the written material is "superimposed" on an image in the sense of "vertical information," which essentially tells the audience what it is already looking at (plate 59): "Now see them in their positions." In plate 57, Foreman admonishes the spectator with the words (barely visible) on the movable screen, "Do not fall prey to that danger."

Written material, like the noises, can at times function as a framing device by calling attention to some aspect of the performance. In *Sophia,* for instance, the music in one scene might have functioned as background but, partly through the use of slides, it was "pulled" into the foreground, as it were, and justified in the context of the scene. Kirby describes the sequence:

> Early in the second act, a man's voice is heard singing a wordless jazz song: "bum-bum-babum." After several moments, a series of slides comes on. They read, in part:
>
> "THE WORKERS LIKE THAT KIND OF MUSIC.
>
> EACH WORKER HAS A SEPARATE RADIO.
>
> THE PEOPLE WHO ARE NOT WORKERS
> PREFER MORE REFINED MUSIC.
>
> THEY DO NOT NEED RADIOS.
> THEY HEAR IT IN THEIR INNER EAR."
>
> Not long afterward, Hannah asks Karl what is on the radio, and the same voice-music is heard. Both characters are motionless while it plays.[23]

In each production slides were used to present written material to a greater or lesser extent depending on the number of "legends" originally written into the script, and how many of these, if any, were delivered by Foreman on the tape. In *Sophia* the frequency of projected written material made the technique a major stylistic element of the performance.

Examples of words painted on set pieces, or cut out of wood as props, were mentioned in chapter 3. The blackboard is another device Foreman frequently uses to present words visually. Twice during the performance of *Sophia* a long, narrow blackboard on casters was rolled onstage, stretching across almost the entire width of the playing area (plate 60). Written in chalk on one end of it was the word "Think" and on the other end "Harder." Because the words appear from left to right, as one normally reads, with an enormous space between them, the intent seems to be the impact of a command without the exclamation point. In *Book of Splendors* the words "Like a . . ." appeared in chalk on a standard, classroom-type blackboard. While one of the performers said, "It drops from my hand like a a a a a," the "teacher" stood next to the blackboard, pointed toward the audience and demanded, "I want *you* to fill in the word!" (plate 45).

Although the noises that accompany every performance are Foreman's primary vehicle for framing lines and activity, a framing device can be anything that punctuates, frames, emphasizes, or brings into the foreground a particular word, object, action or position, and there are many examples of visual framing. In *Total Recall* (plate 5), the curtain of the tabletop proscenium, stage left, hides the face, chest, and upper arms of the performer sitting behind it. The hands are perceived separately from the actor, against the blank background of the curtain. Carefully framed and emphasized, the hands of the miniature stage picture become the focal point of the total stage picture. In *PAIN(T)* there is a freestanding, square, empty picture frame (the lower left corner of plate 29) which contains a grid of strings that divide the area of the picture plane into nine equal squares. An object has been placed directly behind it in plate 25. Like the oldest methods for determining perspective, it is possible to look through the frame, like a pane of glass, and analyze the relationships of the objects (or view) behind it in terms of the discrete areas of the picture plane, delineated by the grid. During the performance, whatever is visible through this frame is emphasized by the nature of the grid.

Mirrors are objects that Foreman uses frequently in his pieces, and many of them can be considered framing devices since a mirror frames whatever it reflects, emphasizing the image by duplicating it (plate 30). A built-in framing device shared by both the *PAIN(T)* and *Vertical Mobility* settings was a small mirror hanging close to the ceiling, facing the audience, and angled toward the floor (plate 24). Spectators could watch the performance in the reflection of the mirror but, because of its size, the mirror reflected only fragments of the total action.

This small mirror plays more than the role of framing device. It is indicative of the importance Foreman places on objects in the sense that, through the built-in mirror, the production is "watching" itself—the mirror is the "eye" of the performance. Objects not only tend to be endowed with animate attributes like the lamps in *Total Recall* (chapter 3), they also tend to become performers like the personified grandfather clock in *Sophia* that was hoisted into the room from the window after "stating," via slide projection, "I'd like to get inside the room."[24]

In some cases, performers become objects and objects become performers simultaneously, as in *Classical Therapy,* the text of which begins:

> (BEN looks at the mirror. It turns and looks back at him. It crosses to him, and bumps into him.)
>
>   BEN
> That proves it's looking back at me.[25]

The "it" is a full-length mirror (plate 61) "worn" by a performer who, standing behind it, is completely covered by cloth except for holes where his arms poke through to become the "arms" of the mirror. Standing next to the mirror is a bookcase. Later in the text, a stage direction describes the activity captured in plate 62:

> ... Door opens. A bookcase enters. The mirror selects a book from out of the bookcase. Opens it and presses it against its own glass front, and tapes it there.
> The bookcase itself takes a book out of its shelves, and throws it across the room. It is, however, attached to the shelf with a rope. And the bookcase then pulls on the rope and hauls the book back. Then casts it out again. This continues as thuds begin.)[26]

In *Rhoda in Potatoland* (plate 36), the largest potato "standing" in the doorway is another example of this object/performer staging technique. The mirror stuck in the potato's head could be considered its "eyes."

Numerous examples of objects rendered both smaller and larger than life-size have been cited in chapter 3. Kirby describes a particularly complex combination of objects in various scales that were presented onstage at the same time in *Sophia:*

> Late in the first act, a kind of cabinet with open doors is rolled into the playing area [plate 63]. In the top section is the model of an exterior scene with a miniature house, a tiny female figure, a toy horse and a small tree. The bottom section contains two different tableaux: an interior scene and flowers in a pot. Although they are all very small, none of the three compartments matches the others in scale.
> While the cabinet is onstage, Max appears and stands at the left, facing the audience [plates 63 and 64]. Attached to his head is a wooden box supported by two long poles. The front of the box is open, its sides slant back in forced perspective, and the model of a room fills it as if it were a miniature stage setting. The back wall of the box has been removed, and Max's eyes can be seen looking into the small room. Cords are hanging from the four front corners of the box, and another performer stretches them to a point some distance in front, where all four lines converge at a single point like reversed lines of perspective.[27]

Visible at the same time are the small, peaked houses on the "cliffs" (see chapter 3) in the background—the stage areas that represent the interior and exterior "places" of the setting are both visible. In this context, the "model cabinet-stage" and "forehead set," as they are referred to in the text, can be considered interior and exterior versions of the setting itself. Certain details suggest this interpretation: A cord attached to the top of the cliffs, stage left, has been drawn downstage and draped loosely over the cabinet, its end dangling in front of the exterior scene, suggesting the mental connection between the two exteriors by literally connecting them through space; the miniature wicker chair in Max's "forehead interior set" is a facsimile of the life-size white wicker chair that appeared earlier as part of the interior setting (place 57); the miniature furniture that hangs on strings from the houses on the cliffs (plate 65) is also made to resemble wicker; Max's eyes and nose visible as the rear wall of his "forehead set" are reminiscent of the performers' heads that appear inside the little houses on the cliffs, nearly filling them. Foreman presents objects in arrangements designed to provide numerous possibilities for interpretation, and multiple perspectives on a particular theatrical event or any element of the event.

While the fundamentals of Foreman's esthetic and approach have been present from the beginning of his production work, individual staging techniques were initiated at various times and developed over the years. Like the use of slide projections for written material, some have been abandoned, at least temporarily. Probably the only technique prevalent in every production, and certainly a dominant stylistic element of all Foreman's work, is his arrangement of performers in tableau compositions with characteristics that distinguish them from other forms of stage picturization.

In his account of the basic staging of *Sophia,* Kirby describes the fundamentals of Foreman's picturization:

> . . . almost all of the scenes are presented as sequences of static pictures. The actor or actors are motionless, posed in position like mannequins displayed in a store window. Often only one actor at a time adjusts his position or moves to alter the stage picture. The new picture remains for a moment or, perhaps, for quite a while, until some clear movement changes the picture again. It would not be completely accurate to say that Foreman's actors "freeze" in position. The term might suggest rigidity and tension. In fact, the performers seem to be quite relaxed, and they hold their poses without exerting any extra or unnecessary force.[28]

These posed performers are sometimes positioned in the same plane, parallel to the proscenium plane, with their bodies turned in such a way that the spectator is presented with an essentially two-dimensional image. Like the strict frontal arrangement of set pieces and props within the playing area (see chapter 3), these tableau compositions emphasize the two-dimensional nature of the picture or proscenium plane of the fourth wall.

Because Foreman's stage pictures often exist solely for such purely formal reasons, they are different from stage picturization as it is usually defined. In traditional theatrical terminology, "picturization" denotes more than the presentation of a playscript in three-dimensional stage pictures. For example, W. David Sievers defines picturization in his textbook entitled *Directing for the Theatre* as that which "should *tell the story,* or picturize the inner relationships in the scene."[29] In *Fundamentals of Play Directing,* Alexander Dean and Lawrence Carra state that to picturize is to "inject meaning into the stage picture."[30] All three authors consider the expression of "the meaning of the moment or scene" as necessary to the definition of picturization.

A picture is a type of composition that may, or may not, depict a story, situation, or the psychological relationships among people. In fact, what Dean and Carra describe as a composition devoid of picturization captures the very essence of Foreman's picturization:

> . . . if a good picture is stripped of its picturization or storytelling elements of emotional relationship of character to character, leaving only its arbitrary line, mass, and form (the composition), an emotional quality or mood of the subject matter will come across to the audience . . . the way to obtain an analysis of the composition in a stage picture is to have each person on the stage eliminate all body expression and relationship to another person— in other words become an inanimate figure.[31]

Foreman's stage pictures are comprised of "inanimate figures" in the sense that his actors make no attempt to project or communicate stories, themes, or psychological/emotional relationships to the audience. Sievers, Dean, and Carra would conclude that Foreman's stage compositions lack the essential element of picturization, when actually his form of picturization is usually merely void of storytelling elements. In addition to its capacity for conveying information and eliciting particular emotional responses, a stage picture might exist for purely formal or esthetic reasons, or to provoke intellectual responses that are completely separate from the subject matter of the composition. Foreman does not limit himself to one or two of these functions. Instead, he exploits all the functional possibilities inherent in the stage picture in order to achieve a variety of specific goals.

For instance, Foreman employs the principles for determining focus in a stage picture, through the lines of the composition, to establish visual patterns that exist completely separate from any interpretation, or meaning, of the picture.

In the special vocabulary of standard stage composition, a distinction is made between "actual" and "visual" lines. The actual lines in the composition are those created by the positions or performers and furniture, while visual lines are the invisible lines that connect the performer with whatever he is looking at. In other words, the eyes of the performer are the starting point of a visual line that extends in the direction of the actor's gaze and terminates at the point (object or person) where the eyes are focused. A combination of actual and visual lines is usually employed to convey information or create a mood.

Both actual and visual lines can define a focal point in a stage picture. If we imagine a triangle of seven performers on a proscenium stage, for example, with one performer positioned upstage center, and the other six forming the two equal sides of an isosceles triangle (the proscenium plane suggests the third side), the apex of the triangle will be the focal point of the stage picture. If, however, everyone looks at a common point in, or outside of, the triangle, then, regardless of the actual lines, the visual lines will determine the focal point.

It would seem that visual lines, although invisible, have more potential for dominance than actual, or visible, lines. For instance, if everyone in the triangle extended a finger and pointed to the same spot, *that* point would dominate the composition, despite the actual or "visible" lines. But suppose that everyone in our isosceles triangle pointed to the same spot outside the triangle, while all looked at another common point inside the triangle. The two dominant points would tend to balance each other, bringing the apex created by the actual line back into play. The eye of the spectator would scan three points of relatively the same "weight." Foreman uses the functional principles for establishing focus in a stage picture to achieve similar effects.

Aware of the power of the visual line to dominate the stage picture, Foreman deliberately used it to accentuate the horizontal "actual" lines of furniture and actor placement in his early production. Of this early work he recalls:

> At the beginning my pieces were based upon the actors in front of the audience, standing in—generally in profile to the audience, looking at each other, dealing completely with each other, and cutting the—ignoring the spectator. Generally, all the lines of force were across the stage, running from one side of the stage to the other.[32]

At least in the first two productions, the general orientation of the body and the head was away from the spectators.

As Foreman's desire to force the spectator to take note of his position in time and space increased, the position of the performers' bodies became more frontal and the "lines of force" began to be directed into the audience area by means of the performers' gaze. The special quality of this approach to the use of visual lines in static, posed compositions, is captured in Kirby's description of *Sophia:*

> In these poses, the eyes always remain as motionless as possible, and, . . . Foreman often places his performers so that they are looking steadily at or toward the audience. Sometimes

a performer's head turns away from the general orientation of the body and faces the spectators. The actors do not "stare." This word, too, might indicate tension. But they gaze fixedly at or beyond the audience, their set or neutral expressions allowing no response and giving no hint of what they actually see.[33]

When looking at or toward the audience, Foreman feels that the performers imply with their gaze, "I am here, where are you?" He adds, "Having to notice where one is, is very exhilarating."[34] This technique is related to the Brechtian alienation effect, and provides another concrete example of a device employed in the staging to distance the viewer from the performance. Furthermore, when an actor looks directly toward the audience, a focal point in the picture is immediately established. The spectator's initial impulse may be to look away, but eyes looking out of a picture create a powerful, almost irresistible, center of attention.

Foreman works with the principles involved in creating visual dominance on the stage in order to induce a "glancing," rather than "staring," physiological response from the spectator. When a single focal point is established on the stage, the spectator tends to look fixedly at it, or stare—his attention is focused and direct. When the techniques for establishing visual dominance are employed simultaneously, the eye tends to move swiftly from one point to another—the spectator's attention is unfocused as the eye glances back and forth.

In one composition in *Rhoda in Potatoland* (plate 41) Manheim gazes toward the audience while pointing to Foreman's head. At the same time, a performer upstage right lifts his left arm and points to another performer who is standing downstage of Manheim, and also looking toward the audience. Strings attached to the floor behind this performer create actual lines running upstage to the nostrils of the gigantic "potatohead" in the rear. Above the nostrils, two enormous eyes look back at the spectator. In this composition, a number of potentially dominant visual elements vie for the center of attention. This composition also demonstrates that although Foreman often uses essentially two-dimensional tableaux and pictures, working on a single plane in a shallow space, he just as frequently uses deep space, with action occurring simultaneously on more than one plane, emphasizing the depth of the playing area.

Many of the devices Foreman uses to dominate the stage picture have become recognizable elements of his style. Performers not only use their fingers to point, often they hold a "pointing device," such as an arrow. In *Classical Therapy* Manheim held a small wooden arrow, pointing to an object, a telephone, held by another performer (plate 66). In another scene, a performer held a long, drooping paper arrow, pointing to his own head (plate 20). In *Vertical Mobility* a performer standing downstage left held a long stick, on the end of which was a stuffed, white glove with the index finger pointing to a performer entering upstage right (plate 67).

Nude performers in a stage picture also tend to dominate the visual field, and Foreman uses nudity extensively. As we saw in the last chapter (page 55), the three women naked from the waist up, in *Book of Splendors,* combined with the men dancing on the railings, made it difficult to notice a striking image presented when the cabinet doors were opened briefly (plate 53).

Even the devices Foreman uses to defuse the visual impact of potential focal points have become familiar stylistic features. For instance, in order to maintain the frontal position of a performer without the eyes creating a focal point, Foreman will have the performer cover his eyes with one or both hands, or wear a blindfold. This is sometimes employed so that it is possible for an inanimate object to become the focal point of the picture. Performers draped or bent over set pieces, or with their backs turned to the audience, are additional ways used to achieve this.

One composition in *Total Recall* has as its focal point a lighted lamp held aloft by an actress (plate 1), who is covering her eyes with her hand. Two of the other three performers onstage are sitting in profile to the audience, looking directly at each other, while the third is bent forward over the window ledge, under the lamp. Light is also the focal point in a composition from *HOTEL CHINA* (plate 10) as Max, wearing a blindfold, sits facing a brightly shining light bult that hangs between him and the spectators.

Foreman's stage compositions do not exist only for establishing multiple centers of attention to elicit a particular physiological response from the spectator. As in traditional theatre, his picturization is also used to relate to dialog. In the following example from the first act of *Sophia,* Kirby, through his description, demonstrates how the scene was presented in three basic pictures:

> Two chairs have been placed facing the audience in the center. Rhoda sits in the one on the left. She faces front, looking toward the spectators, her fingers pressed to her temples at both sides. Sophia enters the door at the left, in the same plane as the chair. She stands motionless just inside the door, looking at Rhoda.

SOPHIA

You don't want my help, probably.

RHODA

I don't believe in your help.

SOPHIA

You are wary of me.

RHODA

Yes.

Sophia walks to the empty chair, sits and turns to look at Rhoda. Rhoda has not moved.

SOPHIA
Do you think I am more beautiful than you are?

RHODA
Oh yes.

A woman enters through the door with two glasses on a tray and crosses to stand beside Sophia.

RHODA
Probably.

SOPHIA
Guess. What. I'm not looking through you Rhoda.

Rhoda and Sophia take glasses of tea, and the girl exists with the tray. The fingers of Rhoda's left hand are still pressed to the side of her head.

SOPHIA
I'm not even looking inside your head. I'm looking at the surface of the side of your head.

Rhoda drops her hand and turns to look at Sophia. The bodies and legs of both seated women face front, their outside hands hold glasses, and their faces, turned toward each other, are seen in profile.

RHODA
Now you're looking into my eyes.

SOPHIA
Maybe. But I'm looking at the surface of your eyes, aren't I?

RHODA
Then I guess I'm looking at the surface of *your* eyes.[35]

Kirby also describes another sequence from *Sophia* in which an elaborate picture is created by the gradual addition of visual elements. He points out that it is an example of picturization used as an independent element, noting "the structure of the scene in time depends upon the growing complexity of the picture."[36]

Late in the second act of "Sophia," Karl has removed his shirt and has lowered his pants around his ankles. He is wearing long underwear. A girl places one end of a long string in his mouth. Holding his arms out at each side with elbows bent and half-opened palms turned up, Karl walks slowly to the center of the playing area, where he stands facing the audience. Stretching the string and touching the other end of it to the floor at some distance from the standing figure, the girl, working very slowly and carefully, begins to mark out a circle [plate 68].

An actress sits on a suitcase directly in front of Karl and strikes a pose, looking into a pocket mirror. In the rear, a brown cross-shaped fixture holding four small shaded lamps is lowered. A small screen with a flower-shaped hole in it is set up in front of Karl. It reaches to his waist, and a ribbon attached to him runs through the hole and stretches away to the left. A man half-reclines on the floor with one leg up in the air, holding the string that runs from Karl's mouth.

Other performers bring on equipment and line up in the same plane as Karl. On either side of him crouches a person with a single red boxing glove pointing outward on a brown wooden "arm." Each "arm" forms the crosspiece of a "T" that stands on the floor; the other ends of the crosspieces turn into wide bands of cloth that continue into Karl's upturned hands. Facing these gloves and aiming inward toward Karl, crouch two actors with red boxing gloves on their hands. Everyone is motionless [plate 69].

A buzzer sounds, and two "boxing matches" begin, one on either side of Karl. The single gloves on the "T"-shaped supports are pushed out and pulled back; the gloved actors shuffle slightly and aim short punches inward, but no contact is made. Another performer moves in and out with a piece of chalk, marking the position of one of the boxer's feet whenever they are momentarily stationary.

Rhoda, who has been lying behind Karl covered by a piece of canvas, crawls out. She is nude. Slowly she creeps forward between Karl and the "fight" on the right. The buzzer sounds; everyone stops and looks at Rhoda. No one moves [plate 70].[37]

(Note that here nudity is used to pull attention away from the dominant action, establishing Rhoda as the focal point in the picture even before everyone stops and looks at her.)

Beginning with *Angelface,* Foreman has consciously and aggressively worked toward breaking down the conventional means for making theatre. Some of the techniques he developed in this process include: visual and aural framing devices; sound-layering; picturization in tableau compositions; a variety of means for superimposing written material; staccato speech using pauses, noises, and verbal punctuation; lights glaring in the spectators' eyes; tape-recorded dialog; the use of extremely loud music and sound; the rendering of objects in scales both smaller and larger than life-size; the use of objects as performers and performers as objects; and direct control of the performance, via the control of all cues for speech and action.

On one level these staging techniques can be regarded as strategies for generating new ways of perceiving the elements of the theatrical event. In 1972 Foreman stated:

When I began making pieces four years ago I invented all kinds of irritating noises, lights in the audience's eyes, broken rhythms. . . . The hostile techniques seem to call up certain resources in the perceptual process which then alter the objects observed. Perhaps it's that more energy flows from perceiver to the object.[38]

Like Gertrude Stein's elimination of internal punctuation in long complicated sentences, Foreman employs "irritating" or "hostile" devices designed to put pressure on the mind, forcing it to work at perceiving and comprehending that which is presented.

Foreman has made significant contributions toward altering traditional ways of experiencing theatre, and it is clear that his unique staging techniques are largely responsible. Since the functional possibility of each device is investigated during the rehearsal period, it is necessary to examine this process in order to understand how these staging techniques are incorporated in the moment-to-moment mounting of a production.

5

Foreman as Director: Rehearsal Procedures and Techniques

A fundamental impulse behind Richard Foreman's approach to theatre is Wagner's concept of a "total artwork," or a *Gesamtkunstwerk*. Foreman is not only concerned with an effective, unified interplay among the elements of theatre in performance, he is also adamant about theatre art as a "total creative process" that does not necessarily involve a group of specialists. He believes that playwrights should be their own directors, explaining, "I am interested in a work of art that . . . is a total creation of a personality,"[1] Writing in 1969 about his reasons for founding the Ontological-Hysteric Theatre in 1967, Foreman stated: "At that point, [I] realized I had my own total vision of the kind of theatre I wanted, and . . .[that] I'd have to do it all myself."[2] Several years later, during an interview with Michael Feingold, Foreman mentioned that he had "always been obsessively interested in all the arts." Doesn't that make specializing difficult?" asked Feingold. "But I don't specialize, really, because in my Ontological-Hysteric Theatre I function as composer, designer, writer, director, dance director . . . everything,"[3] Foreman replied. There is no collaboration in Foreman's work—every Ontological-Hysteric Theatre piece is the product of a single creator.

To negate further the accepted viewzof theatre as an essentially collaborative effort, Foreman insists that in his theatre the staging of a play is a continuation of the writing process. He maintains, "it is important to realize that the following stages are stages of the 'writing' itself, . . . though they occur 'later in time,' . . . 1) the physical act of typing the handwritten manuscript 2) the various problem-solving moments of staging 3) my own experiencing of audience-watching-the-play, ..."[4] From the moment of pen-in-hand writing to opening night, the "process of making the play," he explains, can be "thought of as a certain and continual articulation of alternately passive and active modes. The writing tending towards a more receptive, open, passive receiving of 'what wants to be written' and the staging tending towards more active organization of the 'arrived' elements of the writing—finding ways to make the writing inhabit a constructed environment."[5] His use of the words "tending towards" should indicate that this distinction is not to be taken in the strictest sense.

When Foreman includes the staging as a continuation of the writing process, his intent is not to imply that the staging is a subsidiary element in the creative process. Nor does he elevate the staging above the other processes, though the critics often focus on his role as director, ignoring his contributions as a writer and designer. While he takes each of his tasks equally seriously, and does not consider any one more important than another, it seems clear that the staging is the activity he enjoys most. In an interview with Terry Curtis Fox for *The Village Voice,* Foreman affirmed, ". . . of the esthetic lusts I have, one of the three or four strong ones is moving things around in three-dimensional space. . . . I love to do that."[6] It is during the rehearsal period for each production that Foreman satisfies this particular "lust," for rehearsal time is devoted primarily to arranging people and objects in three-dimensional space.

Each of the Ontological-Hysteric Theatre's first two productions, *Angelface* (1968) and *Ida-Eyed* (1969), was in rehearsal for two weeks, approximately two hours a day. In 1974 when he presented *PAIN(T)* and *Vertical Mobility* in repertory, each received about six weeks of rehearsal time during the three-month rehearsal period: one play—whichever required the most attention—was rehearsed on three successive nights, and the other rehearsed on the remaining two nights. Rehearsals began promptly at 7:00 every weekday night and continued, without interruption until 10:00—a feature typical of the rehearsals for every Ontological-Hysteric Theatre production. As with every Foreman production, weekend rehearsals were rare and only involved one or two performers. By the time he mounted *Rhoda in Potatoland* in 1976, the rehearsal period for a single production was twelve weeks long.

On the surface, Foreman's rehearsal procedures are not very different from those necessary for any traditional theatre production. He works from a previously written script, conducting what appear to be blocking rehearsals, giving oral instructions to the performers, and occasionally demonstrating how to do something. Certain features of his rehearsal process, however, are quite extraordinary. For instance, he stages the entire play to a previously tape-recorded score that includes music and sound effects or noise, as well as dialog. In order to understand the unique nature of Foreman's staging as it develops moment-to-moment in rehearsal, it is necessary to begin by examining the steps taken immediately before rehearsals commence. These steps include: (1) choosing the text; (2) typing the handwritten manuscript; (3) choosing the performers; (4) building the set; and (5) making the tape-recorded score.

Foreman's scripts are culled from the handwritten material that appears in his notebooks. The writing is done in private, before the rehearsals begin (see chapter 2), and the scripted words change very little during the staging. Because Foreman's writing method is "continuous" in its very nature, it does not begin at one point and end at another, producing a particular "play." Furthermore, he discloses, that "when the time comes to mount another play I always have much more material than I can use. . . ."[7] It becomes necessary, therefore, to select, from a great deal of material, that which will become a specific piece. It is crucial to understand, however, that Foreman does not choose a page here and a sequence there, throwing together units of writing from different places in his notebooks. On the contrary, he explains,"At a certain point I pick up one of my notebooks, look casually through it and decide 'Hum . . . go from here to here and I have a play.' "[8] This material, chosen to be staged as a particular play, is always taken in sequence, exactly as it appears in his notebooks, without deletions.

Foreman does not edit the handwritten material he selects because he believes a director must find ways to stage all of the writing. He has always been, he recalls, "very leery of the normal Broadway method of tinkering with the text to make it work—even seeing that done at Yale. . . . I always felt the task of the . . . director was precisely to find those parts that didn't seem to work . . . and find a way to realize that . . . [which] seemed okay on the printed page but somehow [didn't] seem good on the stage."[9] Foreman takes this principle a step further when, in typing the handwritten words into script form for the actors, he comes across material that he rejected during the act of writing.

> My habit is, sometimes, to see a unit I've just written, find it just TOO terrible or simplistic or flat or embarrassing or badly written . . . and cross it out. Then, if that crossed out section happens to fall within those pages I've chosen to stage, I end up feeling guilty about trying to "cast-off" something which did indeed come out of me, no matter how much it embarrassed me, and I decide to stage that crossed out section along with the rest.[10]

He admits that he had to overcome the immediate rejection of material that he thought was not "what mature, successful, sophisticated playwrights write. But I had to learn to accept that [rejected material], and I think I found ways to deal with that in the staging."[11]

This impulse to accept the writing as written has several sources. One of them is related to Foreman's desire to "unlearn" specific techniques, or decrease the impact of previous conditioning. He recalls, for example, that "At Yale, we were taught that plays are not written, they're rewritten. You were supposed to rewrite them so that they would have the manipulative effect upon your audience that you desired. Of course, I find that almost obscene now."[12] It is the manipulation he finds obscene, for even as late as 1977 he was hesitant to discuss his rejection of the process of rewriting:

> It is true—even now I feel frightened to admit this, it's going to be held against me as a sign of "lack of ultimate seriousness"—it is true that I no longer rewrite as I used to. . . . But this is not, I maintain, to stage "unedited" material (though God knows, that would be a perfectly justifiable and important artistic procedure also).[13]

The material is not "unedited" in the sense that it is not a rambling "stream of consciousness," or series of images and ideas captured as they "pop" into his head (see chapter 2). But to cross out units of writing is, in a sense, to rewrite. Even though the motivation behind this form of "rewriting" is not to manipulate the spectator, Foreman avoids the tendency of conscious, critical reflection to alter material generated in an entirely different state of consciousness.

Foreman's conception of the text as the "raw material" of his staging is another reason he does not rewrite and reorder the sequence he selects as the play. "In my works, I'm more interested in using the text as a kind of found material—step one in the creative process."[14] He is aware, of course, that "Foreman the playwright" is providing material for "Foreman the director" to stage. So to help prevent preconceived notions of the staging from interfering with the writing, causing it to stagnate, Foreman accepts the writing as originally written.

> . . . I'm interested in generating texts which are a kind of still slightly unshaped material because I know I'm going to get my hands on them as a director. More and more I'm interested in having my text become day-to-day jottings of where I'm at, almost just keeping a diary. And then subjecting that diary to the most rigorous, disciplined kind of shaping, control, as I stage it.[15]

When he uses the word "diary" to describe what eventually become his texts, it is not in the sense of a daily record of his feelings about events, personal activities, and transactions. If the playwright considers his writing in terms of generating an essentially functionless manuscript, such as a diary, then it is more difficult for the director in him, as it were, to look ahead at the staging, influencing the material in predictable ways. Foreman wants the playwright in him to provide material for the director in him, without the director shaping the writing in ways that limit the ability of the texts to indicate new, previously unimagined directions.

The people who appear in Foreman's plays also function somewhat as "found material." Foreman does not hold auditions when casting his plays because they are not necessary. As he puts it, "I look for a spiritual quality, not technique. Greatest influence in [my] use of actors being [the filmmaker] Robert Bresson."[16] Although he has used professional actors with Broadway experience, Foreman prefers people who have never acted before. Like a script generated without a staged "end product" in mind, nonactors bring no preconceived notions of how to behave on the stage. Foreman accepts volunteers, or telephones people he knows and asks them if they would like to appear in his next production. He wants the casting to be open to as many different kinds of people as possible, but he also notes, "I try to cast people I'd like to spend, oh, twelve weeks with."[17]

Kate Manheim, who has performed in over a dozen Ontological-Hysteric Theatre productions, met Foreman in the fall of 1971 when he appeared at the Anthology Film Archives one day, shortly after she began working there. He was looking for a volunteer replacement for an actress who had dropped out of *HOTEL CHINA* during the rehearsal period. After walking back and forth several times through the office where Manheim was working, Foreman finally approached her and asked shyly, "Would you mind being an angel in my play?" She replied simply, "No, I wouldn't mind."[18] Manheim was literally a "found" element in the production—Foreman did not even know her before asking her to participate.

The setting, too, has a "found" or raw-material dimension to it. It certainly is not a "found space" used in its natural state. It is a carefully constructed environment. But while some props and set pieces are invented and added during the rehearsal period, the basic setting is usually designed and constructed beforehand, and not necessarily with the specifics of a particular text in mind. Rather than build an environment designed to complement and serve a particular play, Foreman constructs a setting with a certain "shape" in mind for a production. He explains that the most important function of the staging lies in "finding ways to make the writing inhabit a constructed environment just as a passively 'arrived' species mutation finds a way, after the fact, to exploit and live in the environment in which it finds itself."[19]

He does consider one or two key moments in a particular text when designing the environment. In *Book of Splendors,* for instance, he remembers that the large, movable step unit (plate 62) was included because of a particular image stemming from an idea for a huge, tiered cake.[20] (Ultimately, it was not used to create that particular kind of image.) The sliding diagonal wall was spawned by a single line of dialog: "It's the room coming towards me" (see page 54, chapter 3). Except for one or two such specific examples in each production, therefore, the set is designed for functional and formal reasons motivated by esthetic, rather than textual, concerns. In this sense the space is a "given" element in the staging process, and not an element derived solely from textual considerations. It is in the act of staging itself that the text and setting come together and are shaped to achieve a *Gesamtkunstwerk.* Foreman states:

> . . . the text gets written, and then the next step is to try to figure out how to make that text resonate using the theatre as a sounding board. To try and find a way to stage it in the given space, so that each line, each gesture, will resonate and be amplified by the space.[21]

Perhaps the most extraordinary prerehearsal activity involves the tape-recording of a sound score. In mounting his productions, Foreman considers this process as a separate creative stage. He gathers the performers and, in one or two sessions, records all of the dialog on tape, and then, he notes, "it takes me about a week to edit the tape, so that we can rehearse to it."[22] During this week of editing, he adds music and noises until he has a complete sound score, explaining, "when I start rehearsing, it's really as if I had an orchestral score, it's really like choreographing—the piece is choreographed to that aural score."[23] It is true that, in a sense, Foreman does not direct the play from the script, because once the dialog is on tape, many other sounds are added to it, producing a finished sound product with its own rhythms. The tape-recorded score becomes a "sound object" involving duration. Foreman has stated, "I stage the play to the tape."[24]

The music included in Foreman's sound score is not homogeneous. The audience never hears an entire piece from beginning to end, but rather "bits and pieces," or short phrases, taken from a variety of musical sources. In addition, Foreman often distorts the music by recording it at a different speed than intended by the record manufacturer, or adding a sound overlay to it. For example, the music that accompanied a dance sequence in *Vertical Mobility* was a section of a banjo instrumental that Foreman recorded at slower than normal speed on one channel, or track, of the tape. He then overlayed an additional sound on a second channel by placing the microphone close to his mouth and repeating a brief whistle on the dominant beat of the banjo music.[25]

He did not decide to use banjo music in *Vertical Mobility* and then search for an appropriate instrumentation. Instead, for every production, he simply purchases anywhere from ten to thirty record albums and then selects from among them. In 1976, during an interview with Ted Shank in Paris while *Livre des Splendeurs* was being presented at the Festival d'Automne, Foreman described how he chooses the music for his productions:

> I tend to just go into record stores and blindly buy things that I think might be interesting. Then it's really amazing how sometimes when I get home—it happened this time again—I put the records on and said, "Shit. I just wasted a hundred dollars buying all these records, they're useless." Then, next day, I'm bored and have nothing to do, so I put on the record again, and hearing it a second time, all of a sudden you hear a section that's . . . aha! It's great! The only time I really appreciate Cagian principles of chance is in getting music for the shows . . . it always works.[26]

In addition to listening for sections that he likes, often he simply drops the needle on the record, and immediately chooses the first phrase, or somewhat longer cut, that he hears, recording it and making a "tape loop" (see page 145, chapter 4). Then he plays the sound from the loop, recording that sound as the loop repeats it over and over again. In choosing the section to record he explains that "when it works best, I just record a little section of it, and I don't really listen to it—I just snip, snip, glue it together, and generally it's okay."[27] In fact, he adds, "I'm stuck with that loop, because [if] I then try to find a better section and make a better loop . . . inevitably . . . [it doesn't work]."[28]

While some additional sound is added to the tape score during rehearsal, most of it is recorded in advance. In preparing the tape score, Foreman literally sits around his loft all day, as he puts it, "editing, adding thuds and things, listening to music, adding music, changing it [by] slowing it up [or] adding noises."[29] Very little of this tape score is altered in rehearsal. For Foreman, "the job of the staging is to take that sound object, and just use it in such a way that it works."[30]

It could be argued that Foreman's prerehearsal activities are not all that different from those that occur in preparing any work before it goes into rehearsal. It would seem, however, that Foreman deliberately "paints himself into a corner," as it were, in making certain choices. Before he begins shaping the performance in rehearsal, he not only decides that he will not adjust, adapt, or alter the text as originally written, but he also casts some performers without knowing what they will be "like" on the stage. Instead of working music and sound effects into the piece during rehearsals, he creates an extensive sound score beforehand and choreographs the performance to it. When the cast gathers to begin the arduous twelve weeks of rehearsals, the set has already been built, and Foreman begins to respond to, and work with, all of these "given" theatrical elements.

Foreman's rehearsals are open to anyone who wants to sit in, and a common reaction from many people who attend them is that the sessions are highly disorganized—a coherent systematic approach seems to be lacking. Observers often do not sense a central, guiding scheme underlying the process and, as a result, the decisions Foreman makes frequently appear to be somewhat capricious. Because Foreman has a reputation, and rightly so, for the rigorous precision of his work, this impression of his rehearsal procedure as somehow chaotic in nature seems anomalous. The reaction of Terry Curtis Fox, after watching a rehearsal, exemplifies a typical response to the experience:

> One of the things that had surprised me when I visited Foreman's theatre was the amount a particular piece changed during the rehearsal process. For all of Foreman's precision, a lot was improvised on the spot—as Foreman watched what happened in front of him—then redone in the context of the full work.[31]

This observation, however, is not entirely accurate and, therefore, somewhat misleading. While it is true that Foreman's approach is largely impromptu— he proceeds and composes extemporaneously—Fox also suggests a "theatre of improvisation" when he states that what is improvised in rehearsal is then "redone in the context of the full work." The implication is that the actors physically improvise activity which is then modified to "fit" the context of the play. Foreman once remarked that after seeing Yvonne Rainer's pieces, and performances by The Grand Union, he "began to feel guilty about allowing the [his] performers . . . so little freedom. Nothing could be further than improvisation from the way I stage my plays."[32]

Foreman controls every aspect of the work—the performers neither improvise nor initiate activity. He merely expects them to write down all of their actions, positions, and pauses; memorize them; and carry them out as precisely as possible. He does not explain "why" an activity must be carried out in one way rather than another, and the performers seldom ask questions or suggest solutions. Rehearsals are rather austere and can be somewhat tedious for the performers since the most distinctive feature of Foreman's staging procedure involves his rigorous attention to, and accumulation of, the most minute details of staging. He admits, "I spend very little time, relatively speaking, working with the actors. I spend a great deal of time on composition, arranging things."[33] During the rehearsals for *PAIN(T)* and *Vertical Mobility,* often what seemed to be an instruction to a performer—"Register how the word relates to the wait [pause]"—was actually Foreman in the process of thinking out loud or talking to himself. His staging process is closer to that of an artist working in private—painting, writing, or sculpting—than that of a theatre director.[34]

PAIN(T) sustained radical changes during the rehearsal period and is a good, if somewhat extreme, example of what an observer might encounter at rehearsals. Foreman tried a different approach to staging each scene almost every night. By the end of the fourth week of rehearsals, he was at a peak of vacillation with the piece. When he came to rehearsal one night, he told the performers that he was going to try some experiments with the fifth scene. The scene involved Rhoda and Eleanor positioned on a bed. The stage direction read: "Now both on a high, rolling table [bed], each head at a different side, legs together and overlapping." The bed was placed center and parallel to the audience, a few feet from the front row, making the space very shallow and crowded. First, Rhoda and Eleanor were to say the lines through long, narrow, cardboard tubes. Foreman watched this for a few minutes, said, "This is no good," and eliminated the tubes. He added music and instructed the performers to look at each other when saying the lines. Next, he discarded the music and told them to look upstage and deliver the lines. Finally, when nothing appeared to be working out, he said, "There is something about these positions that doesn't make sense with these lines." He changed it all again, deleting many of the lines from the text. At the next rehearsal he said, "I've been doing my homework and have finally figured out how to deal with the second part of this play." He added the lines that were deleted at the previous rehearsal, changed the position of the bed, and worked on the scene again (plate 71). It was not until the seventh week of rehearsal that *PAIN(T)* began to take shape and appear as it would in final form.[35]

Improvisation does indeed exist in Foreman's rehearsals, but only the director is involved and, unlike the goal of improvisation in most theatre, Foreman improvises in order to thwart consciously and continuously his own efforts to make a scene or moment "work." Foreman's rehearsal sessions can be characterized as proceeding by "deflection," "digression," or "deviation," where the notion of shaping something to adhere to a predetermined, overall context is irrelevant.

There is a fundamental goal behind this apparent incongruity that seems abstruse only because for centuries theatre art has been dominated by "expressivity"—like language, theatre is believed to possess an intrinsic expressive function. Foreman notes:

> The big trap in theatre, for me, is a kind of fallacy of expressionism, because you are concerned with expressing, which means that you are translating—there is something that you are going to give a kind of secondhand version of because you are expressing something else.[36]

In rehearsal Foreman must struggle to resist the impulse to express an idea or image, and instead find a means through which it can function directly, so that the idea becomes an operation, action, or force in the theatre piece. "Once I have an idea, or an insight," Foreman acknowledges, "a continual problem for me is how to avoid imitating it—how to have it really start functioning as a gesture in the real environment of the theatrical space."[37]

In *Rhoda in Potatoland,* for example, there are recurrent textual references to the act of "comparing." During the first scene of the play, Foreman's voice is heard on tape reciting three sequential lines from the text. In the first, he comments on the activity of Rhoda and Sophia, the two characters on the stage: "They compare their bodies." Next, he points out to the audience that: "It's only by comparing them we will know them." Then he instructs the spectator to: "Compare them in this situation."[38] It seems clear that the initial idea here is related to the fact that, beginning at the most basic perceptual level, we establish fundamental resemblances and differences among things by examining them in relation to one another. Rather than merely devise an image or sequence to express this idea, or make a particular point about it, Foreman works toward setting in motion schemes or systems designed to induce the spectator to make his own comparisons and, by extension, analogies.

For instance, there is a scene later in the play in which Rhoda and Agatha compare themselves to the enormous potato standing in the window (plate

39). They touch the surface of the potato and compare its shape to the roundness of their own behinds. Immediately following this sequence is a cafe scene (see chapter 3). Here, the possibilities for "comparisons" in the tableau (plate 36) are not supported by verbal references from the text. (In fact, the dialog seems somewhat distracting as Hannah discusses a book, as she squats over it, saying that it is titled, "Erotic photographs of the preceding century.")[39] Yet the web of interconnecting visual similarities and intellectual relationships is extremely dense. In addition to the relationships among images and objects in this tableau, pointed out in chapter 3 (see pages 51-52), there are analogies to be derived from similarities between people and objects. When Rhoda crawls to center stage and, remaining on her hands and knees, turns around and arches her back so that her derriere is prominently displayed to the audience, the comparison in the preceding scene, between the roundness of the potato and her derriere, suggests this connection once again. This time, however, the potato has a small, round mirror stuck in the top of its head. The potato is "looking" into the cafe, the mirror is the "eye" of the potato.

This particular potato resembles Rhoda in the roundness of its shape, and it also "sees" and walks. They are like each other in some respects, but do they agree in others? The observer is invited to speculate. Are Rhoda and the potato analogous beings? Are they "homologous," that is, is their similarity attributable to common origin? No. Their relationship is an example of "homomorphy," which is defined as: "similarity of form with different fundamental structure; superficial resemblance between organisms of different groups due to convergence." Foreman has taken the "idea" of comparing people and things to one another and placed it in a context where it functions directly. By creating a larger-than-life-size "potato being" and suggesting an analogous relationship between it and Rhoda, Foreman arouses or stimulates the mind of the spectator to indulge in making comparisons—the nature of these comparisons and analogies is designed to make the spectator aware *that* his mind is working, and realize *how* it is working.

There are many examples from *Rhoda in Potatoland* in which contexts are established for eliciting thought processes related to the "compare/contrast/collate" syndrome (see pages 51-53, chapter 3). But because the functional efficacy of these contexts depends on tactics engendered at different points and developed through time, it is extremely difficult to grasp the structural continuity of a Foreman piece during the rehearsal process. He frequently spends several days on only a few minutes of a production. What is observed, then, is Foreman's struggle with his "continual problem," or predilection for imitation and expression, which persistently arises and must be just as diligently rejected. As a result, one seemingly inexplicable characteristic of Foreman's rehearsal procedure involves the initiation of images and sequences propelled in a particular direction, followed by their sudden obliteration. "The important thing," Foreman insists, "[is] not to succumb to the easy tendency to get carried away in some kind of emotional flow, but to pull oneself to a stop at every moment and re-examine what's there (in the mind as one writes, or in the physical presence of actors and decor as one is staging the piece). . . ."[40]

He describes his staging procedure in terms of what he thinks every visual artist does:

> . . . he puts paint on the canvas and starts slopping it around until it starts looking right. Then it starts going wrong again, and you redo it, and it's wrong, and you redo it. . . . I think you realize, as you go on and on, that the only proficiency you develop is knowing what to reject. You must have the determination to keep trying *anything* to get you out of this terrible problem [of expressivity], and [then] have the ability to realize when, by the grace of God, the right thing shows up.[41]

This "redoing" and "trying anything" is related to the Steinian concept of beginning again and again. "For my purposes," explains Foreman, "that continual rebeginning soon baffles consciously directed effort. Or rather, the effort gets channeled into considerations of process rather than goal."[42] In other words, "consciously directed effort" is required in order to express an idea or image, and, for Foreman, the point is to focus all energy on setting certain processes into operation that will result in, introduce, or generate the truly novel and unexpected. He believes that it is impossible for this phenomenon to occur if the artist proceeds with a specific goal, or end product in mind. In 1976, his answer to a question posed by Ted Shank concerning his 1978 film project, which was still in the money-raising stage, is indicative of his approach to theatre:

> I can't say anything about my plans before I begin them, because it's all a matter of step-by-step constructing and then responding to it. So once the locations are chosen, you're responding to that. Once the music is chosen, you respond to that. Once the actors are chosen, you respond to that. It's sort of an accumulative process rather than just visualizing the end product and then working towards it.[43]

During his "accumulative" staging process, of course, he is also responding to the words of his text which, to some extent, determine the nature of his responses. Foreman has stated that he attempts to stage the process of writing: "I'm basically interested in staging what's going on in my head while I'm writing the play."[44] Hence, he is not interested in staging the text per se, nor does he attempt to express or imitate the meditative state he employs while writing (see chapter 2). "While the texts are carefully written," he points out, "the rehearsal process is a trying of every conceivable alternative to make the text say what I think it secretly wants to say."[45] An interpretation of this statement might read: "The words say what they say, but the text wants to *do* what it says."Taken as a whole, the text is a manifestation of how the mind operates when writing a play. It is not "about" the operations of the consciousness, it directly reflects them. This means, in Foreman's words,

> that the text of any given work is a series of "change of subjects"—which I believe becomes the subject of the work itself as that continual change-of-subject, interruption, re-beginning, reflects the true shape and texture of conscious experience, which recognized and reflected in the work of art puts us in the very "place" where being-human becomes a free and creative way-of-being.[46]

Unlike the receptive, passive, meditative state from which the writing is generated, Foreman is in an active, focused, and highly alert state in rehearsal. In this energetic state, in order to resist staging "ideas about" the nature of consciousness, Foreman employs certain strategies to force all the elements of his theatre to reflect directly how the mind operates. One such strategy involves accepting an initial impulse to stage a moment in a particular way, then determining the exact opposite of that impulse and restaging the moment according to its dictate. He might simply "undo" a sequence, and begin again without any particular scheme in mind.

The most common strategy, however, even when an idea or image is not heading in the direction of expressivity, can be characterized in terms of deflection. Frequently, a sequence of dialog or activity or music will be progressing on a specific course and then, swerve, or suddenly alter its initial direction. More often, an image will slowly and subtly be turned, deflected, or "bent" from a particular course. Foreman sometimes refers to this procedure as a kind of "twisting" of the elements so that each is slightly "off target." It is the strategy of continuous rebeginning that gives each rehearsal session its chaotic aspect. While it is partly due to the nature of deflection that a certain rigor is sensed, the "twisting" of the theatrical elements is related to the "change of subject" nature of consciousness. Foreman believes that "the important thing is to be true to each found 'arbitrary' moment. To see what is found therein as the TRULY 'other,' which allows no emotional identification, but only a 'moment for mental awakening' to the basic 'awkwardness' of the world outside us."[47]

This subtle deflection, or "twisting," he refers to is the most difficult procedure to discern during rehearsals. Yet, during certain sessions, it is possible to sense that it is there, or operating. For instance, the mounting of *Vertical Mobility,* which did not undergo the radical changes that characterized the *PAIN(T)* rehearsals, proceeded smoothly, and Foreman paid a great deal of attention to the slight, subtle movements of each performer. In one scene, Manheim (Rhoda) performed a sequence of words and positions sitting in a chair that directly faced the audience.[48] Foreman worked with her for several hours so that her feet, legs, torso, arms, hands, and head were placed in the essential and most precise positions in relation to the words she delivered. Equally important was the direction in which her eyes were focused with each position. The shifts in position were slight but very exact. For example, Manheim said, "Weight," "Ramp," "Airplane," "Caught," "Ice," "Tilt," "Cave," "Avenue," with pauses between each word.[49] Foreman altered the position of her body in relation to each word—feet to one side, one foot on the chair, head tilted, eyes looking down, legs spread, one hand on opposite thigh, mouth open. At one point he told her to move her lips silently and then said to himself, "This is much better, much more neurotic." Foreman explained to her that the timing had to be exact and the positions precise, because "there is a big difference in the slightest shift in position."

Originally for this scene, the chair was positioned downstage, on the right side. A performer covered completely in white material, like a ghost figure, was placed upstage, on the left side, directly in front of the rear white curtain. Foreman once noted that, "It is hard to know, moment by moment, when to do something because it simply pleases you and when to do something because, whether it pleases you or not, it follows a process or pattern you think important." In the eighth week of rehearsals, Foreman moved Manheim and the chair directly upstage so that they remained on the right side but were placed on the same plane as the ghost figure (plate 24).

While Foreman worked with Manheim on positioning, he added other elements to the scene. The constant, monotonous "tick" of a metronome was heard, and a tape recording of Foreman's voice said: "Notice that each new position of the body implies a different structural extension of the preceding thought. . . ." The performer wearing the ghost costume was given a bell and specific times to ring it. He rang the bell by shaking his entire body under the white material. Foreman added an artificial flower to the top of the ghost costume; later, during a run-through, he left his seat without stopping the rehearsal, walked to the ghost figure, ripped the flower off the costume, and threw it away.

The reason why Foreman discarded the flower after weeks of rehearsal is "anyone's guess," so to speak, and a multitude of such instances occur during the rehearsals for any Foreman production. There are obvious reasons, however, for a number of decisions he makes. During rehearsals for both *PAIN(T)* and *Vertical Mobility,* he added tape-recorded words and speeches to clarify sections he felt needed explanation. After a few weeks of rehearsals, for example, he added a tape of his voice to the beginning of each play: "This play is about making art (pause) from a certain energy (pause) which most people use (pause) most of the time *(PAIN(T)),*" and, "The play focuses on Max who has given up writing . . . *(Vertical Mobility)."* At several points in *Vertical Mobility,* Foreman added, "The important word is . . . showing." The "important word" would change with each repetition depending on which word he wanted to bring into the foreground. The tape allowed Foreman to interrupt the performance and address the spectator directly (see pages 142-43, chapter 4).

Often noises are added during the rehearsal period to provide cues for the performers. At one *Vertical Mobility* rehearsal, Foreman told the actors, "For the change [in position] I'll put in a boing." Until he got around to recording the sound, he shouted "cue!" Eventually, his shouting became part of the piece, and the "boing" was never added. Several times during the performance, Foreman shouted "cue" from his booth behind the bleachers (see footnote 19, chapter 4).

Further examples of decisions that are made for obvious reasons include a distinctive feature of the rehearsal process—the continuous addition of visual framing devices (see chapter 4). In *Vertical Mobility* a performer attached a string to one wall, about three feet from the floor, drew it horizontally across the stage, parallel to the floor, and attached it to the opposite wall. Another performer, lying on the floor, raised his leg so that his toe touched the string. At a rehearsal, Foreman added a frame to the foot by instructing another performer to attach a rectangular piece of white material to the string directly behind the foot, literally framing the foot (plate 72).

Sometimes framing devices are added to framing devices and used simultaneously. A picture and frame were built into the rear wall of the *Vertical Mobility* setting. At one point in the play, the picture popped out of the frame, leaving the frame and a square-shaped opening. Later, a performer stood behind the wall, looking through the opening so that her face was framed. During a rehearsal, Foreman added the beam of a flashlight so that her face was also framed by a small circle of light.

Two flashlights mounted on a board, controlled from above and behind the spectators, were used to spotlight individual faces and objects throughout both performances. In rehearsal, Foreman experimented with aiming the flashlight beams while deciding which elements he wanted to emphasize. For example, in *PAIN(T)* a performer was lying on the floor in the rear of the space with a lighted chandelier on the floor next to him. The lights were dim; there was activity occurring downstage. After several rehearsals, Foreman added a small beam of light around the face of the performer lying in the rear. This device helped to emphasize the depth of the space while, at the same time, framing the face, bringing it "closer."

There is one final reason why Foreman decides to include additional sound or noises during the rehearsal period, that may, or may not, be obvious to some observers. It has to do with a purely subjective sensation of sound, specifically the "tinnitus" quality of spoken language. Because the decision to add a noise or sound after a word or sentence based on tinnitus is entirely dependent on the sound/meaning relationship of the language, Foreman has great difficulty with this procedure when he directs his productions in French. In Paris, he described the problem to Shank:

> In America, when somebody onstage says, "You sat down, you sat down, now you sit down," I can sense, listening to it, that it might have enough weight so, for instance, the stage could be still at that moment. The weight of that statement carries it. Here [France], I know what they're saying, but I can't sense the weight. I feel that, as a result, my direction is just slightly distanced from the text and there's a decorative pattern of the mise-en-scene which isn't locked in quite as tightly to exactly what is being said at each moment. I feel that, but I can't even tell if it's correct . . . but I sense that it's happening.[50]

This notion of "locking the elements together tightly at each moment" is crucial to a fundamental impulse, or drive, behind all of Foreman's staging—the drive is toward clarity. He has stressed this concept in many different contexts stating, for example, that "The realm of art is trying to be clear about its materials which in turn, as you watch it, helps you to be clear about your own watching."[51] Most frequently, however, he discusses "clarity" in relation to his staging:

> As a director, I'm not tinkering to make them [my plays] work better. I'm tinkering to make whatever necessity is there more clearly seen, and to eliminate anything that interferes with the clarity of that moment. Most of my directing is just continual readjustment, mostly spatial, and also in time, in terms of adding thoughts and tics and pauses and whatever. Just framing everything to make whatever is there, in all its contradictoriness and ambiguity, terribly clear at each moment. To make the contradictory polarity of each moment radically clear.[52]

Foreman uses the word clarity not only in the limited sense of intelligibility. He uses it to imply an all-inclusive lucidity, that is, every aspect of each moment is evident on as many different levels as possible, from the perceptual and intellectual to the spiritual. The use of visual and aural framing devices, of course, is one way to achieve clarity on the perceptual level. But framing, as punctuation, is essentially static, and Foreman is equally interested in achieving kinetic clarity.

Foreman employs a variety of means to emphasize movement through space. String, for instance, is often drawn across the playing area to mark the path taken by a performer, moving from one point to another. Originally, the use of string was derived from Foreman's desire to separate and frame specific elements and moments. He states:

> I always start with a basically real situation of some sort. And then I want to isolate things, I want to superimpose the diagrammatic aspect, I want to find ways to frame little details and relationships so that the audience takes joy, as I do, in seeing the intricacy of the way the world is put together, and all the different things coming together in joints.[53]

It was during the rehearsals for one of his commercial productions, *Dr. Selavy's Magic Theatre* (1972), that Foreman began to use string dynamically. He recalls

> the first time I used a lot of string was in *Selavy,* because it was not my work, really. I was using someone else's lyrics, and somehow in the text things were not clear enough for me. And as I started staging it, the space on stage wasn't—because it wasn't reinforced properly by the text—wasn't clear enough. I remember at a certain point midway in the rehearsals saying, " . . . ah, it could be clear, I see. She's making a cross like that. I'll have a string which will emphasize the space that she is creating by making a cross like that."[54]

He also uses a string to "suggest" movement. For example, in *Rhoda in Potatoland,* a white string was stretched horizontally across the proscenium plane, near the first row of spectators, and remained there throughout the performance (plates 36 and 37). Beginning where it was attached to the wall on the right side, about one quarter of the string was painted black. Because the stage floor was also painted black, the black portion of the string became invisible against this black background. Hence, as the spectator's eye moved along the white string, from left to right, the string suddenly disappeared, suggesting that the white line had been propelled from the left and was "still traveling," in a specific direction, toward the right.

The "dotted" black and white strings—white string painted black at equally spaced intervals—also give the impression of movement, like the "running lights" on an electronic billboard that spell out words or depict an image when one bulb at a time is lit in a sequential pattern. The light "moves" from one point to another. In *Vertical Mobility,* a black and white cord, stage left, was used to arouse a sensation of movement from downstage to a vanishing point upstage (plate 24). In *Pandering to the Masses,* "dotted" strings were used to suggest a horizontal movement pattern, intersected by a diagonally moving line (plate 33).

When several strings appear onstage simultaneously, an etching, or line drawing effect is sometimes created because of the "delicate" quality of the strings. In *Rhoda,* Foreman replaced some of the strings with relatively cumbersome tubes, because he wanted some of the lines to be less "elegant," and thereby function less like drawing lines.[55] Note that in plate 73 the section of the white tubing that runs offstage to the left side is painted black, blending it into the black wall (background) behind it, and echoing the same phenomenon created by the white string that seems to disappear on the right side of the stage. Both are present onstage simultaneously and suggest movement in different directions—the tubing emphasizes the depth of the playing area by implying movement from upstage, diagonally, to downstage toward the left, and the string emphasizes the width of the stage by suggesting movement from left to right.

Similarly, stripes painted on set pieces and props can imply movement, or create a sensation of movement, through optical illusion (see page 54, chapter 3). Examples abound in every Ontological-Hysteric Theatre production. The point is that Foreman works with optical and spatial illusions, not only to emphasize the dynamics of movement through space via strings, cords, stripes, and tubes, but also to keep the eye of the spectator "traveling," noticing more than he would if his eyes were focused on only one or two points in the playing area.

Strings and similar devices are used to underscore actual movement through space, as well as arouse the sensation of movement. They are not, however, the only means through which Foreman puts emphasis on his unique way of "moving things around in three-dimensional space." "Rehearsal is all a matter of placement in context," he maintains. "The crucial thing is making each moment completely clear."[56] The word "placement" is more appropriate than the term "blocking" to describe this aspect of Foreman's rehearsal process, because placement is related to his all-encompassing concept of clarity. It is primarily through placement, or his "continual spatial readjustment," that all forms of "interference" are removed and clarity in each moment is achieved. "Placement," he contends, "is nine-tenths of the staging."[57]

On one level, Foreman's placement procedure resembles that of a painter: "I tend to think in a very frontal, picture-plane way."[58] In chapter 4, Foreman's use of picturization was discussed—many of his visual arrangements are composed of tableaux designed to emphasize the two-dimensional nature of the picture, or proscenium, plane. In addition, his set designs are based on the use of right angles so that the walls of his stage settings reinforce the profile and frontal positions of the performers (see pages 39-40, chapter 3). When he places a performer in the playing area, he wants the spectator to be able to see exactly where that actor is placed in spatial relation to every other performer onstage, and all the features of the set.

Accordingly, in moving the performers through space, Foreman often works toward establishing patterns that emphasize the movement itself, and its formal relationship to the area in which it occurs. A dance sequence from *Vertical Mobility* provides an excellent example of this—it was choreographed to the dominant beats of the banjo instrumental described earlier (see page 164). In staging the dance in rehearsal, Foreman arranged four performers standing next to each other, a few feet apart, in the same plane across the stage, facing the audience. A second row of four performers was positioned in the same manner a few feet behind the first row. Foreman paced out the dance for the performers and described it as "a sort of Groucho Marx flapping of the arms, etc. . . ."[59]

The performers were to place their hands on their hips, bend their knees a little, and bend slightly forward from the waist. In this position, they all walked in unison four steps directly to their left. Then, with hands still on hips, they moved (flapped) their elbows back and forth four times. Next, they turned completely around in place using four steps, made another movement with their arms on the count of four, and walked four steps directly to their right (plate 74). They repeated this activity several times, moving from left to right across the stage. Thus, the dance was performed in two planes of the playing space.

After a few rehearsals, Foreman made one change in this dance pattern. A couple of the performers, after performing the pattern described above two or three times, were instructed to take their four steps forward, toward the audience, and their next four steps directly backward, still facing the audience. This was carried out in unison and simultaneously with the other dancers, who continued their movement from left to right. Thus, although the pattern was momentarily extended out of the two single planes, this movement tended to emphasize the horizontal pattern and stress the logical, deliberate division of the playing space. Foreman described the dancers as "large hostile birds" and told them to "glare at the audience in a hostile manner" throughout the dance, "essentially asking the spectators what they are doing about this piece of art they are watching."

Dance sequences are not the only instances in which movement patterns are recognizable. For every production, Foreman establishes patterns for simply moving on and off stage that dominate throughout the performance (see chapter 6). Even small movements and gestures tend to call attention to themselves, demonstrating "how" they are carried out—the opening and closing of doors, for example. Manheim remembers that on the day Foreman asked her to perform in *HOTEL CHINA,* she noticed that when he entered the room he did not just close the door behind him. Instead, after walking into the room, he turned, faced the door and pulled it toward him, closing it before turning to continue through the room. Watching a rehearsal that evening, she noticed that all of the performers were closing doors in the same, somewhat disjointed manner.[60]

Kirby describes how simple movement can be the primary element of a sequence, using an example from the first act of *Sophia:*

> . . . the Mountaineer (or Abominable Snowman), who is wearing a one-piece waterproof suit with a hood and dark glasses, is alone on stage. He is standing motionless, facing front. With a single movement, he throws out the coiled rope he carries onto the floor, holding on to one end as the rope partially uncoils. Rhoda enters, wearing only a blanket and carrying a long thin stick. She aims the stick at the free end of the rope and, working very slowly and carefully, moves the tip along it, following the twists and convolutions. Nothing moves except the long pointer [plate 75].[61]

Kirby also describes a dance sequence from *Sophia,* in which movement is the primary element. But, unlike the dance from *Vertical Mobility,* described above, where movement underscored the width of the stage space, the dancers' movement through space in the sequence Kirby describes emphasizes the depth of the playing area.

> The first act of "Sophia" has almost ended when the performers, who have been holding hands in a long arc and watching the Mountaineer perform a crouching ape-like dance, break into a similar dance to bouncy jazz music. Each person crouches and bends forward. Elbows are held out to the side, away from the body, and the hands are close to the stomach. Most keep their heads up, but no two performers dance in exactly the same way. Some look toward the spectators as much as possible, even when their bodies are turned away. Some move their elbows. Some circle their hands around each other, while others merely move them in time to the music. Gradually, the dancers fill the entire deep space of the playing area [plate 76].[62]

In addition to its obviously contrived aspects, Foreman's placement procedure involves a moment-to-moment responding to the elements in the space. Individual performers can have an effect on the placement process. For example, the performer playing the role of Ida in *PAIN(T)* was replaced by a different performer midway through the rehearsals.[63] Positions were changed somewhat because of the visual differences between the two people. This was true partially because, with the exception of a few deliberately constructed costumes, the performers wore the same clothes in performance that they wore every night to rehearsals. Hence, the colors a performer usually wore affected the way Foreman placed him in the space.

Because the setting for *PAIN(T)* was not complete when rehearsals began, the placement process was also affected by the adding and subtracting of both large set pieces and props. After a few rehearsals, Foreman added a tent structure, shaped like a tower and made from white sheet material. It was hung from the ceiling and extended to the floor with an opening so that a performer could stand inside of it. He tried different ways of using the tent, but eventually it was eliminated and did not appear in the final production. Since it is always true that performers are placed in strict relation to set pieces and props, the placement of performers is restaged if an object is added or discarded.

While the acting style of Foreman's theatre has changed significantly over the years, his general attitude toward the art of acting has been a bone of contention for many of his contemporaries, and there have always been serious misconceptions regarding Foreman's use of performers. One of the earliest such misinterpretations surfaced in the spring of 1969 in a piece published in the *East Village Other* on the second Ontological-Hysteric Theatre production, *Ida-Eyed.* Lita Eliscu described the performance as follows:

Six people motion, talk to and through one another, until the stage is a circus of simultaneous impulses, a clock's inner working all gone crazy, counter and clockwise at the same time (ow). Chairs vibrate, fall over, people announce their intention of doing something but don't. . . . *Paradise Now* and many other avant-garde works are impossible to perform without those people out there [the audience]. *Ida-Eyed* gives off the definite notion that whether or not anyone knew, the chaos on the stage would be reproduced according to the whim and dictate of the actors involved. . . .[64]

The general impression is one of a highly disorganized theatrical event, generated by improvisation among six performers. This, of course, has never been the case. The role of the actors in rehearsal, combined with Foreman's propensity for giving objects and set pieces the same status as live performers in his productions, has led some people to accuse him of treating his performers like objects.

In describing the function of the actors in performance, Florence Falk wrote, "Performers are *merely* persons of masculine or feminine gender whose personal features are deliberately effaced."[65] While it is true that Foreman deliberately strips his *characters* of all personal traits and idiosyncrasies, it is impossible to "efface the personal features" of the *performers* unless you clothe them completely in costume and mask. (Until his 1978 production of *Blvd. de Paris,* the performers often wore their own street clothes in performance.) Foreman places numerous restrictions on the activity of his performers, which automatically determines many characteristics of the acting style. But even in the context of the extreme limitations Foreman imposes, an individual quality, and way of doing things, emanates naturally, and often unconsciously, from each performer.

In addition to the difference that will manifest itself between any two people, even under the most rigidly controlled circumstances, Foreman sensed a difference between his French and American performers, in both general attitude and specific ways of carrying out tasks. He explains:

There is even a difference in the way people handle the props. Americans would bring in a tube, and they'd clunk it down, and that would be it. The French are a little bit more concerned about being graceful, and proper, and correct.

There also seems to be something in the French character that's much more sociable, in a way, than in the American character. With few exceptions, the French don't have that kind of lonely, almost perverse, intense, and very private madness that is part and parcel of a lot of Americans. They don't have the same ability to really be alone onstage and do something, and just do it. They're always speaking about communicating, they're always thinking "I'm doing this and my friends are looking at me."[66]

Of course this difference Foreman senses could merely be the consequence of his own casting decisions, and not the result of inherent qualitative variances. In any case, the qualities he delineates demonstrate the impact of the individual performer on the nature of the work.

Foreman is not a stranger to the traditional approaches to acting. Amy Taubin was a successful "method" actress while she and Foreman were married, and he worked with her and her friends. Before that, in high school and college, Foreman himself played leading roles, generally older men—Willy Loman, Prospero, and Petruchio, among them—in as many as twenty-five plays.[67] Ultimately, he was impressed by Robert Bresson's use of nonprofessional actors because he found their performances genuine, and more interesting than the "overblown" performances in most commercial film.[68]

It was from dance, rather than film, however, that the acting element of Foreman's work derived its greatest influence. Foreman explains that

the great teacher, for me, about acting techniques . . . [was] Yvonne Rainer, not only seeing her performance, but reading what she wrote about dealing with the performer, and finding that what you did was more interesting than the whole reason that you did it.[69]

From Rainer's work, Foreman became interested in channeling the actor's attention and energy on the performance of the action itself, and not the motivation for doing the act. While this is still true of Foreman's approach to acting, other dimensions of the performing have undergone extensive change.

In the early productions of the Ontological-Hysteric Theatre, the "amount" of acting, or its complexity, in the sense of representation, impersonation, and simulation, could be described as "minimal."[70] On an acting/not-acting continuum, the exchange between Rhoda and Sophia that Kirby described from *Sophia* (see pages 155-156, chapter 4) would definitely fall toward the not-acting end. The time/place matrices were weak. The lines, prerecorded and broadcast, were delivered in a flat, unemotional, uninflected manner. During the dialog in each of the three stage pictures that composed the sequence, the women were motionless except for the barely perceptible movement necessary to repeat a few, isolated words related to their tape-recorded lines. If acting is defined as something that is *done* by a performer, then there was no acting in this particular scene. The women represented the characters in a passive, or "received" sense. They did not *do* anything to impersonate, or portray the characters. Their performances tended to be concrete for, while they did not attempt to project their own personalities or "play themselves," they did not actively pretend to be the characters they represented either.

In addition to the six or so titled characters in Foreman's plays, a number of unnamed performers appear in every production. These "crew people," as he calls them, carry props and furniture on and offstage, pull strings across the space and remove them, participate in the dances, appear in the tableaux, and occasionally produce sound effects "live" to accompany the taped score. Although it could be argued that character matrix creates a significant difference in any theatrical context, there was not all that much difference between the performances of the actors representing titled characters and these unnamed crew people, when measured in terms of the amount or complexity of acting.

During rehearsals for *PAIN(T)* and *Vertical Mobility,* in which the performers delivered all their lines live from the stage, Foreman instructed them to deliver the lines flatly and in a normal speaking voice. No attempt was made to project or interpret the lines. Occasionally, in order to inject a moment of color, he gave a performer a specific way to deliver a line, telling him to do it like "a school teacher scolding a child" or "in a singsong manner." In the following production, *Pandering to the Masses,* there was not only a noticeably greater variety of inflection in line delivery, but the performer's gaze shifted more frequently and appeared less fixed and unfocused. In the next Ontological-Hysteric Theatre production, *Rhoda in Potatoland,* the complexity of the acting had increased to the point where Manheim was performing scenes of "hysteria."

Many people attribute this change in the acting style to the influence of Manheim as a performer. Foreman concurs that Manheim's "strong stage personality" became a desirable "interference" in the work, causing it to change.[71]

> There's no question that she has forced certain changes in my work which has made it more accessible. She's interested in all sorts of razzmatazz which I've had to be dragged into reluctantly, but I think it's been very healthy for my work. No question also that it's changing the whole complexion of my casting and that it will continue to do so. Kate clearly has a unique virtuosity that I want to use more and more and that I want from others, which means as the years go by I have to get more and more trained people to do stuff. In the beginning I was just exploiting the fact that I had a lot of performers who were the kinds of people you'd never seen on stage before. You watched their awkwardness. . . . This piece [*Blvd. de Paris*] is all based on an almost cinematographic technique of cutting from one emotion immediately to its violent opposite. Kate spends all night running around from one thing to the other with *no* transitions, which is very difficult. It's a question each night whether she'll get through it.[72]

In a review of the production that Foreman is referring to above, a critic wrote:

> To Foreman and to his admirers, Manheim has grown increasingly expressive, has become an excellent agent for his work. To me she is only an increasingly confident amateur about whom the word "talent" is irrelevant, who is now less doggedly unashamed of being on a stage at all—let alone naked as she often has been—whose movement is now a bit less patent obedience to a director's orders, and who can now make three or four faces more than she used to be able to make.[73]

This, of course, is a value judgment that confuses objective observation with subjective response. The critic obviously equates "good acting" with complexity and, he feels, unless the acting is complex, talent is not required. There is nothing wrong with being able to "make faces"—in some styles it is considered an essential part of acting. How many "faces" Manheim is required to make in a piece is not what determines how well she executes the task. Many people consider Manheim an extraordinary performer—she was presented with an Obie award for her outstanding performance in *Rhoda in Potatoland* at the twenty-first annual *Village Voice* ceremonies honoring achievement in Off Broadway and Off-Off Broadway theatre.

The point here is that the critic implies what many believe to be true, that is, to become an "expressive professional," rather than merely a "confident amateur," the actor must be expressive in a complex way. One way to add to the "amount" or complexity of the acting when expressing something is to become emotionally involved with the character or situation and project that particular quality or emotion. But emotion can certainly be expressed without the emotional involvement of the performer, and the absence of this dimension will not diminish its value in terms of "good" and "bad"—it is merely somewhat less complex.

In *Rhoda in Potatoland,* Manheim performed a sequence on top of a table that was slanted toward the audience in such a way that she had to hang onto the sides to keep from sliding off. The scene began as Manheim walked onto the stage with her hand to her chin and paced back and forth directly in front of the spectators, looking as though she were rather skeptically "sizing them all up." She explains that while she was doing this, "I would think to myself, 'Oh, you're still there.' "[74] This thought would come across as more or less hostile, depending on how she felt about a particular audience on a particular night. In other words, at that moment, Kate Manheim, as performer, was consciously relating to and responding to the spectators' presence. Next, as loud music began to play, she slid onto the table and a large, black, rubber galosh was placed on one of her feet. She acted terribly frightened of it, raising and holding her leg up off the table, as if she were trying to stay as far away from the boot as possible. A potato was then placed on her stomach. From the moment she saw the potato, she became increasingly more hysterical, gyrating her body back and forth wildly, as much as she could while holding onto the table (plate 77). Although she considered her acting in this scene as representing a kind of hysterical fit, she made no attempt to recreate such an emotional state inside herself. She explains that she was creating "just the appearance of such a state"—going through the "motions" of hysteria rather than living through such an experience emotionally. Manheim is continuously aware of the process of performing while she is onstage.

I'm not interested in letting myself get carried away in a role and becoming so absorbed in the character I'm playing that I forget and lose myself. I'm not interested in it all coming so naturally that when I say the lines it's like the person [character] saying them.[75]

In addition, when working on the sequence in rehearsal, she did not think in terms of making the hysteria "believable" in the sense of convincing the spectators that the character was really experiencing such an ordeal. She was not trying to manipulate the spectator's emotions, coercing them into identifying with Rhoda, thereby feeling anxious or sorry for her. When asked how she went about working on the scene, she began by explaining how it was carefully staged and then, "I got used to the scene and I knew that each thing was a cue [like seeing the potato] and I react according to plan."[76] This, of course, does not mean that because she reacts automatically, her acting style is not as good as those using different approaches. On the contrary, her energy level and work with the body make her total performance quite skillful and impressive. The fact that she is not required to become psychologically or emotionally involved with either the character or a scene, merely gives her the opportunity to concentrate on other work—the physical tasks in the hysteria scene particularly, were extremely difficult and strenuous.

Over the years, spectators and critics have commented on Manheim's "presence," the Rhoda "look," and her energy level. The techniques she uses to achieve these qualities were developed during the rehearsal periods for each production, but she developed them quite separately from Foreman's rehearsal process and procedures. She never concerns herself with what the plays are "about." She admits that she does not understand the plays, and she feels it does not matter. She notes, "I do have an understanding, but it's more intuitive—I couldn't explain the plays in the same way Richard would."[77] Like Foreman, she works against ambiguity, explaining, "Just as Richard tries to make each moment of the play clear, I work to make each thing I do completely clear to the audience."[78] In a twelve-week rehearsal period, it is not until three weeks before opening that she begins to think about the character's place in the piece as a whole. "I wait until the run-throughs, until I see where the whole thing is going and then I begin to work with that."[79] Until then, she spends several weeks concentrating solely on memorizing the physical tasks and carrying them out precisely.

Regardless of how many times Foreman changes the placement and activity of each sequence in a play, both he and the actors ultimately work toward clarity in each gesture and moment. In this sense, Foreman functions in the traditional role of the director as a "surrogate audience." Foreman wants the spectator to be able to notice as much as possible, on as many levels as possible, in every moment of the piece. With this in mind, he works toward eliminating anything that might interfere with the numerous possibilities for experiencing his work. He does not function as a surrogate audience in the sense of shaping the piece so that the spectators will "like" it. He is very pleased when the audience responds favorably to the production, but he does not manipulate the elements in rehearsal to this end. Foreman is not concerned only with an "end product." He wants the spectator to notice not only the "art that is made" but also that "art is being made."

He explains that the staging is a manifestation of

all the collisions that result from my own efforts to see and notate clearly, with my awkwardness, with my own built-in problems in perceiving things. And the world not letting me be as enlightened and brilliant and happy as I would like.

So in that sense, the work is all extremely personal. I'm doing it for myself. And then offering it to anybody else that might be encouraged by it, a little bit.[80]

Hence, in rehearsal, Foreman works solely to please himself rather than a prospective audience. "Most theatre is built on people trying very consciously to manipulate the audience's response. I'm certainly not trying to do that. Really, I'm just trying to make an object that I'll end up loving."[81]

Along with the work of many other artists, his pieces have been labeled "experimental theatre." An experiment is defined as a "test, trial, or tentative procedure" carried out in order "to discover or prove something." The experimenting in Foreman's work occurs only in rehearsal. Consequently, when the rehearsal period is over, the testing is over, and his plays are exactly as he wants them to be.

"What interests me most about twentieth-century art," Foreman states, "is that a process is arising where it is no longer a question of 'expressing,' but of finding a way to set processes in operation that really try to introduce novelty into the universe."[82] To understand fully what Foreman means by this statement, it is necessary to examine the structure of his work and its effect.

6

Foreman as Spectator: The Experience of Ontological-Hysteric Theatre

All theatre involves two fundamental, interlocking parts or systems: (1) the presentation, or object of perception—involving all the qualities of the performance itself; and (2) the experience of it, or the spectator's perception of that performance. For the most part, the preceding chapters have focused on Richard Foreman's creative process, and the objective, physical characteristics of his theatre art. In this chapter, emphasis is placed on the spectator and the subjective aspects of the experience, which include a consideration of style, structure, and effect. All of these directly relate to the individual spectator's perceptual and psychological methods-of-operating or subjective states.

In the first chapter, it was established that Foreman is not at all interested in the accessibility of his work to large numbers of people, or "the masses." He is engaged in the creation of a rather esoteric, "coterie art." Because this is true, it seems logical to begin by identifying Foreman's conception of the spectator, discussing the general nature of his intent with regard to that spectator. Who is his audience?

Foreman himself is the principal spectator of Ontological-Hysteric Theatre, as well as its writer, designer, and director. He creates theatre art primarily for himself. Arrogance, however, is not the motivation behind his insistence that he works solely to please himself. On the contrary, his stance is a manifestation of an ethical, or moral, position. When asked about his self-centered approach, Foreman defended himself saying:

> People think that it's very self-indulgent, but I just don't see how else anyone can honestly proceed. How can I guess what would be good for you—what you want, what you would like—and then give it to you? I could proceed that way on a certain level if I wanted to con you, seduce you, do all kinds of other things that I don't think are particularly good for you.[1]

He refuses to gear his theatre art to the conjectured needs of a hypothetical, nebulous group of people, the audience.

The work is self-referential because, he explains, "All I know is what is in my own head, what is my background."[2] At the same time, he does not believe that his experiences are unique, producing work so hermetic that it cannot be fruitfully experienced by others. The point is that, in working for himself, he is the only model for experiencing the work—he does not attempt to second-guess the response of any spectator other than himself. He asserts:

> I have an intention with respect to one member of the audience, who is myself. I would hope that somebody else is on the same wavelength, that I'm not alone on this planet in my obsessions and concerns. I can only hope that some people need what I feel I need, and what I'm trying to make for myself to feed my need.[3]

Mind and Art: Experience Versus Object or Event

Therapy is another dimension of this creator-oriented approach to art. The premise being that, during the creative process, the artist works on himself as much as—if not more than—on the work of art. In the process of creation, the creator changes himself, alters his own consciousness. During a conversation with John Cage and Richard Kostelanetz in December of 1978, published in *Performing Arts Journal,* Foreman pointed out that he was not dissatisfied with his work "because I feel it's as good as anything anyone else has done. I am dissatisfied with what I am because I know that I'm not as good as my plays. To me that's the issue." To which Cage responded, "There's a remark of Thoreau that I think needs to be quoted now. He said, 'It's not important what form the sculptor gives the stone. It's important what the sculpting does to the sculptor.'" "Yes, that's my position," Foreman replied. But Kostelanetz objected, stating: "What we're doing as artists and writers is making things that are superior in perception and intelligence to us: what we do usually extracts from us a cost not only in money but in psychic health." Cage's retort captures the theme and focus of this chapter:

> Since the forties I have thought that wasn't true. So when I read Thoreau's statement I was delighted. The same thing is echoed in that line you're so familiar with: "What is the purpose of making music? To sober and quiet the mind thus making it susceptible to divine influence." Which is another way of saying music is of no importance whatsoever. What is important is the mind of the musician. We're dealing with mind not art. At one time, in the field of music at least, there was a lot of talk about audience participation. And what we've been talking about, if not audience participation, is audience activity.[4]

Foreman has affirmed, on more than one occasion, that "Frankly, my art is a kind of therapy, for myself, but I think that's the best thing art could possibly be."[5] He does not use the term "psychotherapy" because he is not referring to the remedial treatment of mental and emotional disorders. Instead, therapy, in Foreman's usage, implies that art functions as a manner of handling or treating the mind—and its aggregate, the consciousness—which may, or may not, involve a remedial dimension. This function of art is related to the distinction Cage makes between mind and art. He is not referring to the structure of the brain, but to the workings of the mind—audience activity is "mental activity." To reiterate, when Cage states that "We're dealing with mind not art," he means that the subjective perception of art, with its coincident active mental processes, is far more important and significant than the passive object or that which, objectively, is perceived.

Foreman concurs with Cage on this point as well. Although Foreman is the creator of the event experienced, he is more concerned with the subjective facets of experience itself than with the performance object he creates. Hence, Foreman's theatre is necessarily and essentially spectator-oriented—an ostensible contradiction of his creator-oriented, self-centered approach. But even though Foreman is conscious of himself as the *only* spectator in the creation of each piece, he does eventually invite an audience to attend them, and, precisely because he is conscious of himself as spectator/perceiver/observer in the creative process, it is simply by extension that his theatre is ultimately spectator-centered.

In a certain sense, it can be said that all theatre is essentially spectator-oriented and spectator-centered, but here the implication is that the artist is *primarily* interested in (1) the mechanisms that function in the experience of time; and (2) in affecting that experience, altering the usual, predictable experience of most theatre. This is not only what interests Foreman, it constitutes the impulse behind his work, and its fundamental goal.

The Experience of Life-Simulating Theatre

In developing his approach to achieving this goal, Foreman was reacting against an experience of theatre with which he was acutely familiar, describing it in terms of processes and conditions associated with sleep and dream states. Between 1952 and 1961, Foreman saw nearly everything on Broadway. Throughout his teenage years, he attended the theatre every Saturday afternoon and spent the rest of the week daydreaming about the world of the play, immersed in its emotional milieu. While he thoroughly enjoyed this period of involvement with commercial theatre as a spectator, years later he felt that the daydreaming each play induced, in the final analysis, was not desirable, explaining, "I think that kind of daydreaming seduces the perceptual mechanism and puts the will to sleep."[6] Recalling the early work of his contemporary Robert Wilson, Foreman remembers being overwhelmed by the experience, and being bothered by the work for that reason. He explains:

It was overwhelming in a way that I used to find things overwhelming when I was a kid. I remember seeing *Picnic* when I was fifteen, and for a week I just kept thinking about the people and the play and wishing I was in that town and wanting to be with them. And I found Wilson's work seductive in the same way. Overwhelmingly so. . . . I tend to think that to lure people into a dream world can be a very powerful experience, but . . . I think it just increases our tendency to be asleep and to dream. Rather than being very awake in the present.[7]

This waking sleep state Foreman refers to is related to the goal of life-simulating theatre. The spectator is induced to forget where he is and project himself into the illusionary emotional realm of the play. Furthermore, this hypnotism, as it were, is not confined to the time span of the experience of such theatre. It affects everyday life by reinforcing conditioned ways of responding to people, situations, thoughts, and emotions. Foreman contends that,

Most theatre wants you to come out and say, "Wow! Was I knocked out, and was I moved!" What that means is: Wow! The emotional habits that were taught to me by society were again appealed to by this theatre, and I'm more deeply trained than ever to respond in these basically artificial, incorrect ways.[8]

For Foreman, incorrect, artificial ways of responding are those that are taught and learned, becoming habitual and automatic. In 1969 he asserted, "I no longer see any justification for manipulating an audience, putting them through certain preconceived emotional changes that I think only deepen their habitual responses, which are the things that louse them up in life."[9] Eight years later, he reaffirmed his position:

I don't want to reinforce what people already think. I don't want to refrighten them, or reconvince them that they love what they already love. I don't want to deepen the roots of emotional habit.[10]

For Foreman, this is precisely the function of theatre as entertainment.

Foreman believes that "You make entertainment when you give people essentially what they want—what is going to reinforce opinions, feelings, and attitudes that they already have, and enjoy having the fourth, fifth, or eight-hundreth time."[11] He draws an analogy between art and food. "Nobody ever talks about the fact that you are eating art. You're eating art in your head, and some of it is like a continual diet of sweets and sugar that is really going to kill your head."[12] Entertainment is junk food for the mind, and there is nothing wrong with it in occasional doses. But Foreman maintains that persistent exposure to entertainment will do to the head what a steady diet of nonnourishing food will eventually do to the body. In putting the mind to sleep, entertainment encourages man's animalistic propensity for immediate gratification, which Foreman portrays in terms of expectations and rewards:

In classical performance, the audience learns that if they allow attention to be led by a kind of childish, regressive desire-for-sweets, the artist will have strategically placed those sweets at just the "crucial" points in the piece where attention threatens to climax.[13]

Because the spectator's approach to this kind of theatre antedates the experience itself, the response is predictable and, as Foreman explains, the performance " 'works' in your mechanism *as it is*. Of course, the task is to *change* your mechanism as it is."[14]

Theatre as an Instrument for Change

After fairly continuous exposure to conventional theatre as a young man, Foreman began to tire of the experiences provided by such theatre, recalling that "I reached a point where the experience started making me feel bad, sleepy, cut off from the source of my energy."[15] Finally, after years of intending to enter commercial theatre as a playwright, Foreman decided against it, partly because he did not want to contribute to a profession primarily dedicated to leading people into a "postulated, imaginary life . . . in the land of art and dreams. I don't . . . [want my] work used as an excuse to start dreaming. Wake up! Stop dreaming!"[16] Convinced that art should not cater to the perceptual mechanism "as is," Foreman set out to change his own through Ontological-Hysteric Theatre. The impulse was fundamentally to alter consciousness through art, which, Foreman explains:

attempts to create a mode of perception and a level of consciousness that, if applied to the world, then makes the world handleable and solvable. The artist wants to convince himself that he can come to terms with the world—he can deal with the world. Bad art is trying to convince other people, good art is trying to convince yourself. I'm trying to convince myself that, yes, I can see that way, I can see in a way that makes the world handleable, solvable—essentially, desirable.[17]

In this sense, Foreman considers theatre an instrument for change.

In the program notes for his 1978 production, *Blvd. de Paris*, he stated: "Art then as a tool. To perform leverage on the head and its habits. . . ."[18] He does not mean to imply, however, that his theatre functions in the world to achieve specific sociopolitical ends. Instead, Foreman wants his work "to define the kind of self-activity that I think is healthy self-activity—it's like a model of how to use the mind."[19] His initial (and continuing) goal was to create a theatre art that would awaken and exercise his consciousness, forcing the mind to become a "self-generative," rather than merely "reactive," mechanism in the experience of that theatre, thereby setting an example for a more creative approach to everyday living. Thus, Foreman's theatre is useful to him practically in that it provides him with a psychological tool used, not to express ideas about the nature and levels of reality, but rather to explore and better understand the very essence of reality.

Mental Effort and Esthetic Emotion

Foreman's notion of the "reactive" role of the mind in the experience of theatre is related to the nature of literary theatre, which can be characterized as any performance that asks the spectator to "read" it, calling upon many of the same processes that function when reading literature. The theatre experience is "like literature."[20] In literary theatre, the spectator is presented with a stimulus in the form of signs and symbols, arranged in a theatrical syntax, that the mind readily responds to, or "reacts" to, by interpreting the physical signs and translating them into meaning. Most literary theatre is designed to be easily read, thereby requiring little effort on the part of the spectator. It is this relatively effortless perceptual and mental activity, as well as the emotional manipulation that often accompanies it, that Foreman is opposed to.

With this in mind, it is somewhat ironic that in shaping his brand of nonliterary theatre, Foreman wanted his work to induce an experience akin to that evoked by the activity of reading a difficult text. Foreman explains that he begins reading such a text by skimming it, waiting for something to catch his interest. Using this approach, he invariably notices that at some point in his skimming/waiting activity, he stops and finds that he is saying to himself, "Wait a minute! This isn't enough. I have to *make an effort.*"[21] Having made that effort, he occasionally experiences what he describes as an "epiphany"—a sudden manifestation, perception or intuitive grasp of reality or the essential nature or meaning of something. This psychological response is not necessarily a response to the idea being expressed in the text, but rather to the activity of the mind itself when, in the process of struggling to understand, an idea suddenly "organizes itself."[22] What Foreman refers to as an epiphany, Edward de Bono, in his book *The Mechanism of the Mind,* has labeled the "insight phenomenon."[23] When Foreman is self-conscious of this phenomenon, noticing it *as it is occurring,* he experiences a kind of "emotion of the mind," which he often describes in terms of esthetic emotion, or the ecstatic state.

For Foreman, some degree of difficulty is necessary to induce an ecstatic state from the experience of reading. This does not mean, however, that an abstruse literary theatre will necessarily generate esthetic emotion merely because it is difficult to "read." The important thing for the artist, according to Foreman, is to apply pressure to the mind, forcing it to exert effort intentionally. A text alone is limited in its means for applying this pressure. The materials of the theatre, on the other hand, provide a variety of means for introducing perceptual and mental difficulty into the experience of time, forcing the mind to become active, not simply "reactive," in perceiving the event.

Using the materials of the theatre, Foreman attempts to force an intentional mode of "seeing" on himself. He feels that by altering his usual passive modes of perception, he will alter perception itself—by breaking down habitual ways of perceiving, the looking and listening experience of theatre will be altered. "What art *should* do," he maintains, "is to put you in trouble as a perceiving person so that you are forced to reorganize the features presented."[24] This reorganization requires some degree of effort. In reminiscing, Foreman explains:

> I remember in the early days thinking of going to my theatre as like going to a gym, where you would have to make a certain effort, and in so doing, you tone up your body and you feel better. I wanted to make pieces that would make me make a certain effort with my perceptual mechanism, so that it felt more awake, it felt refreshed afterwards.[25]

The Adaptation Response and Theatrical Structure

In shaping a theatre designed to put the perceptual mechanism "in trouble," Foreman manipulated the materials of his art according to a number of theories culled from other disciplines. One such theory was devised by the Swiss psychologist and epistemologist Jean Paul Piaget. Foreman used his knowledge of the principles and functional details of the processes, or system, Piaget identified in the developing child.[26]

Piaget adopted the *constructivist's* view of knowledge acquisition. The constructivist maintains that we do not respond directly to stimuli in our environment but to our perception, or construction, of the stimuli. If learning influences perception, and the evidence most certainly suggests that it does, then learning and cognition may make the world appear as it does—cognitive solutions go beyond sensory data. If it is true that learning plays a part in human development at the perceptual level, then certain aspects of reality (how a person sees the world) depend on the perceiver's unconscious assumptions developed in past transactions with his environment.

Piaget documents this phenomenon in the developing child, describing it in terms of *adaptation,* and noting that there is a fundamental tendency to integrate, or organize, psychological structures into coherent systems. Whenever an individual senses a tension between himself and his environment, the response takes the form of an adaptation, or readaptation, that can be described in terms of *assimilation* and *accommodation.* Attempts to fit new ideas or information into already existing concepts or cognitive structures is the function of assimilation. Accommodation involves the process of continuously modifying existing psychological structures in response to exposure to new ideas or information, or placing old information into new relationships.[27] Processes of assimilation and accommodation maintain the balance, or state of *equilibrium,* that exists between the individual's perceived environment and his cognitive structures. When equilibrium is momentarily upset, the experience of a tension, or *disequilibrium,* results, which generates another adaptation response. Disequilibrium occurs during moments when expectations are not fulfilled or new information is found to be incongruent with currently held beliefs.

Thus, *organization* and *adaptation* (assimilation and accommodation) are two general principles of functioning, but the particular ways in which an individual organizes and adapts his cognitive structures are dependent upon his experience. Moderate levels of disequilibrium lead to reorganization and readaptation of existing psychological structures.

Analogies related to function exist between Piaget's theory of adaptation response and the structure of theatre art. For example, any theatre experience dominated by an information structure is analogous to Piaget's organization and adaptation process in the sense that the spectator attempts to fit together bits of information, presented discontinuously through time, to form a coherent arrangement of parts, or gestalt.[28] The spectator remembers certain details and anticipates others, reshaping the mental pattern as new information is added. New information is assimilated when, in adding it to old information, it "takes," further fleshing out the correct configuration. When a new bit of information is found to be incongruous, it does not "take," and disequilibrium occurs. The existing configuration is then modified or reformed to fit, or conform, to the new information. In the case of literary theatre, it is intended that bits of information eventually "add up," through theatrical syntax, forming a logical, consistent, overall mental configuration of the production, that expresses the central meaning of the drama.

Foreman works with elements of information structure that neither dominate the theatrical structure of his work, nor completely explain it. He understands the mind's tendency to integrate psychological structures into coherent systems, but he presents material designed to evoke varying degrees of disequilibrium that, unlike literary theatre, *thwart,* rather than facilitate, this tendency. Equilibrium is not Foreman's goal. He is not trying to introduce new ideas and meanings to replace old ones. Instead, Foreman attempts to induce levels of disequilibrium, through his theatre, that will assist him in noticing his own mental processes or attempts to adapt, throwing him back on himself, as it were. He is trying to teach himself "to see" in a way that dissipates the power of habitual perceptual modes. He writes:

> Our art then=a learning how to look at 'A' and 'B'
> and see not them
>   but a relation
> that cannot be 'seen.'

You can't look at 'it' (that relation)
  because
it *IS* the looking itself.
That's where the looking (you) *is,* doing the looking.[29]

Foreman stresses that there is not only an A and B involved in the perception of art, but also a C, which cannot be seen because it is the activity of perceiving itself. Yet C is what he wants to learn "to see" in his theatre. To achieve this requires a degree of unlearning, which by definition means "to undo the effect of: discard the habit of." Foreman uses his art to help him reject the habit of fitting everything encountered in both art and life into neat, familiar packages, or systems, based on past experiences. It is the "fitting" itself, or how the mind works, rather than to what ends, that Foreman's theatre is about, and how the mind works in the experience of time is what theatrical structure is all about. Foreman points out:

> . . . (and remember that structure is always a combination of the
> THING
> and the
> PERCEIVING of it) . . .[30]

This combination occurs in the mind of the spectator. Because performance exists primarily in the fourth dimension—time—the experience of any performance is a series of these combinations existing in a series of present moments that slip, one after the other, into the past, from the moment the performance begins to the moment it ends. In chapter 2 the structure of the present moment, or the continuous present, was identified as constituting the basic structural dimension of all of Foreman's texts. Like information structure, however, it does not explain the entire dramatic structure of any one of his productions. Each theatre piece serves as an example of different kinds of structure (formal, landscape, thematic, information, place, and memory/ expectancy, among others) overlaid, one upon the other. A structural analysis of Foreman's work reveals a complex "setting in motion" of certain structural principles designed to affect the experience in particular ways.

Style: A Phenomenological Approach

At this point it should be mentioned that while Foreman's intent, approach, and goals remained decidely and strikingly consistent, he altered some of his methods for achieving his goals as his work developed. Certain stylistic elements changed over the years. For instance, in addition to changes in the acting style, discussed in the last chapter, the tempo of the performances was markedly altered. When the time style, or pacing, changed, the operant structural principles remained the same, but a coincident change occurred in the dynamics of the experience in time, that is, in the structure itself. This, of course, altered the overall effect of each piece. The turning point was heralded by his 1974 production of *PAIN(T)*, and although the changes that occurred were *relatively* subtle, they were nonetheless significant. A review of the differences between pre- and post-*PAIN(T)* productions, in conjunction with a structural analysis, should further elucidate the general nature of the experience of Ontological-Hysteric Theatre.

In comparison to his later productions, Foreman considers his early work the result of a "period of intense hermeticism," which was necessary, he explains, in order "to really reground myself, and to know from where I wanted to start."[31] He began with a strict phenomenological approach, the goal of which consists of the simple practice of an undistorted seeing of that which reveals itself *in* what is seen. This seems easy enough to accomplish, but the premise is that modern society has become so conditioned to understanding the world in terms of sophisticated hypotheses that individuals have all but lost the ability to discern what constitutes the fundamental character of a being. Foreman wanted to emphasize the "isness" of things or the "naked presence of objects,"[32] rather than merely present characters, objects, and words to the senses as source material for the creation of something else—a meaning, for example—in the imagination. Context and pace became two important elements in achieving this.

Taking banal, mundane objects and events of ordinary living, Foreman attempted to place them in contexts in such a way as to render them extraordinary. He created a very subtle form of perceptual syncopation in which both visual material and aural material are presented in contexts that do not quite match our past experience of them. The window in the setting of *Total Recall* (plate 1), for example, is not in congruous proportion to the two doors that are part of the same representation of an interior. If the action were rapidly paced, the spectator might not pay any attention to this, and similar details. But because the action of events on the stage is slowed down significantly, perception is retarded, and a contemplative mode of attention may be initiated. In other words, if the spectator is not overcome by ennui, an intentional form of attention will ensue, in which the spectator ponders that which is being presented to his senses, noticing the mismatching as it is occurring.

The pace is not slow in the filmic sense of slow motion, but rather in the sense of a "snail's pace." A snail is sluggish, that is, not only markedly slow in movement, but also slow to respond to stimulation. The recurrent pauses, of varying lengths, that permeated Foreman's early pieces unrelievedly, retard rather than facilitate perception. Then, within this decelerated experience of time, Foreman presented the spectator with a number of possibilities for combining and internalizing sensory phenomenon, breaking down stale, linear associations, and producing a kind of "vibration." A mental awakening is realized when, given more than one possibility, the spectator "vibrates" between alternatives. The program notes for *Ida-Eyed,* the second Ontological-Hysteric Theatre production, advised the spectator to leave when and as he wished, but quietly so as not to disturb others whenever "his perceptual resources have been so exhausted that he feels compelled to leave the theatre."[33]

This advice for the audience is more than a little presumptuous. It assumes that the desired effect will be achieved and that the spectator might have to leave early because of exhaustion, when it is entirely possible that a spectator might leave early because of boredom. On the other hand, it does indicate two important points related to intent: first that the spectator is fully engaged in some kind of all-consuming activity that could utterly deplete his perceptual means and, secondly, that the piece is structured in such a way that the spectator can leave before it is over and not "miss the ending" in the sense of missing the play's dramatic "completion."

While it is true that, over the years, some audience members have complained that they simply do not sense the momentum Foreman intends in the experience, it is equally true that many people do. During a group discussion following a performance of *Ida-Eyed,* Jonas Mekas told Foreman that,

> I went into your play and I had to use some effort, some force to get into it. I blasted myself into it—most theatre today is so thin you don't need to blast yourself into it, it's like water—and I stayed with it from beginning to end. I was leaning forward in my chair. It was like being completely somewhere else on some very abstract, very formal, on some *mental* plane, and it's this mental aspect that is a special uniqueness of your theatre.[34]

Mekas also pointed out that most of the people in the group discussion had stopped attending the theatre, adding, "and here, suddenly, we face something that interests us, that stirs us, provokes us, pulls us in. Now, why?"[35] Why, indeed, is it that the same work could stir and provoke some spectators and bore others? Personal taste, of course, is part of the answer, but part of it also relates to style and Foreman's attempt to evoke a contemplative state of mind for experiencing the work.

Style and State of Mind

If it is true, as Michael Kirby suggests in his essay "On Style," that "style functions psychologically as a state of mind,"[36] then there is a one-to-one relationship between the objective—sensory style of a performance, or the manner in which it is done—and the subjective—state of mind of the individual spectator. While each of Foreman's staging techniques, for example, has a different, specific effect on the perceptual mechanism, style is general, as is state of mind. Each performance element has its own style, but the style of the performance is dependent upon the orchestration, whether harmonious or disharmonious, of all the elements. Similarly, a state of mind, while singular, implies the sum of the qualities involved in a particular kind of mental existence, at a particular time. It is the mode or condition of mind, the frame or mental set operating in certain circumstances.

State of mind might be described as involving the organizational properties that underlie particular patterns of thought, and the way they function, or the patterns of operation. Structure, then, operates within this frame—the state of mind acts as a "container" for structure, or the "combinations," mentioned earlier, that occur through time. As a frame of reference in the experience of art, state of mind focuses and organizes details, while structure is the specific, dynamic connections the mind makes back and forth during the experience of a performance, in order to establish a mental configuration of that performance as it exists through time.

Kirby points out that each state of mind has its own perceived quality and character. In the productions preceding *PAIN(T)*, Foreman endeavored to induce a contemplative state of mind through the style of his pieces. It may be that this attempt required little effort since, as Kirby notes, "the state of mind of the artist is an organic, stylistic factor and . . . there is one proper or dominant creative attitude implicit in each style."[37] Foreman has written:

> . . . I have been working on the machine of myself for a good many years now—or, to be more exact, I have been working on the somewhat more complex machine "self and circumstance" in order to adjust that machine so that it will, when the starter button of "good-morning" is pushed, turn out a certain product which will have a certain "effect" on a certain kind of human attention—should that "certain kind" of human attention happen to come in contact with the product (my plays) in question.[38]

Foreman's extensive use of esthetic meditation in generating his texts was discussed in chapter 2, and should explain, at least in part, why a contemplative state might ultimately result from his production style.

The state of mind that accompanies Foreman's "self and circumstance" generating machine, might also help to explain the complexity of the work. In his radio interview with Foreman, Kirby stated:

> Certainly your work is tremendously complex—it exists on many levels. I think one thing we've indicated here is the dimensions of it, the way so many things seem to come together— the intellectual, the visual, the philosophical, and the physical.[39]

This "coming together," or fusion, of multiple dimensions in a single work might be directly related to Foreman's creative attitude, or state of mind, as well as his approach.

In any case, the dimensions of Foreman's work are not sensed at all by some audience members, and this is not necessarily indicative of a failing on the spectator's part, but rather the result of a particular state of mind induced by the performance style. In Foreman's early work, a contradiction existed in his style that could generate either one of two possible states of mind.

Style and the State of Ennui

If Foreman's goal was a contemplative state of mind, then one might assume a degree of tranquility to be generated by the production style. After all, contemplation is the act of considering or regarding steadily, or with continual attention, which requires a certain amount of concentration. While it is true that he staged his early plays in a series of static pictures (see chapter 4) within a decelerated time frame, the quality of which was indeed tranquil, at the same time, the style of other performance elements was often extremely aggressive toward the spectator. Bright lights glaring into the eyes of the audience, accompanied by sudden, very loud noises, for instance, are capable of interrupting attempts to concentrate, and can be quite irritating to the perceptual mechanism.

Whether or not these potentially aggravating stylistic elements are overcome by the individual spectator and a contemplative state is allowed to dominate the experience is entirely subjective, of course, and depends upon a number of variables, including past experience and present expectations. Interestingly, although Foreman was aware of the two possibilities for subjective states, he did not abandon his irritating techniques in order to insure a contemplative one, admitting that he "enjoyed watching the 'weaker' members of the audience give up."[40] This, however, was not the motivation for keeping them, as he indicated by adding to that last statement, "But what moved me was the discovery—for myself anyway—that the effort to endure and see what was going on *behind* various painful and distractive phenomena invested the events, words, et cetera with a rather new . . . quality."[41] For Foreman, his hostile staging techniques, as he refers to them, are necessary for invoking the intentional effort he feels is necessary to perceive or experience the work in fresh, new ways. When he began in 1968, he felt that "if there was a certain amount of aggression you had to overcome to go into the work, to find out what was behind the bright light or the buzzer, then it evoked in you a certain energy of perception. . . ."[42]

The perceptual tolerance of the audience is taxed and some physical discomfort may result. If, in addition to this, an audience member expects the recognizable situations that Foreman presents to develop in familiar ways, when they do not, it is possible that the spectator's patience will "wear thin." If the spectator also anticipates, and looks forward to, an empathic experience, when every means is taken to prevent both characters and events from generating empathy/identification (see chapters 2 and 4)—making it nearly impossible for the spectator to project himself psychically into the presentation—feelings of frustration, discomfort, and impatience may overwhelm the spectator, ultimately resulting in a general state of ennui. The style has produced an affective state, or a feeling, of weariness and tedium. Kirby maintains every style produces an affective state, that is, "Each state of mind produces a particular emotional tone that is part of its character."[43]

Style and the Contemplative State

Because Foreman's staging techniques and the way he structures his pieces make projection and identification extremely difficult, the spectator is sharply distanced from the presentation and must, as Mekas put it, "blast" himself into the experience. Foreman described this phenomenon in terms of his experience of New American Cinema films:

> I don't see how you can sit there and let it flow over you. If I let that happen to me, I'd go out of my skull with impatience. But if I force myself to start noticing and savoring all of my problems in looking at the film, under that influence I leave the theatre—not in love, because I think you leave an adventure movie in love with that world of adventure—not in love, but full of energy, and ready to see the world outside the theatre with that new energy.[44]

In other words, like New American Cinema films, Foreman's theatre does not *do* anything to the spectator, so he must act upon it. He is not lured into the work, and when he is not able to empathize, identify, or project, he is either bored or he acts—he thinks. Foreman's sensory, perceptual style—involving his acting, movement, auditory, and, especially, picture and time style—is as capable of inducing and maintaining a rigorous contemplative state as it is a state of ennui. After his second Ontological-Hysteric production, Foreman characterized his auditory and time style as follows:

> Most important, the non-inflected lines are always partially obliterated and/or sustained by some repetitive sound system that is going on behind them. A tape loop of thumps or the text itself at a different speed, anything to provide a basic contrast in performance between the moments when there is speaking (which must be moments of FULL sound, as if the whole spectrum of possible sound were implied) interlaced by hundreds of moments of utter silence and, often, stillness. That's the effect—a snatch of full, awkward brief and

unsustained activity and sound, followed immediately by a long silence in which nothing moves but the actor's breathing, perhaps his hand twitches. The audience just sits and waits, then another full awkward moment, then another silence, back and forth, on and on.

. . . there are like three hundred pauses in the play, and the reason those pauses are there is because one has to collect one's thought.[45]

Foreman's static pictures (see chapter 4) comprise, or are contained by, these long moments of stillness and silence, during which the picture can be contemplated because the spectator is given time to think.

Perceptual Automatizing

There are different kinds of thought, however, and not all thought requires extended periods of time. Some occurs rapidly. For example, each new picture presents the perceptual mechanism with a novel stimulus. Vision must be translated into perception. The intensity and rate at which the brain processes the information in the picture are related to the degree of conscious perception experienced. Charles Furst, author of *Origins of the Mind: Mind/Brain Connections,* recently performed an experiment with eye movements, which, it is generally believed, reflect visual processes occurring in the brain. He writes:

> I wanted to discover what happened to the pattern of eye movement as people viewed the same pictures over and over again. I found that as the scenes became more familiar, two things happened: the rate of eye movement decreased and the patterns of movement in response to each scene became more stereotyped and predictable. People seem to adopt automatic, consistent ways of moving their eyes over scenes once the visual objects become known.[46]

This tendency, or perceptual "automatizing," indicates that the increase in stereotyping of the sense perceptions results in a decrease in the intensity and rate of perceptual processing in the brain. Furst concludes that:

> This decrease in rate frees the machinery of consciousness for other tasks. Brain efficiency and mindlessness are thus two sides of the same coin.[47]

This "mindlessness" is precisely what Foreman is referring to when he calls for an "emptying of the mind" in the experience of art, "so that the mind is more alert, more awake."[48] In other words, a different reflex or response is elicited as each new picture presents the perceptual mechanism with a novel stimulus, the effect of which rapidly disappears when the response becomes habitual. The eyes scan the same image, extended through time, over and over. The predictable pattern of eye movements indicates that the image has become so familiar that it can be retained while the consciousness turns to other matters—the mind has been emptied, as it were. All of this happens quickly, but when the image is static and no new data are being "sent" from the stage to fill the mind, the "other matters" that the consciousness turns to are forms of self-generating thinking, that is, ruminative thought or meditative reflection. Of his theatre, Foreman states:

> You don't use your mind the way you do in George Bernard Shaw's theatre. What happens to your mind in the experience of my theatre, hopefully, is an emptying of mind, rather than a filling of it with ideas that you can really chew on.[49]

In everyday life, it is crucial that perceptual automatizing occurs instantaneously. Because consciousness is inherently limited in capacity, some form of perceptual inattention must function in conjunction with attention so that the mind can deal with matters that are of immediate importance. As Furst points out, "We can't afford to notice the way our socks feel on our feet."[50] Although the same perceptual principles are involved in the experience of theatre, they do not function in exactly the same ways as in everyday life. Foreman's picturization, for example, elicits the perceptual automatizing response but then no new matters of importance are immediately presented— in a sense, we *can* afford to notice the way our socks feel on our feet.

Psychic Intensification

Kirby has suggested that "contemplation may provide intensification through redundancy."[51] The pose of an actor in one of Foreman's static pictures, for instance, often implies movement. If the amount of time the spectator is given to consider all of the possibilities inherent in this implied movement far exceeds that necessary for such consideration, then, as the eyes scan the composition, Kirby notes, "they may repeatedly send the same data, resulting in several identical messages."[52] He suggests that these multiple identical messages—that result from unconsciously making the same calculations many times, as the same data are contemplated—strengthen each other, intensifying the effect.

Unlike most situations in everyday life, Foreman's contemplative staging encourages a certain kind of ruminative thought in which the mind is allowed repeatedly to go over data calmly and slowly, considering various sensory and intellectual combinations, and weighing a variety of possibilities. When the visual field, for example, includes more than one image, each rendered in a different scale (see pages 145-46, chapter 4), the eye and mind are free to scan the picture/field, making comparisons, considering the degree of fusion that exists among images of contradictory scale held simultaneously in the field as a whole, or concentrating on details. This kind of thought is made possible by

Foreman's time style. The hundreds of pauses he uses slow down the rate of change in the perceptual field, providing intervals of extended periods of relative stillness and silence, during which a kind of ruminative thought may occur.

Kirby believes that this retardation of flow in Foreman's pieces can cause a psychic intensification, which can be thought of as "intensification through analogy." He explains:

> When the mind is involved with a crisis situation [such as a car skidding out of control ahead of us while we are driving along an expressway], things often seem to be happening in slow motion. The mind responds so actively that the progress of the skidding car seems retarded; each detail seems more sharply defined than it would be normally. A performance done in slow motion can create, by analogy, the same sense of crisis. The amount of information and the complexity of detail perceived are much greater than would be registered *unless* the mind were responding rapidly to a crisis situation. Even when the occurrences observed are not dangerous or threatening, the retardation of flow creates psychic intensification.[53]

It would seem that such a mental state would be conducive to realizing Foreman's phenomenological goal of an awareness of the "isness" or naked presence of objects. In 1969, he wrote about "the use of artistic technique as a means to RETARD perception ... making the act of perception present to the spectator. Making the object perceived more phenomenologically present to the spectator."[54]

In the same year, Mekas pointed out that this "crisis-like" kind of acute presence can be sensed in auditory, as well as visual, phenomena in Foreman's productions. He spoke of "a presence" of words: "The words are treated so royally that they become like objects—'every each of them.' "[55] Language is an important element of Foreman's theatre and yet, by its very nature, it would seem most resistent to a phenomenological treatment. Foreman has written that "the old language is always (we are habituated to it) always more 'powerful,' more 'seductive' to our mental mechanisms, than the new insight."[56] Foreman's style of disjunctive sound used in the delivery of dialog (see chapter 4) certainly contributes to the special presence and effect of speech in his pieces, but the writing itself is also a determining factor. One distinctive feature of Foreman's texts involves an extensive use of repetition leading to a kind of "cinematic" style. Gertrude Stein also employed this technique, which she characterized as the "continuous succession" of a statement. Each statement, formed in the present, is succeeded by another, slightly different statement, like the consecutive frames of a film that create an image that seems to extend itself in the present for a given period of time. Thus, like his picturization, Foreman's use of language also has a contemplative quality, in that it does not have the rapid "flow" of facts added to facts, as in an information structure.

Information and the Tendency of Meaning to Dominate Experience

Each Foreman play, however, does have an information structure, that is, "Information is passed from one element to another, sometimes across long units of time. Things explain each other to varying extents, and remembered facts can be joined with new information to arrive at new meanings," as Kirby points out in his discussion of *Sophia*.[57] The difference lies in the kind of information structure that exists in Foreman's productions. Because *Sophia,* for example, does not have a plot or story, the progression, or series of connected facts, crucial to story and plot development is unnecessary. Information structure can exist without each bit of information adding up or connecting to some extent with every other bit of information. Foreman uses elements of information structure as a "triggering" device, among other things. He deliberately works with the mind's propensity for functioning in certain ways. Information is used as a stimulus for initiating a particular mental process, in much the same way that the sight or odor of food may be used as a trigger for eliciting the physiological response of salivation.

Largely because of conditioning, when meaning exists in a production, it generates mental activity that tends to overwhelm and dominate other processes. When the mind arrives at a meaning, it usually attempts to interpret other material in terms of the new-found meaning. The tendency is to assume that if some moments convey meaning, or some elements have purport or signification, then they must overflow or connect with other moments and elements. The mind instinctively searches for evidence to confirm the interpretation suggested by what may well be merely an isolated instance of meaning. The result might be that meanings are projected into material not intended to be interpreted in one way or another at all.

Following a performance of *Rhoda in Potatoland,* one spectator reported an experience of "reading" the entire production and was surprised to discover that the story she felt she had no difficulty following consistently from beginning to end was not, objectively, presented. In this case, the mind was so persistent in making logical sense out of the experience that the imagination completely took over. The inclination for mentally processing everything "syntactically" overwhelmed sensory relationships to the point where the intellectual component not only dominated the experience, but ultimately bore little relationship to that which, objectively, was being presented. This is an extreme example, but it demonstrates the mind's potential proclivity toward organizing psychological structures into coherent, familiar, recognizable systems based on past experience.

To the extent that the mind searches for information to support an overall interpretation of the performance, the event is structured in a particular way. Structure is subjective. One experience is not better or worse than another, it is simply different. Foreman works with certain structural principles to manipulate his own mental structures in particular ways, but how each individual spectator processes the material presented is subjective and depends on expectations as well as experience. The concern here is with *intent* to involve certain ways of responding, rather than with either individual response or universal response.

Foreman calls the meaning/information processing mechanism into play precisely in order to interrupt or block it, rather than propel it into the future. He explains, "I try to get into the greatest difficulty possible. Syntactically, logically, rationally, narratively. 'Train-of-thought' trouble and blockage is cultivated."[58] He purposefully begins with a seemingly "naturalistic scenario," as he calls it, and "realistically conceived characters," and then tries to teach himself not to be "blocked" when he sees the naturalistic, realistic aspects dissolve.

> The whole point is to dissolve . . . you do start with that [naturalistic scenario] . . . but to dissolve it . . . not to end up knowing about it because I think knowing about it is getting fixated on it, is getting refixed in all the grooves of association and habit and so forth that gets us into all kinds of troubles in life.[59]

Foreman does not literally begin one of his plays in a realistic style and then "dissolve" or break it down by gradually switching to his contemplative style. Unlike a life-simulating play that often begins with expository dialog designed to familiarize the spectator with the world of the play, conveying information about time, place, situation, and character, Foreman presents information in a manner that requires the viewer to assemble it. Equally unlike realistic theatre, the complete assembly of bits of information tells the viewer very little about the characters or the situation they are in. Foreman is emphatic about wanting to involve the spectator in "the game of putting the piece together,"[60] but the puzzle pieces, so to speak, frequently do not quite fit together and, when they do, a full-blown picture is seldom the result. He explains:

> You want to make a field, you want to make a composition, you want to make a shape, you want to make a time, in which, if the viewer isn't bored out of his skull, he must focus his intentional vision. He must, in a sense, structure what he sees. He must try, in a sense, to make something out of materials that he is given.[61]

At the same time, he does not make it easy for the spectator to "make something out of what he sees" for, while the mind of the perceiver is busily manipulating the received data, attempting to make sense out of them, the object of perception is just as busily generating ever-more-elusive combinations of its elements that stymie attempts to integrate them into a coherent, consistent gestalt.

Structure: The Experience of Sophia

We can demonstrate the structural continuity or the dynamics of the mechanisms functioning in the experience of one of Foreman's plays by using Kirby's detailed description of the opening scenes of *Sophia,* cited in chapter 4 (see pages 138-39), and imagining a spectator attending the performance. Before *Sophia* begins, expectancy is generated. Because there is no front curtain, the audience can see the setting and may wonder how it will be used. Each person has a program that not only generates expectancy by listing the performers who will appear, it also reminds the spectator of the title— *Sophia=(Wisdom) Part 3: The Cliffs*—he may anticipate the presentation of something having to do with cliffs.

Whatever the thought pattern, it is suddenly, abruptly interrupted and the mind is erased, as it were, by the loud sound of the buzzer that begins the play. A long-term expectancy is automatically generated by any beginning, that is, the audience expects a performance of some duration to follow. This expectancy is quickly thwarted, however, by the words, "Not yet," which suggest that the performance has not yet begun, and also triggers a "When?" response from the spectator. The play's three formal beginnings, in which both short- and long-term expectancies are generated and terminated, were discussed in chapter 4. Expectancy, however, is not all that functions in holding the experience of this sequence together through time. Other mechanisms are working, and several elements are introduced that begin to function structurally as the performance continues.

The use of a buzzer, for example, is neither a conventional nor a realistic means for beginning a play. It does, nonetheless, have certain structural implications in that sound is often used to begin activity in everyday life. The sound of a shot from a starting gun signals the beginning of a race, and when we encounter a telephone answering machine, we are told to "begin speaking at the sound of the tone," to cite just two examples. Because the buzzer was used initially to begin the performance, even though it is used the second time in conjunction with the end of the third scene, it may actually function to signal the beginning of the fourth, and final, "beginning" of the performance. Repetitions of the buzzer throughout the production function to interrupt thought patterns so that the spectator can "begin again" in contemplating the piece, and because of this, it is a powerful device in the structure of the present moment (as is "Not yet," which is also repeated during the piece). The very nature of a sudden, loud noise within a contemplative context stops mental activity short, and prevents the mind from propelling itself into the future.

Within the second formal beginning of the play, peformers crawl under a canvas to form "a brown mass that rises into hills in several places" (plate 56). Memory is triggered and a connection is made if the spectator recalls "The

Cliffs" in the title and associates it with the "mountainous object," or image of hills, before him in the space. Two "places," rendered in different scales, are superimposed in that the hills exist within what had already been established as the interior of a room. Once the image is formed, Kirby states, "Nothing moves for quite a while," so that the spectator is given time to contemplate the relationship between the two places. In the third beginning, a table and white wicker chair are placed directly in front of "the hills" so that the scale contradictions are further emphasized as the two places are more tightly fused into one image.

When the performers emerge from underneath the canvas and take it off stage, the audience is told to "imagine the cloth slowly descending over everything." This instruction is in the form of written material presented via a slide projection on the screen hanging over the playing area. Until this point, the experience has been one of looking at people and objects, and listening to sounds, music, and words. Now the spectator is engaged in reading which, because it is a visual rather than an aural experience of words, has a very different effect on the perceptual mechanism. Reading is similar to contemplating a picture in that they are both forms of visual activity, but information is received entirely differently from these two visual sources and each generates a different type of thought.

Slide projections are not only a major stylistic element in *Sophia,* as mentioned in chapter 4, they are also a significant structural device. This is so partly because the frequent repetition of any element functions to hold the experience together through time, but more importantly because the projections serve to trigger mental activity in the present moment, as well as forward and backwards across time. When the audience is told to "imagine the cloth," it is only the first of numerous instances where slides are used to instruct the spectator to think. Before long, a certain momentum can be sensed. For example, immediately following the direction to "imagine the cloth," an assertion is announced:

ASSERTION

THERE IS NOTHING ELSE INTERESTING.
ONLY ASSERTION IS INTERESTING.

These two statements are themselves assertions—assertions about assertion. The second statement is repeated immediately but in a different area or place, on a different screen, one that is tall, narrow, and wheeled onto the stage. In the statements that appear on it, the viewer is first warned, "Do not fall prey to that danger," and then told to "Think of an assertion." The buzzer is heard and when the play "begins again," yet another kind of pressure is exerted on the mind as the spectator hears a voice from the loudspeaker say:

Two simultaneous assertions, notice. (The
  performer says, "simultaneous.")
Now that painting ("Now" "that") is no
  longer interesting, perhaps
something else ("something") will be
  interesting in the same way.
A slide appears on the raised screen: "Painting a wall is still interesting."
The first voice heard from the loudspeakers
says, "People are more interesting than props: Do
you agree with that statement?"

The pressure to *notice* is intensified because live and recorded words are being spoken at the same time (echoing the supposed simultaneity of the assertions being made), and instead of the anticipated two assertions, three are actually made. Two are heard and one is read. The spectator is then asked to formulate an opinion regarding the final assertion.

In a sense, the play can be understood as a series of assertions to be questioned by the audience. The momentum generated by this kind of thinking might continue if the spectator considers the activity that follows in this context. If not, toward the end of the scene that follows, the same tall, narrow screen is wheeled onstage and the words REMEMBER "ASSERTION" appear on it.[62] In remembering, the mind jumps back across time and, at the same time, may anticipate further references to assertion in the future. Perhaps the assertions will eventually "explain" the presentation.

The momentum in *Sophia* exists in the dense web of associations and dissociations that are triggered in the mind. Shortly after REMEMBER "ASSERTION" is projected, for example, the image of a man appears on the same screen wearing mountain-climbing gear. The spectator may try to associate this information with the cliffs—perhaps the mountain-climber is the clue to understanding the action. One of the characters, Sophia, moves to the screen and presses her body against the image, in the same manner that Max, in the first scene, pressed his body against the door. In the next line of dialog the audience learns that Sophia is a goddess, and another association is possible, that is, in ancient mythology the gods and goddesses lived on mountain tops.

In the next scene, the curtain that defined the back wall of the room is removed and the "cliffs" of the stage setting (alluded to in a variety of ways since the beginning of the performance) are revealed with little peaked "houses" on top of them (see page 46, chapter 3). Later in the performance, miniature wicker doll furniture, attached to strings, dangles from the little houses over the cliffs (plate 65).[63] This image echoes, and reverses the scale of, the image at the beginning of the play when life-size furniture was placed in front of the hills formed by performers huddled underneath the canvas. In that rendition, the furniture against the cliffs dwarfed them, while in the second version, the miniature furniture against the cliffs makes them appear enormous. The spectator may recall the relationship of cliffs to furniture in the first image of the play and compare it to the relationship in the second. At the same time, the head of a performer is visible in each of the houses on top of the cliffs, nearly filling it. The houses and furniture are proportionate to each other, but neither is proportionate to the actors, and another kind of thought process is triggered. As Kirby points out:

> Either the houses on the cliffs are accepted as life-size and the heads that fill them become gigantic, or the heads are accepted as life-size and the houses become miniature. Like an optical illusion these relationships change, and the mind instinctively searches for information to support and confirm one choice or the other.[64]

Images recur throughout the performance, and the connections among them structure the performance in formal, rather than chronological ways. Like Max pressing his body against the door and Sophia pressing against the screen, the mountain-climber presses his body against the wall of the room and Ben presses against the cliffs. Near the end of the play another image of hills and houses is created when brown papier-mâché "hills" are placed along a bench (plate 78) and miniature houses, a church, and trees are placed on top of them. A crew person, lying on the floor, "walks" a tiny doll along the bench, at the "bottom of the hills," echoing the actors walking along the bottom of the cliffs of the stage setting, with the peaked houses on top, during the performance.

The way the mind works on these visual, pictorial relationships is quite different from the way it handles the associations generated by the various kinds of subject matter presented in *Sophia*. Interspersed throughout the performance are several references to biblical characters and events, for example, presented through dialog, direct address, stage symbols, and metaphors. Christ's miracle of the "multiplication of the loaves and fishes" which, incidentally, occurred on a mountain side, is suggested through dialog:

(Pause. RHODA slowly uncovers the basket and shows it to SOPHIA. The ringing noise, which gets louder. SOPHIA and RHODA sit on the ground, as if dazed.)

SOPHIA

(Silence. She points.)
I could make something out of that lunch.

RHODA

Oh, angel.

SOPHIA

I really could. I could make something out of that lunch.
(She stops pointing.)[65]

A few short scenes later, written material projected on the screen informs the spectator that the mountain-climber, like Christ, can heal through touch:

Legend: THERE IS NOBODY FOR HIM TO HEAL. LOOK AT HIS HANDS. HE IS READY TO LAY THEM ON THE FOREHEAD OF THE SICK PERSON BUT THE SICK PERSON IS NO LONGER INSIDE THE HOUSE.[66]

This could be connected with the resurrection of Lazarus for when Christ arrives to heal him, he is told that Lazarus is no longer in the house. He has died and is already buried.

At another point in the play, Rhoda is onstage, wearing only a blanket, when Ben enters with an apple. A stage direction indicates how the angel driving Adam and Eve from Paradise with a sword was represented:

. . . RHODA turns and looks at him. She takes the apple from him and the blanket slips from her, and she prepares to bite.)

CROWD

Ahhhh.

(She stops and looks off. Waits. SOPHIA enters where she is looking. SOPHIA has a sword. She places the point so it rests on the apple.)

CROWD

Ahhhhhh.[67]

(SOPHIA, RHODA and BEN now slowly shuffle off without dropping their poses or relation to each other.)

CROWD

There is nothing more to know about the lives of unhappy people.

Recurrent references to biblical characters and events establish one of the many themes related to specific kinds of subject matter in *Sophia,* just as connections made among recurrent images, like the different versions of hills or cliffs, establish visual themes. While the overlapping of verbal and visual ideas and references is extensive, generating complex intellectual relationships that exist simultaneously on several different levels, *Sophia* is not an example of literary theatre. There is no message to be read from the thematic material—nothing is being said, or sent, through the themes in the play. In many ways *Sophia* is structurally similar to life-simulating theatre in that places and characters are established and recur, relationships evolve to varying extents, expectations are triggered, information is generated, and identifiable themes emerge. The difference is that all of these kinds of structure coexist and overlap each other, feeding into each other in varying degrees, but not to the point of creating a coherent, overall meaning. Just as certain elements frequently relate to each other, strengthening each other to greater or lesser extents, there are just as many instances of verbal and visual material that is dissociated.

MOUNTAIN-CLIMBER
Now I have you in my power, huh.
(Pause.)
Oh Rhoda, Rhoda. You don't understand me.
(Behind the room, on the cliffs, the houses light up.)

RHODA
I can't see them. My own house interferes with my vision, not a house complete, a room. I was very quick to correct myself.
(Pause.)
I hurt myself yet, so my mind itself is more perceptible, don't you think.[68]

In each of his productions, Foreman employs the entire range of associative and dissociative thinking, or the varying degrees of logic and illogic generated by intellectual connections, as well as alogical, or purely sensory, relationships that are incapable of generating either positive or negative mental energy.[69] The process, not the end product, of thinking is of utmost importance to Foreman, and he uses every means he can imagine to trigger any and all kinds of mental operations. In the plays from *Angelface* through *PAIN(T)*, these mental operations, or structure, existed within a contemplative framework determined by the style of the productions.

Style and the Redistribution of Attention

Although they differed somewhat in magnitude, specific content, and emphasis, any one of the productions preceding *PAIN(T)* could be used as an example of Foreman's early style, since his style remained distinctively consistent from production to production. *PAIN(T)* can be considered a turning point because, in contrast to *Vertical Mobility* (presented in repertory with *PAIN(T)*), individual stylistic elements were beginning to change noticeably, but these changes were not yet radical enough to alter the contemplative state associated with all of Foreman's previous productions.

In *PAIN(T)*, the beginnings of change in the use of space and the acting style were evident (see chapters 3 and 5). Most significantly, however, the pace was somewhat faster, in that tableau compositions changed more frequently and were not held quite as long. It seems feasible that the style of either the acting or the setting could change without altering the overall contemplative quality of Foreman's work. But since a slow velocity or rate of thought is essential to the contemplative state, a significant acceleration of that rate would necessarily cancel out the possibility for ruminative thought. Although the tendency toward an accelerated production pace was evident in *PAIN(T)*, it was not until the following Ontological-Hysteric Theatre piece, *Pandering to the Masses: A Misrepresentation,* that the pacing or time style changed significantly enough to produce a change in the state of mind coincident with Foreman's previous production style.

Florence Falk described the general characteristics of Foreman's visual and time styles in *Pandering,* and their general effect:

> Visual patterns overlap, are superimposed, or repeated, so that the eye (and mind) wander over a constantly shifting theatre-scape or field. As soon as one formal arrangement has, in Foreman's words, "seduced the senses," it is disassembled, rearranged, or discarded altogether. . . . The eye is not allowed to rest long enough on any form to be satisfied but is forced to readjust as forms continually shift and change location, and group themselves into new patterns that do not possess any stable center. As a result, foreground and background become ambiguous locations and perceptual experience tends to become more diffuse.[70]

This new approach to timing, combined with significant changes in the acting and scenic styles, effected a distinct change in the overall style of Foreman's work. Through this new style—especially in comparison to his previous production style—Foreman virtually bombarded the spectator with rapidly changing visual and auditory stimuli.

If it is true that a given style produces a particular state of mind, then a change in style will produce a change in that state of mind. Just from Falk's brief description it is clear that in *Pandering* Foreman had abandoned his desire to induce a contemplative state of mind for experiencing the work. But then contemplation, per se, was never his goal, but rather a certain redistribution of attention brought about through moments of disequilibrium. The change in style was merely an attempt to accomplish this goal by different means.

This redistribution or "different kind of human attention" Foreman frequently makes reference to can be understood in terms of what Anton Ehrenzweig has described as *differentiation,* or a focusing of attention, and *dedifferentiation,* or a dispersing of attention.[71] Differentiation involves the freedom to choose to look or listen to one thing rather than another, while dedifferentiation involves freedom from having to make a choice at all. Dedifferentiation is what Foreman was referring to during the conversation with Post-Modern dancers in 1972 (see pages 55-56, chapter 3) when he described a mode of attention in which conflicting events could be held simultaneously in a nondirected, wide-angled, meditative kind of attention. A redistribution of attention occurs in performance when the spectator "oscillates," as Ehrenzweig puts it, between this unfocused, dedifferentiated form of attention and the focused, differentiated mode. Taking his cue from Ehrenzweig, Foreman feels that this oscillation between focused and unfocused modes of perception not only brings about a redistribution of attention, but also affords the spectator the opportunity to engage in a kind of mental gymnastics not available, as such, in everyday life.

The shortcoming of the contemplative state as a frame or container for the kind of attention Foreman wants to apply to his performances is related to its most important feature—time. Certainly it is possible to achieve a redistribution of attention within a contemplative context, but it would seem that the experience of varying degrees of disequilibrium necessary to accomplish such a mode of attention could be heightened or intensified within a more excited or active state. The contemplative state generates a certain unity and coherence by virtue of its decelerated rate of thought that may dissipate, somewhat, the impact of moments of disequilibrium. Foreman acknowledges that "in the universe there is a continual straining towards coherence,"[72] or what Piaget identified as the fundamental tendency for individuals to integrate psychological structures into coherent systems. Therefore, no matter how intense the contradictory relationships established among elements are, given enough time, the mind will tend to equilibrate them, dissipating the tension created by states of disequilibrium. Within a contemplative context the spectator may, perhaps, choose to ignore certain relationships while focusing on others. Foreman points out:

> Most people think, "Oh, I've got to work hard to keep it all together, to make sense." No! I think that, as a matter of fact, the task is to try and punch a few little holes in this continual insistence of the universe that there shall indeed be coherence.[73]

In order to poke holes, as it were, in this tendency toward unity and coherence, Foreman increased the rate of flow in both the visual and auditory fields of his productions. This increased rate functioned to put ever more pressure on the perceptual mechanism and, hence, the mind. Rapidly changing stimuli exert more pressure by virtue of speed alone, that is, material must be seized and comprehended quickly, before it slips away. Unlike the leisurely consideration made possible by a series of static pictures presented in a slowly changing visual field, moving images, and static pictures that change in rapid succession, combined with rapid changes in auditory material as well, force the mind to work harder if details are to be grasped. In addition, equilibration of the tension generated by moments of disequilibrium is more difficult simply because there is less time to respond—attempts at assimilation and accommodation are initiated instinctively, but often there is not enough time to complete them and establish a state of equilibrium. ·

An increase in the rate of flow in the perceptual field, of course, does not guarantee that a redistribution of attention will occur, since, under any circumstances, the spectator can always choose to focus on some elements to the exclusion of others. Hence, within this accelerated time frame, Foreman manipulates certain environmental factors in specific ways in an attempt to encourage the spectator to scan the entire field, rather than become fixated on a select number of details.

In the field of psychology, environmental factors are those aspects of the physical surroundings that can be varied, such as illumination, noise level, and temperature. They directly affect, and can even impair, sensory receptors. Foreman works with the principles that govern receptivity under particular conditions to pull attention in several directions simultaneously. On the auditory level, for example, one would assume that since loud sounds have high density, they would automatically cancel out softer sounds and, for the most part, this is the case. There are instances, however, when softer sounds can actually seem more acute against a background of louder sound. In other words, if a sound signal is embedded in a noise field of greater intensity and sufficiently different frequency characteristics, the auditory loss could conceivably enhance signal detection.

During one sequence in *Book of Splendors: Part II* the spectator could hear three different sound patterns, simultaneously, emanating from four different sources—loudspeakers positioned in different places in the space (see page 146, chapter 4). The loudest sound was Foreman's voice speaking the following lines from the text, very slowly:

(The Scene Changes)

Tape: LATER, ALONE AND UNDISCOVERED
THEY TREAT EACH OTHER MORE GENTLY.

(The Beach)

Tape: HE FINDS HIMSELF IN PARADISE. THE
TWO WOMEN ARE ENTERTAINING EACH OTHER ON THE
BEACH.[74]

At the same time, the spectator could hear a series of soft or subdued tones produced, perhaps, by chimes or a xylophone. The sequence proceeded slowly—as each tone was sounded, it was held so that the reverberation continued until the next tone was heard. This musical sound pattern produced a serene, lulling effect, that may have reinforced the verbal allusions to "paradise" and "the beach."

The third sound pattern was also speech but barely audible. The spectator could detect a woman's voice speaking rapidly, but lyrically. Each word spoken was distinct but the volume was so low that it was necessary to strain in order to hear it. Because of the effort required, the spectator could have simply ignored it, but the quality of the voice was so intriguing that attention was probably pulled toward the sound—the tendency was to make the effort to hear it. The voice was Gertrude Stein's, taken from a recording of her reading selections from her work. (In writing about Stein, those who knew her not only describe her physical appearance, but also frequently comment on the unusually deep, mellow, yet commanding quality of her voice.) It was virtually impossible to discern what Stein was saying without concentrating on the sound. Having made the effort, however, each word seemed sharper, more clipped and distinct somehow, against the other two sound patterns that were significantly louder. The combined effect was one of an allegro speech pattern (Stein's voice) against an andante speech pattern (Foreman's voice) and an andante musical composition.

During this sound sequence, which lasted just under sixty seconds, two actresses faced each other, holding each other's arms at the elbows, and danced slowly upstage. As the lights dimmed, they seemed to fade into the distance. Thus, the spectator was not only straining to hear what Stein was reciting, but was also straining to see the two women as they slowly "disappeared." The frustration engendered by attempts to hear and see intriguing, but obscured, sounds and images might trigger or induce one, or both, of the two responses intended: (1) attention is pulled in so many disparate directions simultaneously that a redistribution of attention occurs— the spectator oscillates between focused and unfocused modes; and/or (2) the strain is such that it results in an ecstatic state—the spectator becomes aware of his own perceptual and mental effort to grasp the event before him and is thrown back on himself, as it were.

Perceptual manipulation, however, is not the only kind of manipulation Foreman employs to elicit the response he desires. Although he is fundamentally opposed to it, Foreman does use emotional manipulation, particularly to the extent that it is capable of functioning through music. He feels that music is very seductive and that the ecstatic state is intensified when it exists in opposition to some kind of temptation to succumb to the desire for gratification. He uses music as a means for "emotionalizing the viewer so that the emotion can be conquered." Furthermore, he explains:

> Passivity and detachment [esthetic distance] are not very interesting unless there is something strong from which to be detached. It's a straw man. Anybody can set up a scene and have it be passive, beautiful, detached, and lovely. The question is, can you maintain detachment and intellectual lucidity in the face of very strong emotion, very strong colors, very strong sensorial activity—that's the achievement.[75]

So, for example, the spectator might be presented with some very rhythmical, "toe-tapping" kind of music and then, just as he begins to get caught up in the beat, Foreman interrupts it.

> Many people come to my shows and say that they are very frustrated because, "just when a musical number is about to get really interesting, the buzzer comes and you stop it, and—

continually—you're not giving us a chance to get into these things." Just like anybody else, I know that I can be seduced by a big musical number, but that's not enough. I want to stop so I can see myself getting seduced and realize what the implications of that are.[76]

Thus, an emotional response may be triggered, via an enticing musical number, but the spectator is not given time to indulge himself in it.

A similar effect is achieved through visual imagery insofar as Foreman is successful in exploiting sexual impulses and prurient or voyeuristic tendencies. In *PAIN(T)*, for example, numerous tableaux consisted of Manheim and her sister, Nora, naked and in positions that were sexually implicit, if not explicit. At the same time, through techniques of "hiding and revealing," Foreman made it extremely difficult for the spectator to see the two women. Hence, within his new production style, Foreman worked to place the spectator in a kind of rapidly alternating "pull and push" situation, where at one moment the spectator can sense himself being seduced, or pulled into the emotional and intellectual realm of the play, and in the next moment he feels himself being pushed back or away from it.

The Relational Perspective

In one sense, the change in Foreman's production style can be seen as a shift in emphasis from his initial hermeticism—in which words and objects were isolated, carefully framed or bracketed and presented to the spectator for consideration—to what Piaget refers to as the "relational perspective."[77] It is important to stress at the outset that this is not a substantive shift but a shift in emphasis, since Foreman has always been committed to the tenets of the relational perspective, which hold that it is the relations among elements that count. The whole, and the elements that make up the whole, are secondary while the procedures and processes by which the whole is formed are primary.

Although concern for the "isness" of things was retained, Foreman began to work with much more complicated contexts as he became increasingly interested in the fact that no perception, thing, or operation exists in isolation—all are woven together in a complex web. In Foreman's work, the focus shifted from objects themselves to the conditions under which they retain their identity and the nature of the temporal, spatial, and causal network that contains them. Foreman considers this web or network to be the ultimate reality and, as he continued to work, his production style evolved to reflect this.

In individual scenes, Foreman builds on an image, adding performers, set pieces, and props until the visual field is filled with detail. Then, just as the spectator begins to become familiar with a sequence, it is interrupted or dissolved and replaced by another complex web of relationships among people, objects, words, sounds, music, and activity. It is this web and its continuous displacement that characterizes Foreman's later productions. He feels that the theatre event should provide a field for discovering a kind of attention that reflects the unfocused nature of the world perceived as a web of interrelated energies, explaining, "The only thing that counts is the moment-to-moment progression of the total field—there is a total amount of input at every moment and that's what the work is about."[78]

Foreman attempts to create a visual and aural field for generating the kind of artistic "output" that sparks the senses and intellect of the spectator to an awake, alert, attentive form of conscious perception. The interconnected "energies" in the total field, then, consist not only of the web of relationships between text, performer, and constructed environment, but also of the energy generated by the mind of the spectator who actively uses his perceiving mechanism to experience the piece. Instead of creating a situation in which the spectator passively receives input from the stage, Foreman's desire is to fill the space with input and output, "energy," flying in all directions.

This energy exists—in both positive and negative forms, and in varying degrees of intensity—during successive moments of disequilibrium designed to aid the viewer in "standing under," as opposed to understanding, the experience. Standing under experience can be understood in terms of a kind of duo-consciousness, or the ability of the mind to be in two "places" simultaneously—you not only see, but also see yourself seeing. The idea is to be able "to ride" the energy generated by, and during, the experience. Foreman explains:

> People want to be able to leave the play carrying a message and that means they have gone back to sleep because the message is like a fossil—the remains of the real energy. You have to learn to ride the energy process without this obsessive need to be able to name it, know exactly what it is and have it under control. That is the only way to be creative and I assume all people want to be creative, not by making art, necessarily, but in their work and relationships.[79]

Foreman's productions not only reflect what he considers to be the most creative way to use the mind, they are also designed to trigger, induce, or encourage a kind of mental liberation crucial to creativity. He believes art

> should begin the process of freeing men by calling into doubt the solidity of objects—and laying bare the fact that it is a web of relations that exists, only; that web held taut in each instance by the focal point of consciousness. . . . I show the traces of such web intersections—and by seeing that, you are "reminded" to tune to your own. . . . for when you see the web relatedness of all things—which is in a certain ever-alive relation to "your own web" of consciousness—you then are no longer a blind, hypnotized worshipper of "objects"—but a free man.[80]

Foreman creates contexts not available in nature in order to put pressure on the mind to "wake up" to its own processes. There are no potatoes seven feet tall, for example, to be encountered in nature, and while the way the mind works when comparing Rhoda to such a potato is exactly like the way it works in distinguishing among objects and people in everyday life, in life the mind is not, at the same time, "looking at itself" or aware that it is functioning in a particular way. There are connections and relationships that could be discovered in everyday life if the consciousness were in a different "place," and not operating solely on the level necessary to carry on mundane existence. It is to this end that Foreman works.

In 1974, he stated that "time has already proven that there are at least some other human beings who find that the work gives them a great deal of intellectual and emotional energy, and if there are three or five or twenty, that's really enough."[81] While that number greatly increased with the productions that followed, in a sense it really does not matter how many people appreciate his work. Richard Foreman makes art for himself in an attempt to stretch, widen—ultimately, change—the structure of his own consciousness or the mind's configuration. In the final analysis, Foreman remains the Ontological-Hysteric Theatre's principal spectator.

Conclusion

In a review of Richard Foreman's fourth Ontological-Hysteric Theatre production *HčOhTiEṅLâ (or) HOTEL CHINA* (1971-72) published in *Changes,* Victoria Schultz wrote: *"HOTEL CHINA* is made up of a succession of bizarre, surrealistic illogical events that do not connect for the purpose of carrying forward a narrative pattern."[1] Over the years, the single word most frequently used by reviewers to describe Foreman's work has been "surreal." This is understandable to a certain extent since elements of the illogical and irrational, which characterize Surrealism historically, are present in Foreman's productions. However, the tendency has been to lump Foreman's pieces together with Robert Wilson's and discuss them as up-to-date examples of Surrealism. The problem with categorizing Ontological-Hysteric Theatre as Surrealist is that in order to make Foreman's work fit this classification, it would be necessary to ignore many aspects of the work that bear no relationship to Surrealism and are, in fact, in opposition to it.

Foreman's roots are in theatre and, before founding the Ontological-Hysteric Theatre, he was immensely erudite, as he puts it, in all aspects of the historical, theatrical avant-garde. Elements of Symbolism (especially the quality of the initial acting style, and early tableau compositions, in which performers were placed in strict profile to the audience) and Expressionism (for example, the notion that Foreman's plays are monodramas that represent the workings of his mind as it speaks to, or addresses, different aspects of itself) can also be found in Foreman's productions. There are many precedents for his work and, therefore, no single model can suffice in explaining it entirely.

There is another reason why this is true. It should be clear from the preceding chapters that Foreman is also familiar with disciplines that are not directly related to the arts, such as the natural sciences (especially physics), the behavioral sciences (especially psychology), and philosophy. The philosophical underpinnings of Foreman's work, alone, are enough to distinguish it from the majority of the theatre done today and in the past. His work is embedded in complex philosophical concepts, although it does not attempt to express them, nor do they explain the work completely. Philosophical concerns are inherent in his approach and, like certain qualities and theories culled from the historical avant-garde they help to elucidate the work to a definite, but limited, extent. The point is that Foreman's work is more than the sum of its parts and, in an analysis of it, the differences between Ontological-Hysteric Theatre and its precedents are most significant. (The influences on Foreman are so numerous that such an analysis is not possible here. It is the subject of another work that, hopefully, will be attempted in the future.)

Recently, Bonnie Marranca coined the phrase "Theatre of Images," in her book of the same title, in an attempt to distinguish among forms that have evolved in the last twenty years. While the phrase has many advantages, the convenience of it as a catch-phrase among them, it tends to muddy the issue somewhat, especially considering the artists and groups Marranca includes in her definition. For example, in the introduction to her anthology (which includes scripts by Foreman, Wilson, and Lee Breuer of Mabou Mines) Marranca states that the Theatre of Images is meant to separate literary from nonliterary theatre. Yet she includes Mabou Mines, a group that works extensively, if not exclusively, in forms of literary theatre. (It is impossible to use the script she includes of Breuer's *The Red Horse Animation* as a source for determining the literary or nonliterary nature of the production since the text appears in comic book form. The reader must accept, on faith, her statement that, "at the theatrical level, *Red Horse* remains non-literary,"[2] a somewhat difficult leap to make from her previous statement that "Mabou Mines is . . . concerned with . . . story telling techniques."[3])

More to the point, Theatre of Images continues the tradition of lumping Foreman and Wilson together as examples of the same phenomenon. This pairing, of course, is not completely unfounded. Indeed, on January 1, 1970, a review of Wilson's production *The Life and Times of Sigmund Freud* appeared in *The Village Voice* written by Foreman, in which he discusses Wilson's work in precisely the same terms in which he discusses his own work.[4] But, again, it seems that it is the differences that are most interesting, as well as important.

Theatre of Images indicates that the artist is *primarily* an image-maker and, while Foreman is unquestionably an ingenious image-maker, he also works extensively with language. Marranca does include "aural and verbal images" in her definition but it is difficult to comprehend an "aural image" unless it is in the verbal sense of describing or portraying an image in language which, obviously, Foreman is not involved in. It is evident from chapter 2 that even though Foreman's theatre can not be "read," and language does not dominate his images, language is of equal importance, often carrying equal weight in the experience. Furthermore, almost every moment of Foreman's productions is permeated with sound and, as seen in the discussion of aural dedifferentiation in chapter 6, Foreman consciously uses sound as a crucial experiential dimension of his theatre art—his theatre is not *primarily* one of images.

In addition, and perhaps more significantly, an important definition of the word "image" is a "mental picture of something not actually present." Wilson works extensively with this area of "imagery," focusing particularly on the products of the individual spectator's imagination. While the spectator is perceiving the performance on his "exterior screen," Wilson designs his productions to call the "inner screen" into play, so that images that usually occur only during the sleep state overlap the waking images of the performance, both occurring simultaneously. Foreman, on the other hand, uses specific devices to "erase" the mind, as it were, snapping it back into full, lucid consciousness. He sounds his loud, harsh buzzer to help the spectator resist being seduced by a particular provocative image.

On a very fundamental level, many of the impulses, methods, and goals of Foreman's work are quite different from those of Robert Wilson. Both artists have only been working for about ten years and, perhaps, it is simply too soon to label their work in terms of current tendencies or past movements.

At the time of this writing, Foreman is in Italy where he is mounting his sixteenth Ontological-Hysteric Theatre production, using Italian actors and Kate Manheim. Last season, 1978-79, in New York he cancelled the opening of what would have been his sixteenth piece, after three months of rehearsals. The reason he gave involved work on his first feature-length film, which was in the editing stages at the time. The film, entitled *Strong Medicine,* has since been completed. See Appendix A for a "Complete Chronology of Plays by Richard Foreman" (specifically pages 224-25) for updated information on Foreman's work through the summer of 1981.

Appendix A

Complete Chronology of Plays by Richard Foreman*

—1968:

ANGELFACE   Presented by the Ontological-Hysteric Theatre at the Cinematheque (80 Wooster Street), New York City, April, 1968.

ELEPHANT STEPS   Music by Stanley Silverman. Commissioned by the Fromm Music Foundation. Presented at Tanglewood, Lenox, Mass., by the Berkshire Music Festival, July-August, 1968. Second production at Hunter College Opera Theatre, New York City, April, 1970.

—1969:

IDA-EYED   Presented by the Ontological-Hysteric Theatre at the New Dramatists Workshop, New York City, May, 1969.

RHODA-RETURNING

REAL MAGIC IN NEW YORK   Music by Stephen Dickman. Concert production at the Cinematheque, May, 1970.

SOPHIA=(WISDOM): Part 1   (Produced by Theatre for the New City, New York City, November, 1974, under the direction of Crystal Field.)

—1970:

TOTAL RECALL (SOPHIA=(WISDOM): Part 2)   Presented by the Ontological-Hysteric Theatre at the Cinematheque, December, 1970—January, 1971.

MAUDLIN NOTATIONS

All produced plays were designed and directed by Richard Foreman unless otherwise indicated.

FOREST: (SUBTITLED DEPTH)

TWO VACATIONS

HOLY MOLY

LINES OF VISION

—1971:

HčOhTĭEñLå (or) HOTEL CHINA

Presented by the Ontological-Hysteric Theatre at the Cinematheque, December, 1971—January, 1972.

EVIDENCE

Privately printed notebooks in which LINES OF VISION and HOTEL CHINA were originally written. The first 30 pages were staged and presented by the Ontological-Hysteric Theatre as EVIDENCE, at Theatre for the New City, April, 1972.

(A selection entitled 15 MINUTES OF EVIDENCE was presented by the Playwrights' Cooperative, New York City, May, 1975, under the direction of Kate Davy.)

DREAM TANTRAS FOR WESTERN MASSACHUSETTS

Music by Stanley Silverman. Presented by Lyn Austin and Oliver Smith at the Lenox Arts Center, Lenox, Mass., August, 1971.

SOPHIA=(WISDOM) Part 3:
 THE CLIFFS

Presented by the Ontological-Hysteric Theatre at the Cinematheque, December, 1972—January, 1973.

—1972:

DAILY LIFE

One scene, retitled HONOR, presented by the Playwrights' Cooperative at the Cubiculo Theatre, New York City, May, 1973.

OP/RA: AN ISOMORPHIC REPRESEN-TATION OF THE GRADUAL DISMEM-BERMENT FROM WITHIN OF WESTERN ART IN WHICH A NEW UNITY THAT OF CONSCIOUSNESS ITSELF EMERGES

HOTEL FOR CRIMINALS

Music by Stanley Silverman. Commissioned by the National Opera Foundation. Produced at the Exchange Theatre, New York City, January, 1975.

DR. SELAVY'S MAGIC THEATRE

Music by Stanley Silverman. Lyrics by Tom Hendry. Presented by Lyn Austin, Lenox Arts Center, Lenox, Mass., July, 1972. Also presented at the Mercer-O'Casey Theatre in New York City, November, 1972—April, 1973.

AFRICA

CLASSICAL THERAPY or A WEEK UNDER THE INFLUENCE . . .

Presented by the Ontological-Hysteric Theatre for the Festival d'Automne, Paris, France, September-October, 1973.

PARTICLE THEORY

Presented by the Ontological-Hysteric Theatre at Theatre for the New City, April-May, 1973.

THE REM(ARK)ABLE CABIN-CRUISER: (DEPTH)

—1973:

INSPIRATIONAL ANALYSIS

VERTICAL MOBILITY (SOPHIA= (WISDOM): Part 4)

Presented by the Ontological-Hysteric Theatre, New York City, April-May, 1974.

WALLED GARDEN (LANGUAGE)

LIFE OF THE BEE (I've Got der Shakes)

AFRICANNS-INSTRUCTIS

—1974:

PANDERING TO THE MASSES: A MISREPRESENTATION

Presented by the Ontological-Hysteric Theatre, New York City, January-March, 1975.

PAIN(T)

Presented by the Ontological-Hysteric Theatre, New York City, April-May, 1974 (in repertory with VERTICAL MOBILITY).

RHODA IN POTATOLAND (HER FALL-STARTS)

Presented by the Ontological-Hysteric Theatre, New York City, December, 1975—February, 1976.

THINKING (ONE KIND)

Presented by the Drama Department of the University of California, San Diego, March, 1975.

—1975:

OUT OF THE BODY TRAVEL

Presented as a video piece at the American Dance Festival, New London, Connecticut, July, 1975.

SEANCE

PLACE+TARGET

END OF A BEAUTIFUL FRIENDSHIP

RADIANT CITY

LIVRE DES SPLENDEURS

Presented at the Festival d'Automne, Paris, France, October, 1976.

—1976:

BOOK OF SPLENDORS: PART TWO
  BOOK OF LEVERS):
  ACTION AT A DISTANCE

Presented by the Ontological-Hysteric Theatre, New York City, March-May, 1977.

The Threepenny Opera (Brecht)
  (Director)

Produced by the New York Shakespeare Festival and presented at Lincoln Center, opened in June, 1976.

—1977:

BLVD. DE PARIS

Produced by the Ontological-Hysteric Theatre, New York City, January-March, 1978.

CITY ARCHIVES

Color video piece produced by the Walker Art Center, Minneapolis, Minnesota, July, 1977.

SLIGHT

(Directed by Stuart Sherman. Presented by the Playwright's Group Festival 3, New York City, March, 1977.)

—1978:

STRONG MEDICINE

Feature-length film (filmed in New York City, July-August, 1978).

Stages (Ostrow)
  (Director)

Written and produced by Stuart Ostrow. Presented at the Belasco Theatre, March, 1978.

AMERICAN IMAGINATION

Music by Stanley Silverman. Produced by the Music Theatre Performance Group, New York City, May, 1978.

—1979:

MADNESS AND TRANQUILITY

Produced by the Ontological-Hysteric Theatre but never opened (rehearsed from November, 1978 to January, 1979).

LUOGO + BERSAGLIO (PLACE + TARGET)

Produced by Teatro di Roma, Rome, Italy, December, 1979 and Milan, January, 1980.

—1980:

MADAME ADARE

Music by Stanley Silverman. Produced by the New York City Opera, Lincoln Center, October, 1980.

—1981:

PENGUIN TOUQUET

Produced by the Ontological-Hysteric Theatre and the New York Shakespeare Festival, New York City, January-February, 1981.

Don Juan (Molière)
  (Director)

Produced by the Tyrone Guthrie Theatre, Minneapolis, Minnesota, June-August, 1981.

Appendix B

List of Characters and Performers

ANGELFACE
New York City
April, 1968

Max	Ken Kelman
Walter	Prentiss Wilhite
Agatha	Eleanor Herasmachuck
Karl	Larry Kardish
Walter II	Ernie Gehr
Weinstein	Mike Jacobson
Rhoda	Judy Kardish

TOTAL RECALL
(SOPHIA=(WISDOM): Part 2)
New York City
December, 1970—January, 1971

Ben	Mike Jacobson
Leo	Bob Fleischner
Rhoda	Judy Fyve
Sophia	Margaret Ladd
Little Girl	Alexandra Stone

HčOhTĬEńLå (or) HOTEL CHINA
New York City
December, 1971—January, 1972

Max	N.E. Deinau
Karl	Bob Fleischner
Karl II	Ernie Gehr
Rhoda	Sarah Boothe
Eleanor	Judy Fyve
Angel	Kate Manheim
Ben	Andrew Noren
Hannah	Kate Manheim
Ida	Jan Penovich
Hannah II	Ann Clark
Little Girl	Diana Paris

SOPHIA=(WISDOM)
Part 3: THE CLIFFS
New York City
December, 1972—January, 1973

Max(Leo)	Bob Fleischner
Ben	Andrew Noren
Hannah	Margot Breier
Sophia	Linda Patton
Rhoda	Kate Manheim
Karl (Snowman)	Jim Hoberman
Workers	Myron Adams
	Jim Boerlin
	Gregory Gubitosa
	Iris Newman
	Bill Plympton
	Allegra Scott

CLASSICAL THERAPY or A
WEEK UNDER THE INFLUENCE . . .
Paris, France
September-October, 1973

Rhoda	Kate Manheim
Ben	Gerard Neut
Max	Remy Chaignard
Eleanor	Anemone
Karl	Christian Ducray
Hannah	Nicole Guichaoua
Leo	Bernard Tourtelier
Crew Persons	Odile Michel
	Sanna de Kerviler
	Elke Gerard
	Martine Carlier

VERTICAL MOBILITY
(SOPHIA=(WISDOM): Part 4)
New York City
April-May, 1974

Max . . . . Bob Fleischner
Rhoda . . . . Kate Manheim
Ben . . . . Jim Jennings
Sophia . . . . Donna Germain
Crew Persons . . . . Marcy Arlin
John Matturri
Gregory Gubitosa
Stuart Sherman

PAIN(T)
New York City
April-May, 1974

Rhoda . . . . Kate Manheim
Eleanor . . . . Nora Manheim
Ida . . . . Mimi Johnson
Max . . . . Stuart Sherman
Sophia . . . . Hanneke Henket
Crew Persons . . . . Bob Fleischner
Norma Jean Deak
Charles Bergengren
Gregory Gubitosa

RHODA IN POTATOLAND
(HER FALL-STARTS)
New York City
December, 1975—February, 1976

Rhoda . . . . Kate Manheim
Max . . . . Bob Fleischner
Sophia . . . . Rena Gill
Waiter . . . . Gautam Dasgupta
Admirer . . . . John Matturri
Hannah . . . . Ela Troyano
Eleanor . . . . Camille Foss
Agatha . . . . Cathy Scott
Crew Persons . . . . Tim Kennedy
Phillip Johnston
Charley Bergengren

PANDERING TO THE MASSES:
A MISREPRESENTATION
New York City
January-February, 1975

Max . . . . Bob Fleischner
Leo . . . . Stuart Sherman
Rhoda . . . . Kate Manheim
Ben . . . . John Erdman
Black Magician . . . . Charles Bergengren
Eleanor . . . . Aline Lillie Mayer
Sophia . . . . Sheila McLaughlin
Crew Persons . . . . Camille Foss
Ellen Mills LeCompte
Gregory Gubitosa
Richard Levine
Gail Conrad
Suzanne Oshry
Susan Siegel
John Matturri

BOOK OF SPLENDORS: PART TWO
(BOOK OF LEVERS): ACTION AT
A DISTANCE
New York City
March-April, 1977

Rhoda . . . . Kate Manheim
Hannah . . . . Peyton
Ben (Max) . . . . John Erdman
Max (Ben) . . . . Robert Schlee
Eleanor . . . . Cynthia Pattison
Crew Persons . . . . Charles Bergengren
Phillip Johnston
Louis Belogenis
Camille Foss
Anna Jordan
Francois Thiolat

BLVD. DE PARIS (I'VE GOT
THE SHAKES)
New York City
January-March, 1978

Rhoda . . . . Kate Manheim
Man . . . . John Erdman
Devil . . . . Robert Schlee
Lady in Black . . . . Peyton
Crew Persons . . . . Cynthia Pattison
Charles Bergengren
Camille Foss
Francois Thiolat
Louis Belogenis
Larry Tighe
Mayra Levy

Notes

Introduction

1. Richard Foreman, *Angelface,* in *Richard Foreman Plays and Manifestos,* ed. Kate Davy (New York: New York University Press, 1976), p. 19.

2. Interview with Richard Foreman, New York, New York, October, 1976.

3. Richard Foreman, Lecture to P. Adams Sitney's graduate film class, Department of Cinema Studies, New York University, New York, 9 November 1973.

4. Michael Kirby, Radio Interview with Richard Foreman, New York, New York, 11 January 1974.

5. Michael Feingold, "An Interview with Richard Foreman", *yale/theatre* 7 (Fall, 1975), p. 14.

6. Blurb appearing on the album jacket of the recording of *Elephant Steps,* Columbia Records, New York, 1974.

7. Feingold, "Interview with Foreman," p. 14.

8. Robb Baker, "The Theatre of Richard Foreman: Hysterical Cool," *The Soho Weekly News,* 9 January 1975.

9. Arthur Sainer, "The scene lately seen (1)," *The Village Voice,* 8 July 1971, p. 46.

Chapter 1

1. Richard Foreman, "How I Write My (Self: Plays)," *The Drama Review* 21, 4 (December, 1977), p. 6.

2. Ibid., p. 8.

3. Ted Shank, Interview with Richard Foreman, Paris, 22 September 1976.

4. Michael Feingold, "An Interview with Richard Foreman," *yale/theatre* 7 (Fall, 1975), p. 9.

5. Interview with Amy Taubin, New York, New York, 9 December 1974.

6. Foreman, "How I Write," p. 9.

7. Feingold, "Interview with Foreman," p. 8.

8. Ibid., p. 7.

9. Foreman and Taubin were married until 1971.

10. Feingold, "Interview with Foreman," p. 8.

11. Foreman, "How I Write," p. 9.

12. Interview with P. Adams Sitney, New York, New York, 23 November 1974.

13. Taubin, Interview.

14. Ibid.

15. Interview with Richard Foreman, New York, New York, 18 December 1974.

16. Information on Foreman's involvement with the New American Cinema movement was obtained from private interviews in New York City, in 1974, with Richard Foreman (18 December); Ernie Gehr (17 December); Richard Foreman and Ken Jacobs (22 November); Ken Kelman (18 November); Jonas Mekas (20 November); P. Adams Sitney (23 November); and Amy Taubin (9 December). Unless otherwise noted, all further references to events and dates were derived from these interviews.

17. Foreman, Interview.

18. Feingold, "Interview with Foreman," p. 11.

19. Foreman provided this additional insight in a letter to me after reading chapter 1 of this work.

20. Richard Foreman, as quoted in "The Talk of the Town," *The New Yorker,* 27 January 1973, p. 24.

21. Foreman, Interview with Foreman and Jacobs.

22. Ibid.

23. Kelman, Interview.

24. Sitney, Interview.

25. Mekas, Interview.

26. Foreman, Interview with Foreman and Jacobs.

27. Foreman, Interview.

28. Jonas Mekas, *Movie Journal: The Rise of the New American Cinema 1959-1971* (New York: Collier Books, 1972), p. 212.

29. Taubin, Interview.

30. P. Adams Sitney, *Visionary Film: The American Avant-Garde* (New York: Oxford University Press, 1974), p. 396.

31. Kelman, Interview.

32. Feingold, "Interview with Foreman," p. 8.

33. Foreman, "How I Write," p. 9.

34. Foreman, Interview.

35. Feingold, "Interview with Foreman," p. 11.

36. Foreman, "How I Write," p. 9.

37. Jacobs, Interview with Foreman and Jacobs.

38. Foreman, Interview with Foreman and Jacobs.

39. Mekas, Interview.

40. Feingold, "Interview with Foreman," p. 10.

41. Ibid., p. 7.

42. Taubin, Interview.

43. Feingold, "Interview with Foreman," p. 12.

44. Richard Foreman, Unpublished notes written in the summer of 1969, obtained from the personal files of Richard Foreman and Jonas Mekas (Anthology Film Archives).

45. Richard Foreman, "Richard Foreman Comments," entry on Richard Foreman in *Contemporary Dramatists,* ed. James Vinson (London: St. James Press, 1973), p. 247.

46. Feingold, "Interview with Foreman," p. 12.

47. Richard Foreman, Group Discussion, with Ernie Gehr, Ken Kelman, Jonas Mekas, P. Adams Sitney, Michael Snow, Amy Taubin, and Joyce Wieland participating, New York, New York, Spring, 1969.

Chapter 2

1. Richard Foreman, "How I Write My (Self: Plays)," *The Drama Review* 21 (December, 1977), p. 9.

2. Michael Feingold, "An Interview with Richard Foreman," *yale/theatre* 7 (Fall, 1975), p. 20.

3. Gertrude Stein, *The Autobiography of Alice B. Toklas,* in *Selected Writings of Gertrude Stein,* ed. Carl van Vechten (1946; rpt. New York: Vintage Books, 1972), p. 177.

4. Richard Foreman, Group Discussion, with Ernie Gehr, Ken Kelman, Jonas Mekas, P. Adams Sitney, Michael Snow, Amy Taubin, and Joyce Wieland participating, New York, New York, Spring, 1969.

5. William James, *The Principles of Psychology,* vol. 1 (New York: Holt, 1890), p. 185.

6. Ibid.

7. William James, as quoted by Elizabeth Sprigge in *Gertrude Stein: Writings and Lectures, 1909-45,* ed. Patricia Meyerowitz (Baltimore: Penguin Books, 1967), p. 14. See James's essay "The Stream of Consciousness," in *The Modern Tradition: Backgrounds of Modern Literature,* ed. by Richard Ellmann and Charles Feidelson, Jr. (New York: Oxford University Press, 1965).

8. For an in-depth study of Stein's conception of "being existing," novelty, and creative vision, see the second chapter of Allegra Stewart's work *Gertrude Stein and the Present* (Cambridge: Harvard University Press, 1967).

9. Gertrude Stein, "How Writing is Written," in *How Writing is Written,* ed. Robert Bartlett Haas (Los Angeles: Black Sparrow Press, 1974), p. 155.

10. Gertrude Stein, "The Autobiography of Rose," in *How Writing is Written,* p. 39.

11. Foreman, "How I Write," pp. 10-11.

12. Ibid., p. 8.

13. Gertrude Stein, "Plays," in *Lectures in America* (1935: rpt. New York: Vintage Books, 1975), pp. 104-5.

14. Gertrude Stein, "Composition as Explanation," in *What are Masterpieces* (1940; rpt. New York: Pitman Publishing Corp., 1970), pp. 37-38.

15. Gertrude Stein, "A Transatlantic Interview, 1946," in *A Primer for the Gradual Understanding of Gertrude Stein,* ed. Robert Bartlett Haas (Los Angeles: Black Sparrow Press, 1973), p. 20.

16. Donald Sutherland, *Gertrude Stein: A Biography of Her Work* (New Haven: Yale University Press, 1951), p. 174.

17. Richard Foreman, "Richard Foreman Comments," entry on Richard Foreman in *Contemporary Dramatists,* ed. James Vinson (London: St. James Press, 1973), p. 247.

18. Richard Foreman, Unpublished notes written in the summer of 1969, obtained from the personal files of Richard Foreman and Jonas Mekas (Anthology Film Archives).

19. Stein, "Plays," p. 112.

20. Ibid., p. 113.

21. Ibid., p. 112.

22. Ibid.

23. Ibid., p. 104.

24. Ibid., p. 93.

25. Ibid., p. 115.

26. Ibid.

27. Stein, "Transatlantic Interview," p. 16.

28. Stein, "Plays," p. 122.

29. Ibid., p. 21.

30. Ibid., p. 23.

31. Ibid., pp. 6-7.

32. Ibid., p. 6.

33. Ibid., p. 7.

34. Ibid., p. 20.

35. Ibid., p. 22.

36. Ibid., p. 11.

37. Ibid.

38. Richard Foreman, *Rhoda in Potatoland,* in *Richard Foreman: Plays and Manifestos,* ed. Kate Davy, (New York: New York University Press, 1976), p. 212.

39. Foreman, "How I Write," p. 12.

40. Ibid.

41. Kate Davy, "Foreman's *PAIN(T)* and *Vertical Mobility,*" *The Drama Review* 18, 2 (June, 1974), p. 28.

42. *Richard Foreman: Plays and Manifestos,* p. 174.

43. Michael Kirby, "Richard Foreman's Ontological-Hysteric Theatre," *The Drama Review* 17, 2 (June, 1973), p. 32.

44. Foreman, "How I Write," p. 22.

45. Richard Foreman, "Ontological-Hysteric Manifesto II" (July, 1974), in *Richard Foreman: Plays and Manifestos,* p. 135.

46. Gertrude Stein, "Poetry and Grammar," in *Lectures in America,* pp. 220-21.

47. William James, "The Stream of Consciousness," in Ellmann and Feidelson, pp. 719-20.

48. Feingold, "Interview with Foreman," p. 20.

49. Foreman, "How I Write," p. 14.

50. Ibid.

51. Gertrude Stein, as quoted by Janet Flanner in her forward to *Two: Gertrude Stein and Her Brother, and Other Early Portraits (1908-1912)* (New Haven: Yale University Press, 1951), p. xvii.

52. P. Adams Sitney, entry on Richard Foreman in *Contemporary Dramatists,* ed. James Vinson (London: St. James Press, 1973), p. 248.

Chapter 3

1. See *The Theatre of Images,* ed. Bonnie Marranca (New York: Drama Book Specialists, 1977), pp. 3-11.

2. Michael Kirby, Radio Interview with Richard Foreman, New York, New York, 11 January 1974.

3. Ibid.

4. Ibid.

5. Richard Foreman, *Total Recall,* in *Richard Foreman: Plays and Manifestos,* ed. Kate Davy, (New York: New York University Press, 1976), p. 38.

6. Ibid., p. 48.

7. Ibid.

8. Interview with Richard Foreman, New York, New York, Summer, 1977.

9. *Richard Foreman: Plays and Manifestos,* p. 35.

10. Ibid., p. 57.

11. Ibid., p. 33.

12. Ibid., p. 39.

13. *Ida-Eyed,* the second Ontological-Hysteric Theatre production, was presented at the New Dramatists Workshop.

14. The character holding the beam in plates 7 and 11 is "HANNAH," played by Kate Manheim who appears as "RHODA" in subsequent productions.

15. *Richard Foreman: Plays and Manifestos,* pp. 96, 97, 99, 101.

16. *Richard Foreman: Plays and Manifestos,* p. 111.

17.   Michael Kirby, "Richard Foreman's Ontological-Hysteric Theatre," *The Drama Review* 17, 2 (June, 1973), p. 6.

18.   Ibid.

19.   Ibid., p. 10.

20.   Ibid., p. 6.

21.   Ibid., p. 14.

22.   Kirby, Radio Interview with Foreman.

23.   Ibid.

24.   Interview with Richard Foreman, New York, New York, March, 1974.

25.   *Richard Foreman: Plays and Manifestos,* p. 206.

26.   *Sophia=(Wisdom): Part I* was produced by Theatre for the New City, under the direction of Crystal Field, in November, 1974.

27.   Kirby, "Foreman's Ontological-Hysteric Theatre," p. 7.

28.   Kirby, Radio Interview with Foreman.

29.   *Book of Splendors: Part I* was presented for the Festival d'Automne in Paris (September-October, 1976).

30.   Interview with Foreman, Summer, 1977.

31.   Ted Shank, Interview with Richard Foreman, Paris, 22 September 1976.

32.   *Richard Foreman: Plays and Manifestos,* p. 218.

33.   Interview with Foreman, Summer, 1977.

34.   Ibid.

35.   Kirby, Radio Interview with Foreman.

36.   Stephen Koch, "Performance, A Conversation," *Artforum* XI, 4 (December, 1972), p. 55.

37.   Ibid.

38.   Interview with Foreman, Summer, 1977.

39.   Ibid.

40.   Terry Curtis Fox, "The Romance of Intellect," *The Village Voice,* 2 January 1978, p. 77.

Chapter 4

1.   Arthur Sainer, "Someone trips, an angel smiles," *The Village Voice,* 6 January 1972.

2.   Michael Smith, "theatre journal," *The Village Voice,* 4 May 1972.

3.   Michael Kirby, "Richard Foreman's Ontological-Hysteric Theatre," *The Drama Review* 17, 2 (June, 1973), pp. 7-9.

4.   Richard Foreman, "How I Write My (Self: Plays)," *The Drama Review* 21, 4 (December, 1977), p. 13.

5. Richard Foreman, Group Discussion with Ernie Gehr, Ken Kelman, Jonas Mekas, P. Adams Sitney, Michael Snow, Amy Taubin, and Joyce Wieland participating, New York, New York, Spring, 1969.

6. Ibid.

7. Ibid.

8. Kirby, "Ontological-Hysteric Theatre," p. 10.

9. Interview with Richard Foreman, New York, New York, March, 1974.

10. Michael Kirby, Radio Interview with Richard Foreman, New York, New York, 11 January 1974.

11. Terry Curtis Fox, "The Romance of Intellect," *The Village Voice,* 2 January 1978, p. 77.

12. Kirby, Radio Interview with Foreman.

13. Kirby, "Ontological-Hysteric Theatre," p. 18.

14. Richard Foreman, *HOTEL CHINA,* in *Richard Foreman: Plays and Manifestos,* ed. Kate Davy, (New York: New York University Press, 1976), p. 97.

15. Kate Davy, "Foreman's *PAIN(T)* and *Vertical Mobility*," *The Drama Review* 18, 2 (June, 1974), p. 36.

16. The recording was made in France by the RCA Corporation, from the original Victor recording, and distributed under the series title of "Black and White," Vol. 89. The title of the album is "Tiny Parham and his Musicians, vol. 1 (1928-29)."

17. *Richard Foreman: Plays and Manifestos,* p. 117.

18. Kirby, "Ontological-Hysteric Theatre," p. 10.

19. The exceptions are *PAIN(T)* and *Vertical Mobility* when he sat above and in back of the bleacher section.

20. Kirby, "Ontological-Hysteric Theatre," p. 15.

21. Kirby, Radio Interview with Foreman.

22. Ibid.

23. Kirby, "Ontological-Hysteric Theatre," pp. 17-18.

24. Ibid., p. 19.

25. *Richard Foreman: Plays and Manifestos,* p. 149.

26. Ibid., pp. 150-51.

27. Kirby, "Ontological-Hysteric Theatre," p. 20.

28. Ibid., p. 10.

29. W. David Sievers, *Directing for the Theatre* (Dubuque, Iowa: William C. Brown Co., Publishers, 1965), p. 117.

30. Alexander Dean, Lawrence Carra, *Fundamentals of Play Directing* (New York: Holt, Rinehart and Winston, Inc., 1965), p. 173.

31. Ibid., pp. 173-74.

32.   Kirby, Radio Interview with Foreman.

33.   Kirby, "Ontological-Hysteric Theatre," pp. 10-11.

34.   Foreman, Interview.

35.   Kirby, "Ontological-Hysteric Theatre," pp. 11-12.

36.   Ibid.

37.   Ibid.

38.   Stephen Koch, "Performance, A Conversation," *Artforum* XI, 4 (December, 1972), p. 55.

Chapter 5

1.   Michael Feingold, "An Interview with Richard Foreman," *yale/theatre* 7, 1 (Fall, 1975), p. 26.

2.   Richard Foreman, Unpublished notes written in the summer of 1969, obtained from the personal files of Richard Foreman and Jonas Mekas (Anthology Film Archives).

3.   Feingold, "Interview with Foreman," pp. 11-12.

4.   Richard Foreman, "How I Write My (Self: Plays)," *The Drama Review* 21, 4 (December, 1977), p. 12.

5.   Ibid., p. 6.

6.   Terry Curtis Fox, "The Romance of Intellect," *The Village Voice,* 2 January 1978, p. 77.

7.   Foreman, "How I Write," p. 11.

8.   Ibid., p. 14.

9.   Feingold, "Interview with Foreman," p. 27.

10.   Foreman, "How I Write," p. 23.

11.   Feingold, "Interview with Foreman," p. 27.

12.   Robb Baker, "The Theatre of Richard Foreman: Hysterical Cool," *The Soho Weekly News,* 9 January 1975.

13.   Foreman, "How I Write," p. 11.

14.   Baker, "Hysterical Cool."

15.   Ibid.

16.   Foreman, Unpublished notes.

17.   K.S., "Richard Foreman: 'Responding to life in my one leaf-like moment,'" *Brown University Bulletin* (obtained from Richard Foreman's personal files).

18.   Kate Davy, "Kate Manheim as Foreman's Rhoda," *The Drama Review* 20, 3 (September, 1976), p. 38.

19.   Foreman, "How I Write," p. 6.

20.   Interview with Richard Foreman, New York, New York, Summer, 1977.

21.   Ted Shank, Interview with Richard Foreman, Paris, 22 September 1976.

22.   Ibid.

23. Ibid.

24. Ibid.

25. Kate Davy, "Foreman's *PAIN(T)* and *Vertical Mobility,*" *The Drama Review* 18, 2 (June, 1974), p. 34.

26. Shank, Interview with Foreman.

27. Ibid.

28. Interview with Richard Foreman, New York, New York, March, 1974.

29. Shank, Interview with Foreman.

30. Ibid.

31. Terry Curtis Fox, "Cinema is Ontological-Hysteria at 24 Frames a Second," *The Village Voice,* 4 September 1978, p. 75.

32. Stephen Koch, "Performance, A Conversation," *Artforum* XI, 4 (December, 1972), p. 56.

33. Baker, "Hysterical Cool."

34. All descriptions of the rehearsals for *PAIN(T)* and *Vertical Mobility* were taken from my article on Foreman's rehearsal techniques which appeared in a special "Rehearsal Procedures Issue" of *The Drama Review* 18, 2 (June, 1974), pp. 26-37, hereafter referred to as "Rehearsal Procedures," *TDR.*

35. Ibid.

36. Richard Foreman, Panel discussion on "Schizo-Culture" with Francoise Kourilsky, Frantisek Deak, and Stephen Koch participating, Columbia University, New York, 14 November 1975.

37. Richard Foreman, Lecture to P. Adams Sitney's graduate film class, Department of Cinema Studies, New York University, New York, 9 November 1973.

38. Richard Foreman, *Rhoda in Potatoland,* in *Richard Foreman: Plays and Manifestos,* ed. Kate Davy, (New York: New York University Press, 1976), p. 207.

39. Ibid., p. 244.

40. Foreman, Unpublished notes.

41. Shank, Interview with Foreman.

42. Koch, "Conversation," p. 56.

43. Shank, Interview with Foreman.

44. Davy, "Foreman's *PAIN(T)* and *Vertical Mobility,*" p. 28.

45. Ibid., p. 32.

46. Foreman, "How I Write," p. 14.

47. Foreman, Unpublished notes.

48. "Rehearsal Procedures," *TDR.*

49. *Richard Foreman: Plays and Manifestos,* p. 172.

50. Shank, Interview with Foreman.

51.   Davy, "Foreman's *PAIN(T)* and *Vertical Mobility*," pp. 26-27.

52.   Baker, "Hysterical Cool."

53.   Feingold, "Interview with Foreman," p. 23.

54.   Ibid.

55.   Interview with Foreman, Summer, 1977.

56.   Davy, "Foreman's *PAIN(T)* and *Vertical Mobility*," p. 29.

57.   Ibid., p. 28.

58.   Ibid., p. 33.

59.   "Rehearsal Procedures," *TDR.*

60.   Davy, "Manheim as Rhoda," p. 38.

61.   Michael Kirby, "Richard Foreman's Ontological-Hystric Theatre," *The Drama Review* 17, (June, 1973): pp. 15-16.

62.   Ibid., p. 17.

63.   "Rehearsal Procedures," *TDR.*

64.   Lita Eliscu, "Ontological-Hysteric Theatre," *East Village Other,* 27 May 1969.

65.   Florence Falk, "Ontological-Hysteric Theatre: Setting as Consciousness," *Performing Arts Journal* 1, 1 (Spring, 1976), p. 55.

66.   Shank, Interview with Foreman.

67.   Foreman provided this information in a letter to me after reading chapter 1 of this work.

68.   Michael Kirby, Radio Interview with Richard Foreman, New York, New York, 11 January 1974.

69.   Feingold, "Interview with Foreman," p. 25.

70.   For a complete analysis of the acting/not-acting continuum, see Michael Kirby's article "On Acting and Not Acting," *The Drama Review* 16, 1 (March, 1972), pp. 3-15.

71.   Shank, Interview with Foreman.

72.   Fox, "Romance of Intellect," p. 77.

73.   Stanley Kauffmann, "Arts and Lives: Stanley Kauffmann on Theater," *New Republic* 178 (25 February 1978), p. 39.

74.   Davy, "Manheim as Rhoda," p. 45.

75.   Ibid.

76.   Ibid., p. 46.

77.   Ibid., p. 42.

78.   Ibid.

79.   Ibid.

80.   Baker, "Hysterical Cool."

81.   Davy, "Foreman's *PAIN(T)* and *Vertical Mobility*," p. 37.

82. Foreman, Panel discussion, "Schizo-Culture."

Chapter 6

1. Ted Shank, Interview with Richard Foreman, Paris, 22 September 1976.

2. Interview with Richard Foreman, New York, New York, March, 1974.

3. Shank, Interview with Foreman.

4. John Cage, Richard Foreman, and Richard Kostelanetz, "Art in the Culture," *Performing Arts Journal* IV, 1-2 (Summer, 1979), pp. 78-79.

5. Richard Foreman, Lecture to P. Adams Sitney's graduate film class, Department of Cinema Studies, New York University, New York, 9 November 1973.

6. Ibid.

7. Robb Baker, "The Theatre of Richard Foreman: Hysterical Cool," *The Soho Weekly News,* 9 January 1975.

8. Richard Foreman, Panel presentation for a symposium on "Schizo-Culture" with Francoise Kourilsky, Frantisek Deak, and Stephen Koch participating, Columbia University, New York, 14 November 1975.

9. Richard Foreman, Group Discussion, with Ernie Gehr, Ken Kelman, Jonas Mekas, P. Adams Sitney, Michael Snow, Amy Taubin, and Joyce Wieland participating, New York, New York, Spring, 1969.

10. Richard Foreman as quoted by Mike Steele in "Avant-garde director shakes arts world," *Minneapolis Tribune,* July 31, 1977, p. 1D.

11. Michael Kirby, Radio Interview with Richard Foreman, New York, New York, 11 January 1974.

12. Foreman, Lecture.

13. Stephen Koch, "Performance, A Conversation," *Artforum* XI, 4 (December, 1972), pp. 53-54.

14. Terry Curtis Fox, "The Romance of Intellect," *The Village Voice,* 2 January 1978, p. 77.

15. Foreman, Lecture.

16. Koch, "Conversation," p. 58.

17. Foreman, Lecture.

18. Richard Foreman, "NOTES ON THE PROCESS OF MAKING IT: WHICH IS ALSO THE OBJECT," program notes for 1978 production of *Blvd. de Paris (I've Got the Shakes).*

19. Interview with Richard Foreman, New York, New York, Summer, 1977.

20. See Michael Kirby's essay "On Literary Theatre," *The Drama Review* 18, 2 (June, 1974), pp. 103-13.

21. Cage, Foreman, Kostelanetz, "Art in the Culture," p. 74.

22. Foreman, Lecture.

23. See *The Mechanism of the Mind* by Edward de Bono (New York: Simon and Schuster, 1969), pp. 163-75.

24. K.S., "Richard Foreman: 'Responding to life in my one leaf-like moment,'" *Brown University Bulletin* (obtained from the personal files of Richard Foreman).

25. Michael Feingold, "An Interview with Richard Foreman" *yale/theatre* 7, 1 (Fall, 1975), p. 15.

26. See *Structuralism* by Jean Piaget, translated by Chaninah Maschler (New York: Harper and Row, Publishers, 1971), and "Piaget's Theory," by Gerald E. Gruen in *International Encyclopedia of Psychiatry, Psychology, Psychoanalysis, and Neurology,* ed. by Benjamin B. Wolman, Vol. VIII (New York: Aesculapius Publishers, Inc., 1977), pp. 395-402.

27. Assimilation and accommodation are complementary processes that occur simultaneously and are functionally invariant, that is, they are present in every act, at every level of development.

28. Michael Kirby is responsible for delineating a structural theory of performance and an approach to structural analysis for theatre art. See his article, "Structural Analysis/Structural Theory," *The Drama Review* 20, 4 (December, 1976), pp. 51-68.

29. Richard Foreman, "14 Things I Tell Myself," written for publication in *Tel Quel* (No. 68, Paris). Unpublished version obtained from the personal files of Richard Foreman.

30. Richard Foreman, "How to Write a Play: (in which i am really telling myself how, but if you are the right one i am telling you how, too)," *Performing Arts Journal* 1, 2 (Fall, 1976), p. 84.

31. Feingold, "Interview with Foreman," p. 13.

32. Interview with Foreman, March, 1974.

33. Lita Eliscu, "Ontological-Hysteric Theatre," *East Village Other,* 27 May 1969.

34. Foreman, Group Discussion.

35. Ibid.

36. Michael Kirby, "On Style," *The Drama Review* 15, 3a (Summer, 1971), p. 15.

37. Ibid.

38. Richard Foreman, "How I Write My (Self: Plays)," *The Drama Review* 21, 4 (December, 1977), p. 7.

39. Kirby, Radio Interview with Foreman.

40. Koch, "Conversation," p. 55.

41. Ibid.

42. Feingold, "Interview with Foreman," p. 15.

43. Kirby, "Style," p. 14.

44. Foreman, Lecture.

45. Foreman, Group Discussion.

46. Charles Furst, "The Brain: Automating Attention," *Psychology Today,* August, 1979, p. 112. Also see Furst's book *Origins of the Mind: Mind/Brain Connections* (Englewood Cliffs, New Jersey: Prentice Hall, 1979).

47. Ibid.

48. Foreman, Group Discussion.

49. Ibid.

50. Furst, "The Brain," p. 112.

51. Michael Kirby, "Richard Foreman's Ontological-Hysteric Theatre," *The Drama Review* 17, 2 (June, 1973), p. 28.

52. Ibid.

53. Ibid.

54. Richard Foreman, Unpublished notes written in the summer of 1969, obtained from the personal files of Richard Foreman and Jonas Mekas (Anthology Film Archives).

55. Foreman, Group Discussion.

56. Foreman, "NOTES," program notes for *Blvd. de Paris.*

57. Kirby, "Foreman's Ontological-Hysteric Theatre," p. 23.

58. Foreman, "NOTES," program notes for *Blvd. de Paris.*

59. Foreman, Unpublished notes.

60. Richard Foreman, as quoted by Mel Gussow in "Stage: Avant-Garde at Home in Lenox," *The New York Times,* 8 August 1972.

61. Foreman, Lecture.

62. Richard Foreman, *Sophia=(Wisdom) Part 3: The Cliff,* in *Richard Foreman: Plays and Manifestos,* ed. Kate Davy, (New York: New York University Press, 1976), p. 114.

63. Ibid., p. 117.

64. Kirby, "Foreman's Ontological-Hysteric Theatre," p. 31.

65. *Richard Foreman: Plays and Manifestos,* p. 115.

66. Ibid., p. 120.

67. Ibid., p. 119.

68. Ibid., pp. 120-21.

69. See Kirby's discussion of both associational and dissociational continua in "Richard Foreman's Ontological-Hysteric Theatre," pp. 26-27.

70. Florence Falk, "Ontological-Hysteric Theatre: Setting as Consciousness," *Performing Arts Journal* 1, 1 (Spring, 1976), pp. 54-55.

71. See Chapter II entitled "The Two Kinds of Attention" in Anton Ehrenzweig's book *The Hidden Order of Art: A Study in the Psychology of Artistic Imagination,* Berkeley and Los Angeles: U. of California Press, 1971, pp. 21-31.

72. Shank, Interview with Foreman.

73. Ibid.

74. Richard Foreman, *"Book of Splendors: Part II (Book of Levers) Action at a Distance,"* playscript published in *Theatre* 9, 2 (Spring, 1978), p. 81.

75. Kirby, Radio Interview with Foreman.

76. Shank, Interview with Foreman.

77.   Piaget, *Structuralism*, p. 9.

78.   Interview with Foreman, Summer, 1977.

79.   Ibid.

80.   Richard Foreman, "How to Write a Play (in which i am really telling myself how, but if you are the right one i am telling you how, too)," *Performing Arts Journal* 1, 2 (Fall, 1976), p. 86.

81.   Interview with Foreman, March, 1974.

Conclusion

1.   Victoria Schultz, "Arts: Theatre: *Hotel China,*" *Changes,* February 15, 1972.

2.   Bonnie Marranca, ed. *The Theatre of Images* (New York: Drama Book Specialists (Publishers), 1977), p. 117.

3.   Ibid., p. 113.

4.   Richard Foreman, " 'The Life and Times of Sigmund Freud,' " *The Village Voice,* 1 January 1970, p. 41.

Bibliography

Books

Benmussa, Simone, and Kralik, Erika, eds. *Le Théâtre de Richard Foreman*. Paris: Gallimard, 1973.

Davy, Kate, ed. *Richard Foreman: Plays and Manifestos*. New York: New York University Press, 1976.

Dean, Alexander, and Carra, Lawrence. *Fundamentals of Play Directing*. New York: Holt, Rinehart and Winston, Inc., 1965.

De Bono, Edward. *The Mechanism of the Mind*. New York: Simon and Schuster, 1969.

Ehrenzweig, Anton. *The Hidden Order of Art: A Study in the Psychology of Artistic Imagination*. Berkeley and Los Angeles: University of California Press, 1971.

Furst, Charles. *Origins of the Mind: Mind/Brain Connections*. Englewood Cliffs, New Jersey: Prentice Hall, 1979.

Gruen, Gerald E. "Piaget's Theory." *International Encyclopedia of Psychiatry, Psychology, Psychoanalysis, and Neurology*. Edited by Benjamin B. Wolman. Vol. VIII. New York: Aesculapius Publishers, Inc., 1977.

James, William. *The Principles of Psychology*. Vol. I. New York: Holt, 1890.

_____. "The Stream of Consciousness." *The Modern Tradition: Backgrounds of Modern Literature*. Edited by Richard Ellmann and Charles Feidelson, Jr. New York: Oxford University Press, 1965.

Marranca, Bonnie, ed. *The Theatre of Images*. New York: Drama Book Specialists (Publishers), 1977.

Mekas, Jonas. *Movie Journal: The Rise of the New American Cinema 1959-1971*. New York: Collier Books, 1972.

Meyerowitz, Patricia, ed. *Gertrude Stein: Writings and Lectures, 1909-1945*. Baltimore: Penguin Books, 1967.

Piaget, Jean. *Structuralism*. Translated by Chaninah Maschler. New York: Harper and Row, Publishers, 1971.

Sievers, W. David. *Directing for the Theatre*. Dubuque, Iowa: William C. Brown Co., Publishers, 1965.

Sitney, P. Adams. *Visionary Film: The American Avant-Garde*. New York: Oxford University Press, 1974.

Stein, Gertrude. *The Autobiography of Alice B. Toklas*. New York: Harcourt, Brace and Company, Inc., 1933.

_____. "The Autobiography of Rose." *How Writing is Written*. Edited by Robert Bartlett Haas. Los Angeles: Black Sparrow Press, 1974.

_____. "Composition as Explanation." *What are Masterpieces*. 1940; rpt. New York: Pitman Publishing Corp., 1970.

_____ . "How Writing is Written." *How Writing is Written.* Edited by Robert Bartlett Haas. Los Angeles: Black Sparrow Press, 1974.

_____ . *Lectures in America.* 1935; rpt. New York: Vintage Books, 1975.

_____ . *Narration: Four Lectures.* 1935; rpt. New York: Greenwood Press, 1969.

_____ . *Picasso.* Boston: Beacon Press, 1938.

_____ . "A Transatlantic Interview." *A Primer for the Gradual Understanding of Gertrude Stein.* Edited by Robert Bartlett Haas. Los Angeles: Black Sparrow Press, 1973.

_____ . *Two: Gertrude Stein and Her Brother, and Other Early Portraits (1908-1912).* New Haven: Yale University Press, 1951.

Stewart, Allegra. *Gertrude Stein and the Present.* Cambridge: Harvard University Press, 1967.

Sutherland, Donald *Gertrude Stein: A Biography of Her Work.* New Haven: Yale University Press, 1951.

Van Vechten, Carl, ed. *Selected Writings of Gertrude Stein.* 1946; rpt. New York: Vintage Books, 1972.

Vinson, James, ed. *Contemporary Dramatists.* London: St. James Press, 1973.

Weinstein, Norman. *Gertrude Stein and the Literature of the Modern Consciousness.* New York: Frederick Ungar Publishing Co., 1970.

Journals and Magazines

Cage, John; Foreman, Richard; and Kostelanetz, Richard. "Art in the Culture." *Performing Arts Journal,* IV, 1-2 (Summer, 1979), 70-84.

Davy, Kate. "Foreman's *PAIN(T)* and *Vertical Mobility.*" *The Drama Review,* 18, 2 (June, 1974), 26-37.

_____ . "Foreman's 'Pandering.' " *The Drama Review,* 19, 1 (March, 1975), 116-17.

_____ . "Kate Manheim as Foreman's Rhoda." *The Drama Review,* 20, 3 (September, 1976), 37-50.

_____ . "Richard Foreman's Ontological-Hysteric Theatre: The Influence of Gertrude Stein." *Twentieth Century Literature,* 24, 1 (Spring, 1978), 108-26.

_____ . "Richard Foreman's Scenography: Staging the Ontological-Hysteric Théâtre in a SoHo Loft." *Théâtre Crafts,* 12, 4 (May/June, 1978), 31-33, 56-62.

Dumur, Guy. "Théâtre: Sauts dans le temps." *Le Nouvel Observateur,* 1er octobre, 1973, p. 77.

"entretien avec RICHARD FOREMAN." *Chroniques de l'art vivant,* No. 43, octobre, 1973, pp. 31-33.

Falk, Florence. "Ontological-Hysteric Theatre: Setting as Consciousness." *Performing Arts Journal,* 1, 1 (Spring, 1976), 51-61.

Feingold, Michael. "An Interview with Richard Foreman." *yale/theatre,* 7, 1 (Fall, 1975), 6-29.

Founes, Claudie, and Piet, Patrick. "Richard Foreman et l'Ontologic Hysteric Theatre: LE LIVRE DES SPLENDEURS." *Liberation,* 24 septembre, 1976.

Foreman, Richard. *Book of Splendors: Part II (Book of Levers) Action at a Distance.* Playscript published in *Theater,* 9, 2 (Spring, 1978), 79-89.

_____ . "The Carrot and the Stick." *October,* 1, 1 (Spring, 1976), 22-31.

_____ . "Critique: Glass and Snow." *Arts Magazine,* February, 1970, pp. 20-22.

_____ . "How I Write My (Self: Plays)." *The Drama Review,* 21, 4 (December, 1977), 5-24.

_____ . "How to Write a Play: (in which i am really telling myself how, but if you are the right one i am telling you how, too)." *Performing Arts Journal,* 1, 2 (Fall, 1976), 84-92.

Furst, Charles. "The Brain: Automating Attention." *Psychology Today,* August, 1979, p. 112.

Gill, Brendan. "Echt Brecht." *The New Yorker,* May 10, 1976, p. 103.

_____ . "Off Broadway: Paris Nights and Frights." *The New Yorker,* January 13, 1975, p. 65.

Gousseland, Jack. "Theatre: L'insolence américaine." *Le Point,* No. 52, 17 septembre, 1973, p. 73.

Kauffmann, Stanley. "Arts and Lives: Stanley Kauffmann on Theater." *The New Republic,* 178 February 25, 1978, pp. 38-40.

_____. "Stanley Kauffmann on Theater: Ontological-Hysteric Theatre." *The New Republic*, January 27, 1973, pp. 26, 35.

Kirby, Michael. "On Acting and Not Acting." *The Drama Review*, 16, 1 (March, 1972), pp. 3-15.

_____. "On Literary Theatre." *The Drama Review*, 18, 2 (June, 1974), pp. 103-13.

_____. "On Style." *The Drama Review*, 15, 3a (Summer, 1971), pp. 11-20.

_____. "Richard Foreman's Ontological-Hysteric Theatre." *The Drama Review*, 17, 2 (June, 1973), pp. 5-32.

_____. "Structural Analysis/Structural Theory." *The Drama Review*, 20, 4 (December, 1976), pp. 51-68.

Koch, Stephen. "The Histrionics of Despair." *World*, July 18, 1972, pp. 78-79.

_____. "Performance, A Conversation." *Artforum*, XI, 4 (December, 1972), pp. 53-58.

Kroll, Jack. "Mack Is Back." *Newsweek*, May 17, 1976, p. 74.

_____. "Theatre of Crisis." *Newsweek*, May 8, 1972, pp. 116-17.

_____. "Well That's Life." *Newsweek*, December 4, 1972, p. 70.

"LE LIVRE DES SPLENDEURS de Richard Foreman." *Le Nouvel Observateur*, 27 septembre, 1976.

" 'le livre des splendeurs' de Richard Foreman." *Rouge*, 23 septembre, 1976.

Leverett, James. "Richard Foreman and Some Uses of Cinema." *Theatre*, 9, 2 (Spring, 1978), 10-14.

Marranca, Bonnie. "Richard Foreman: genius of avant-garde theater." *Changes*, February, 1975, pp. 36-37.

_____. "Theatre." *Changes*, June, 1974, p. 34.

Oliver, Edith. "Off Broadway." *The New Yorker*, January 19, 1976, p. 46.

_____. "Off Broadway: La Vie en Rose." *The New Yorker*, December 9, 1972, pp. 109-10.

Perec, Georges. "Théâtre: 'O, images, vous suffisez à mon bonheur.' " *La Quinzaine Litteraire*, du 1er 15 octobre, 1973.

"Richard Foreman: 'Responding to life in my one leaf-like moment.' " *Brown University Bulletin*. Obtained from the personal files of Richard Foreman.

Schultz, Victoria. "Arts: Theatre: *Hotel China*." *Changes*, February 15, 1972.

Stasio, Mario. "A Theatre of the Mind." *Penthouse*, May, 1976, pp. 46-47.

"Talk of the Town." *The New Yorker*, January 27, 1973. pp. 23-25.

Wittenberg, Clarissa K. "Art Now 74: A National Arts Festival Comes to Washington." *Memo*, June 1-15, 1974, pp. 10-11.

Newspapers

Baignères, Claude. "Fondateur du théâtre ontologique Richard Foreman ouvre son 'Livre des splendeurs.' " *Le Figaro*, 1 septembre, 1976.

Baker, Robb "Foreman's Rhoda and Her Brave New (Funny) World." *The Soho Weekly News*, January 30, 1975.

_____. "Keep-Away." *The Soho Weekly News*, March 10, 1977, p. 24.

_____. "*PAIN(T)* & *Vertical Mobility*." *The Soho Weekly News*, April 4, 1974.

_____. "The Theatre of Richard Foreman: Hysterical Cool." *The Soho Weekly News*, January 9, 1975.

Barnes, Clive. "Papp's 'Threepenny' Echoes Original." *The New York Times*, May 3, 1976.

_____. "Stage: Leers, Love Songs and Lunacy." *The New York Times*, November 24, 1972.

Bass, Milton R. " 'Doctor Selavy's Magic Theatre.' " *Berkshire Eagle*, August 3, 1972.

Beltzer, Lee. "Foreman's Splendors." *The Villager*, March 10, 1977.

Cournot, Michel. "Théâtre: AU FESTIVAL D'AUTOMNE: 'Une semaine sous l'influence de . . ' " *Le Monde*, 23-24 septembre, 1973, p. 21.

Eder, Richard. "Comic Tyrant In a Self-Invented, Peculiar World." *The New York Times*, March 20, 1977. p. 3.

Eliscu, Lita. "Ontological-Hysteric Theatre." *East Village Other,* May 27, 1969.

Falk, Florence. "Kate Manheim: Theme and Variations within an Erotic Landscape." *The Soho Weekly News,* December 22, 1977, pp. 23-25.

Feingold, Michael. "Everybody's Incomprehensible." *The Village Voice,* September 12, 1974, pp. 61-71.

——. "The Potato's the Thing." *The Village Voice,* December 29, 1975, pp. 105-6.

——. "Richard Foreman: 'I Want to Thrill and Elate Myself.' " *The Village Voice,* January 13, 1975, p. 80.

——. "The Two by Four Is a Whorehouse Again." *The Village Voice,* May 10, 1976.

Foreman, Richard. "The Life and Times of Sigmund Freud." *The Village Voice,* January 1, 1970, p. 41.

Fox, Terry Curtis. "Cinema is Ontological-Hysteria at 24 Frames a Second." *The Village Voice,* September 4, 1978, p. 75.

——. "The Romance of Intellect." *The Village Voice,* January 2, 1978, p. 77.

Galey, Matthieu, "Le Livre des splendeurs de Richard Foreman: Tout de même une idée." *le QUOTIDIEN de paris,* 25-26 septembre, 1976.

Godard, Colette. "Richard Foreman au Festival d'Automne: Les faux pas de la logique." *Le Monde,* 16 septembre, 1976.

——. "Théâtre 'LE LIVRE DES SPLENDEURS,' de Richard foreman." *Le Monde,* 24 septembre, 1976.

Gussow, Mel. "Stage: Avant-Garde at Home in Lenox." *The New York Times,* August 8, 1972.

——. "Stage: Two by Foreman." *The New York Times,* April 3, 1974.

——. "Stage: Zesty Pandering." *The New York Times,* January 16, 1975.

——. "Theatre: New Shocks, 'Splendors.' " *The New York Times,* March 4, 1977.

Henahan, Donal. "But Doctor, You Must Be Kidding!" *The New York Times,* August 20, 1972.

Highwater, Jamake. "Threepenny Doesn't Sing (But Richard Stolzman Zings)." *The Soho Weekly News,* July 15, 1976.

Jenner, Cynthia Lee. "Artsboard: 108 Plays Later." *The Villager,* July 22, 1976.

——. "Inside-Out Play." *The Villager,* January 22, 1976.

Lahr, Anthea. "Stanley Silverman: 'I Want to Write Tacky Brechtian Operas.' " *The Village Voice,* January 13, 1975, p. 80.

Lahr, John. "Intellectual Vaudeville." *The Village Voice,* January 20, 1975, p. 82.

Lester, Elenore. *"Threepenny Opera." The Soho Weekly News,* May 13, 1976.

Marcabru, Pierre. "Le Livre des splendeurs de Richard Foreman: Une curiosité." *Le Figaro,* 25-26 septembre, 1976.

Marranca, Bonnie. "Quo Vadis, Richard Foreman?" *The Soho Weekly News,* December 25, 1975.

Mekas, Jonas. "Movie Journal." *The Village Voice,* June 13, 1974, p. 91.

Mignon, Frédéric. "Le Théâtre RICHARD FOREMAN AU RECAMIER." *Combat,* 27 septembre, 1973.

Moore, Carman. "Dance to read, music to touch." *The Village Voice,* December 14, 1972.

Munk, Erica. "Book of Splendors." *The Village Voice,* March 21, 1977.

Novick, Julius. "All in Favor of Decadence. . . ." *The Village Voice,* January 13, 1975.

——. "Nobody's Laughing at This Threepenny." *The Village Voice,* May 10, 1976.

Rockwell, John. "The Magic Theatre of Richard Foreman." *The New York Times,* February 8, 1976, pp. 1, 5.

Sainer, Arthur. "A Hot Tip for a Bitter Winter." *The Village Voice,* January 21, 1971.

——. "A Little August in the Berkshires." *The Village Voice,* September 2, 1971.

——. "The Buzzers Are Back." *The Village Voice,* January 20, 1975, p. 84.

——. "Dead god and winking angel." *The Village Voice,* December 21, 1972.

——. "Let Us Now Praise Famous Potatoes." *The Village Voice,* December 29, 1975.

_____ . "Only mental, where's my foot gone?" *The Village Voice,* August 10, 1972, p. 48.

_____ . "The scene lately seen (1)." *The Village Voice,* July 8, 1971, p. 46.

_____ . "Someone trips, an angel smiles." *The Village Voice,* January 6, 1972.

_____ , and Smith, Michael. "Bubbles of joy in a sober field." *The Village Voice,* April 11, 1974.

Schechner, Richard. "If Heidegger Wrote Soaps, He'd Be Richard Foreman." *The Village Voice,* February 23, 1976.

Schonberg, Harold C. "Light Music To Be Taken Seriously." *The New York Times,* January 26, 1975.

Shank, Ted. "From Soho to Paris and Back Again." *The Soho Weekly News,* January 27, 1977, pp. 17-19.

Smith, Michael. "theatre journal." *The Village Voice,* May 4, 1972.

Steele, Mike. "Avant-garde director shakes arts world." *Minneapolis Tribune,* July 31, 1977, pp. 1D, 8D.

Syna, Sy. "Richard Foreman's Latest Opus." *Wisdom's Child,* March 21, 1977, p. 15.

Wetzsteon, Ross. "Obie Awards: Off-Off Broadway Extends From Beckett to Box Office." *The Village Voice,* June 7, 1976.

_____ . "Harsh, Bitter, Brutal—the Real 'Threepenny' Comes to New York." *The Village Voice,* May 10, 1976.

Unpublished Materials

Davy, Kate. Interview with Richard Foreman. New York, March, 1974.

_____ . Interview with Richard Foreman. New York, Summer, 1974.

_____ . Interview with Richard Foreman. New York, December 18, 1974.

_____ . Interview with Richard Foreman. New York, June 20, 1975.

_____ . Interview with Richard Foreman. New York, October, 1976.

_____ . Interview with Richard Foreman. New York, Summer, 1977.

_____ . Interview with Ernie Gehr. New York, December 17, 1974.

_____ . Interview with Ken Jacobs and Richard Foreman. New York, November 22, 1974.

_____ . Interview with Ken Kelman. New York, November 18, 1974.

_____ . Interview with Kate Manheim. New York, February 22, 1974.

_____ . Interview with Kate Manheim. New York, April 3, 1976.

_____ . Interview with Jonas Mekas. New York, November 20, 1974.

_____ . Interview with P. Adams Sitney. New York, November 23, 1974.

_____ . Interview with Amy Taubin. New York, December 9, 1974.

Foreman, Richard. "14 Things I Tell Myself." Article written for publication in *Tel Quel* (No. 68, Paris). Unpublished version obtained from the personal files of Richard Foreman.

_____ . Group Discussion. Ernie Gehr, Ken Kelman, Jonas Mekas, P. Adams Sitney, Michael Snow, Amy Taubin, and Joyce Wieland participating. New York, Spring, 1969.

_____ . Lecture delivered at New York University in the Department of Cinema Studies. November 9, 1973.

_____ . Lecture delivered at New York University in the Graduate Drama Department, Fall, 1974.

_____ . "NOTES ON THE PROCESS OF MAKING IT; WHICH IS ALSO THE OBJECT." Program notes for 1978 production of *Blvd. de Paris (I've Got the Shakes).*

_____ . Panel discussion for a symposium on "Gesture and Language: The Semiotics of the New American Theatre," with Lee Breuer, John Guare, Ted Hoffman, Rosette C. Lamont, Bonnie Marranca, and Andrzej Wirth participating. New York: The Graduate School and University Center of the City University of New York, December 8, 1975.

_____ . Panel discussion on the work of Michael Snow. New York: Museum of Modern Art, February 23, 1976.

————. Panel presentation for a symposium on "Schizo-Culture," with Frantisek Deak, Francoise Kourilsky, and Stephen Koch participating. New York: Columbia University, November 14, 1975.

————. Unpublished notes written in the summer of 1969. Obtained from the personal files of Richard Foreman and Jonas Mekas (Anthology Film Archives).

Kirby, Michael. Radio Interview with Richard Foreman. New York, January 11, 1974.

Shank, Ted. Interview with Richard Foreman. Paris, September 22, 1976.

Index